The Legislative Themes of Centralization

The Legislative Themes of Centralization

From Mandate to Demise

JEFFREY G. AUDIRSCH

☙PICKWICK *Publications* • Eugene, Oregon

THE LEGISLATIVE THEMES OF CENTRALIZATION
From Mandate to Demise

Copyright © 2014 Jeffrey G. Audirsch. All rights reserved. Except for brief quotations in critical publications or reviews, no part of this book may be reproduced in any manner without prior written permission from the publisher. Write: Permissions. Wipf and Stock Publishers, 199 W. 8th Ave., Suite 3, Eugene, OR 97401.

Pickwick Publications
An Imprint of Wipf and Stock Publishers
199 W. 8th Ave., Suite 3
Eugene, OR 97401

www.wipfandstock.com

ISBN 13: 978-1-62032-038-9

Cataloguing-in-Publication Data

Audirsch, Jeffrey G.

The legislative themes of centralization : from mandate to demise

xvi + 224 p. ; 23 cm. Includes bibliographical references.

ISBN 13: 978-1-62032-038-9

1. Bible. Deuteronomy—Criticism, interpretation, etc. 2. Bible. Deuteronomy—Theology. 3. Law (Theology)—Biblical teaching. I. Title.

BS1275.52 A92 2014

Manufactured in the U.S.A.

To Alicia

Ecclesiastes 4:9–12

Contents

Preface | ix
Abbreviations | xi

1. Introduction | 1
   Excursus: Methodological Considerations | 11
2. Approaching the Concept of Centralization | 22
3. The Abrogation of Idolatry | 42
4. The Israelite Concept of Tithing | 81
5. The Israelite Festivals | 103
6. The Judiciary Officials | 125
7. Priesthood in Israel | 139
8. Centralization and the Integrated Methodology | 161
9. Conclusion | 183

Bibliography | 187

Scripture Index | 209

Preface

IN 2010, I SUBMITTED my dissertation to the faculty at New Orleans Baptist Theological Seminary. That original work, "From Tetrateuch to Enneateuch: A Reassessment of the Deuteronomic Concept of Centralization," examined the diachronic and synchronic aspects of the six legislative themes associated with the Deuteronomic mandate. The current monograph is a revision of my dissertation. Since completing the dissertation, my views of Deuteronomy have shifted somewhat. In many ways, this monograph represents that shift. I still advocate an "integrated methodology," that is, a blending of diachronic and synchronic readings of the biblical texts. For purposes of clarity, I have included an excursus on "Methodological Considerations," which I believe fleshes out my approach more clearly. I hope this revision and expansion will be beneficial for readers and, more importantly, provide validity to the method.

In ch. 2, I have tried to limit the history of research to the Deuteronomic concept of centralization. I did not turn over every stone in my summation and assessment. That being said, I am certain that arguments and contributions have been overlooked, and for this I apologize. One of the most drastic changes is found in the diachronic and exegetical work of chs. 3–7. As stated above, in my initial research I examined the six legislative themes related to the Deuteronomic concept of centralization. In this monograph I have removed my original discussion on kingship. Although the kingship laws in Deut 17:14–20 play a prominent role in the book, and though they are related to the centralization mandate peripherally, I have decided to focus on the five legislative themes that are directly related to the mandate. In chs. 3–7, emphasis is given to the diachronic and exegetical aspects of various texts to these five themes. At times, I emphasize the

Preface

diachronic more so than the exegetical and at other times vice versa. The decision to do so is determined by the individual texts.

Given the volume of texts examined, I regret that deeper diachronic assessment was not given for several texts. I am aware that my interaction with scholarly contributions will be found wanting by some. That said, I preferred a macro understanding (i.e., emphasis on the metanarrative) of the five themes over and against a microanalysis. While on the topic of the five legislative themes, the nature of chs. 3–7, unfortunately I must say, can be disjointed in places. Hopefully this will not take away from the overall scope and purpose of my work. The biggest change is found in ch. 8, particularly in my implications of the study. It is within the implications that my shift in understanding Deuteronomy can be identified. Lastly, I have included a slightly more in-depth bibliography that will provide readers with other works in the areas of my research.

A work like this one cannot be accomplished alone. Thus, I am grateful for the direction by my doctoral mentors Dr. Archie England and Dr. R. Dennis Cole. To date, both of these men continue to give me direction and thoughtful criticism. A special word of thanks is due to Dr. Walter Brown for his doctoral seminar in biblical law. It was in this seminar that I was introduced to the magisterial world of Deuteronomy. The unique blend of law, narrative, and theology captivated me then and continues to challenge me today. I am grateful to Pam Cole for her keen eye and meticulous attention to details. Her editorial insights made my work much improved. Naturally, any errors are mine. As for the current revision, I would like to extend my appreciation to the library staffs at Shorter University and Columbia Theological Seminary. The revisions and updating of my dissertation could not have been accomplished without their help. Additionally, I would like to thank R. Anthony Purcell for his hours of dialogue, review, and critique. Last, I want to thank my family for their love and support. To my son Gideon, I am grateful for your unconditional love even in my absence as I worked on meeting the deadline. And, to my loving wife Alicia, I want to thank you for your patience and sacrifice. It was your encouragement and support that motivated me to complete the original work and now the revision. Your love and compassion inspires me and I am a better man for it.

Jeffrey G. Audirsch
Rome, GA

Abbreviations

AASF	Annales Academiae scientiarum fennicae
AB	Anchor Bible
ABD	*Anchor Bible Dictionary*
ABRL	Anchor Bible Reference Library
AnBib	Analecta biblica
Ant	*Jewish Antiquities* by Josephus
AOTC	Abingdon Old Testament Commentaries
AP	Aramaic Papyri
ATANT	Abhandlungen zur Theologie des Alten und Neuen Testaments
ATD	Das Alte Testament Deutsch
BA	*Biblical Archaeologist*
BASOR	*Bulletin of the American Schools of Oriental Research*
BBB	Bonner biblische Beiträge
BBET	Beiträge zur biblischen Exegese und Theologie
BBRSup	Bulletin for Biblical Research Supplement
BDB	*A Hebrew and English Lexicon of the Old Testament*
BETL	Bibliotheca ephemeridum theologicarum lovaniensium
BEvT	Beiträge zur evangelischen Theologie
BFCT	Beiträge zur Förderung christlicher Theologie
BH	Biblical Hebrew
Bib	*Biblica*
BibInt	*Biblical Interpretation*
BIS	Biblical Interpretation Series
BJRL	*Bulletin of the John Rylands University Library of Manchester*

Abbreviations

BN	*Biblische Notizen*
BRev	*Bible Review*
BRB	*Bulletin for Biblical Research*
BRS	Biblical Resource Series
BSac	*Bibliotheca Sacra*
BT	*The Bible Translator*
BTB	*Biblical Theology Bulletin*
BZ	*Biblische Zeitschrift*
BZAW	Beihefte zur Zeitschrift für die alttestamentliche Wissenschaft
CBC	Cambridge Bible Commentary
CBQ	*Catholic Biblical Quarterly*
CH	Chronicler's History
Colloq	*Colloquium*
CurBS	*Currents in Research: Biblical Studies*
DB	*Dictionary of the Bible*
DCH	*Dictionary of Classical Hebrew*
DDD	*Dictionary of Deities and Demons in the Bible*
DH	Deuteronomistic History
DOTHB	*Dictionary of the Old Testament: Historical Books*
DOTP	*Dictionary of the Old Testament: Pentateuch*
DSFLS	Distinguished Senior Faculty Lecture Series
Dtr	Deuteronomistic editor
Dtr^1	First redaction of the DH
Dtr^2	Exilic redaction of the DH
EdF	Erträge der Forschung
EncJud	*Encyclopaedia Judaica*
ESV	English Standard Version
EvT	*Evangelische Theologie*
ExAud	*Ex auditu*
FAT	Forschungen zum Alten Testament
FOTL	Forms of the Old Testament Literature
FRLANT	Forschungen zur Religion und Literatur des Alten und Neuen Testaments
GBS	Guides to Biblical Scholarship

Abbreviations

GDNES	Gorgias Dissertations: Near Eastern Studies
HALOT	*Hebrew and Aramaic Lexicon of the Old Testament*
HAT	Handbuch zum alten Testament
HB	Hebrew Bible
HCSB	Holman Christian Standard Bible
HKAT	Handkommentar zum Alten Testament
HSM	Harvard Semitic Monographs
HTIBS	Historical Texts and Interpreters in Biblical Scholarship
HTR	*Harvard Theological Review*
HUCA	*Hebrew Union College Annual*
HvTSt	*Hervormde teologiese studies*
IB	*Interpreter's Bible*
IBC	Interpretation Bible Commentary
IBHS	*Introduction to Biblical Hebrew Syntax*
IBT	Interpreting Biblical Texts
ICC	International Critical Commentary
IDB	*Interpreter's Dictionary of the Bible*
IDBSup	*Interpreter's Dictionary of the Bible: Supplementary Volume*
Int	*Interpretation*
IOS	*Israel Oriental Studies*
ISBL	Indiana Studies in Biblical Literature
ITL	International Theological Library
JAOS	*Journal of the American Oriental Society*
JBL	*Journal of Biblical Literature*
JBQ	*Jewish Bible Quarterly*
JETS	*Journal of the Evangelical Theological Society*
JNES	*Journal of Near Eastern Studies*
JNSL	*Journal of Northwest Semitic Languages*
JPST	JPS Torah
JPSTC	JPS Torah Commentary
JQR	*Jewish Quarterly Review*
JSOT	*Journal for the Study of the Old Testament*
JSOTSup	Journal for the Study of the Old Testament: Supplement Series
JTS	*Journal of Theological Studies*

Abbreviations

KJV	King James Version
LAI	Library of Ancient Israel
LBI	Library of Biblical Interpretation
LBS	Library of Biblical Studies
LD	Lectio divina
LHB	Library of Hebrew Bible
LOS	London Oriental Series
LXX	Septuagint
Maarav	*Maarav*
MT	Masoretic Text
NAC	New American Commentary
NASB	New American Standard Bible
NCBC	New Century Bible Commentary
NEchtB	Neue Echter Bibel
NIB	*New Interpreter's Bible*
NICOT	New International Commentary on the Old Testament
NIDOTTE	*New International Dictionary of Old Testament Theology & Exegesis*
NIV	New International Version
NIVAC	NIV Application Commentary
NKJV	New King James Version
NRSV	New Revised Standard Version
OBO	Orbis biblicus et orientalis
OBT	Overtures to Biblical Theology
OTG	Old Testament Guides
OTL	Old Testament Library
OTS	Old Testament Studies
OtSt	Oudtestamentische Studiën
OTT	*Old Testament Theology* (Gerhard von Rad)
PH	Primary History
Proof	*Prooftexts: A Journal of Jewish Literary History*
R^{JE}	Redactor of the Jahwist and Elohist
ResQ	*Restoration Quarterly*
RevExp	*Review and Expositor*

Abbreviations

RSV	Revised Standard Version
SBLDS	Society of Biblical Literature Dissertation Series
SBLSP	*Society of Biblical Literature Seminar Papers*
SBLStBl	Society of Biblical Literature Studies in Biblical Literature
SBLSymS	Society of Biblical Literature Symposium Series
SBS	Stuttgarter Bibelstudien
SBTS	Sources for Biblical and Theological Study
Semeia	*Semeia*
SFSHJ	South Florida Studies in the History of Judaism
SHBC	Smyth and Helwys Bible Commentary
SJOT	*Scandinavian Journal of the Old Testament*
SJT	*Scottish Journal of Theology*
SPOT	Studies on Personalities of the Old Testament
SSN	Studia semitica neerlandica
TB	Theologische Bücherei
TDOT	*Theological Dictionary of the Old Testament*
ThStKr	*Theologische Studien und Kritiken*
TS	*Theological Studies*
TWOT	*Theological Wordbook of the Old Testament*
TynBul	*Tyndale Bulletin*
VT	*Vetus Testamentum*
VTSup	Supplements to Vetus Testamentum
WBC	Word Biblical Commentary
WMANT	Wissenschaftliche Monographien zum Alten und Neuen Testament
WTJ	*Westminster Theological Journal*
WW	*Word and World*
ZAW	*Zeitschrift für die alttestamentliche Wissenschaft*
ZDPV	*Zeitschrift des deutschen Palästina-Vereins*
ZPEB	*Zondervan Pictorial Encyclopedia of the Bible*
ZTK	*Zeitschrift für Theologie und Kirche*

1

Introduction

AT ITS CORE, THE book of Deuteronomy is theological. For centuries, scholars have gravitated to the riches of the book. The theologies inherent to the book transcend Deuteronomy and extend into other books of the Hebrew Bible (HB) and the New Testament.[1] The richness of the book continues to attract and challenge scholars. To date, no consensus has been reached concerning the authorship, date, and province of the book.[2] On the other hand, most scholars agree on the basic literary message of the book.

Deuteronomy represents the transition point between the wilderness experience and the Israelites' inhabitance of the land of Canaan. The Sinaitic covenant between Yahweh, Moses, and the Israelites emphasized obedience and monotheism (Exod 19:5).[3] The old generation of Israelites

---

1. In recent years, interest in Deuteronomy has grown among New Testament scholars. See Wilson, *Blessing for the Nations*; Bekken, *The Word is Near You*; Moyise and Menken, eds., *Deuteronomy in the New Testament*; Waaler, *The Shema and the First Commandment*; and Lincicum, *Paul and the Early Jewish Encounter with Deuteronomy*.

2. Describing the scholarly contributions to Deuteronomy and the so-called DH, Robert Polzin opined, "It is my pessimistic view that almost two centuries of research on Deuteronomy and the other books it introduces—research that began with de Wette's ground-breaking work on Deuteronomy (1805) and culminated in Martin Noth's modern classic (1967)—have produced no hypothesis that can be described as historically or literarily adequate." See Polzin, *Moses and the Deuteronomist*, 13. Due to the nature of this book, the scholarly theories of authorship, date, and province will not be examined in detail. When appropriate, attention will be given to issues related to these areas.

3. Throughout the monograph I will use the personal name for Israel's god. I am aware of the interplay between Yahweh and Elohim within the Pentateuch, but for the

The Legislative Themes of Centralization

did not heed the words of Yahweh and became defiant against Moses and Aaron. As a result, the old generation slowly perished during the wilderness experience. The abhorrent sins of the old generation transgressed the Sinaitic covenant (Num 14:1–45) and resulted in a farewell address by Moses to the new generation of Israelites. Deuteronomy was this farewell address and demanded the renewal and restoration of the covenant between Yahweh and the Israelites. After the tumultuous years of wandering, Moses and the new generation found themselves encamped in the land of Moab on the brink of the land of Canaan. Just east of the Jordan River, Moses proclaimed his farewell address through three sermons.[4] Thus, the purpose of Deuteronomy was to connect Yahweh's covenantal promise at Mount Sinai with the new generation's deposition to obey the law (cf. Josh 24:19–28).

For the last two centuries, the traditional literary message of Deuteronomy has been overshadowed by the historical-critical interpretations of the book. For scholars, the covenantal characteristics in Deuteronomy have served as points of contention due in part to the book's rich and unique blend of history, law, and theology. Much of the dialogue has surrounded the Deuteronomic law code (chs. 12–26).[5] The Deuteronomic law code, self-titled "this book of the law" (ספר התורה הזה),[6] in many ways represents a "new literary genre" void of any parallel within the broader legal spectrum—the Pentateuch and the ancient Near East (ANE) legal corpuses.[7]

---

purposes of clarity, I will only use proper name Yahweh when discussing the various texts.

4. The final four chapters transition the leadership from Moses to Joshua, yet, more importantly theses chapters prepare the people for life in the land of Canaan without their religious leader Moses.

5. Biblical law does not occupy an isolated place in the Tetrateuch (Genesis–Numbers) nor the Pentateuch (Genesis–Deuteronomy). The law codes in the HB are imbedded into every facet of Israelite life (i.e., social and religious settings). Ze'ev W. Falk provided an explanation of the unique relationship between biblical law and religion, particularly during the monarchy. See Falk, *Hebrew Law*, 8–16.

6. The designation of "this law" (התורה הזה) is most definitely in reference to an inanimate object, possibly the *urdeuteronomium*. Textual evidence suggests that the author(s) use "this law" (התורה הזה) to describe some form of Deuteronomy (Deut 1:5; 4:8; 17:18, 19; 27:3, 8, 26; 28:58, 61; 29:20, 28; 30:10; 31:9, 11, 12, 24, 26; 32:46; Josh 1:8). The only exception to "this law" (התורה הזה) occurring outside Deuteronomy is in the book of Joshua. In Josh 1:8, Joshua, Moses' successor, declares that the people should meditate on the words of "this book of the law" because it will make the way of the people prosperous (i.e., obedience equals blessing; cf. Deut 28:1–14). Scholars have long debated the structure of the *urdeuteronomium*.

7. See McBride, "Polity of the Covenant," 236.

Introduction

Even amidst the historical-critical uncertainties, Deuteronomy is still considered the lynchpin and/or centerpiece of the HB since it functions as the capstone of the Tetrateuch and as the introduction to the so-called Deuteronomistic History (DH).[8] The unique position of Deuteronomy has played an important role in various studies concerning the HB.[9] Due in large part to the complexities of theology and history in the book, historical-critical methodologies have become the tour de force when studying Deuteronomy, as well as in the Tetrateuch and the so-called DH.[10]

The emergence of Deuteronomy as the apex of modern critical thought in the Pentateuch and the so-called DH can be traced to Wilhelm Martin Leberecht de Wette. He was the first modern scholar to argue that Deuteronomy represented a sui generis since it looked back on the material in the Tetrateuch and provided the theological foundation of the Former Prophets. His seminal argument theorized that "the book of the law" (ספר התורה) discovered in the temple during Josiah's reign (2 Kgs 22:8) was an *urdeuteronomium*.[11] Proponents of de Wette's theory have equated the concept of centralization of the cult in Deuteronomy, that is the sanctioned mandate to worship Yahweh in a future centralized location, with the abolishment of all the local shrines and high places during the religious purging and social reforms of Josiah (2 Kgs 22–23). The actions of Josiah ratified the centralized worship of Yahweh to the temple in Jerusalem while simultaneously

---

8. I prefer the designation "so-called DH" over and against the traditional identification of DH. This preference is based on the conclusions made in this study and the works of others (see ch. 8). That being said, when summarizing the contributions of other scholars, if she/he uses the designation DH, I will retain her/his usage.

9. For example, see Römer, "Le Deutéronome," 66–67; Alexander, *From Paradise*, 266–67; and Childs, *Introduction to the Old Testament*, 204. Siegfried Hermann went a step further when he proposed that Deuteronomy was the theological center of the Bible. See Hermann, "Die Konstruktive Restauration," 166–67.

10. The discussion concerning the relationship between the Pentateuch and the so-called DH has been described as a "battlefield." See Römer, "Cult Centralization," 168.

11. Wette, "Dissertatio critica qua Deuteronomium"; idem, *Opuscula Theologica*, 149–68. A more comprehensive look into the life of de Wette can be found in Rogerson, *W. M. L. de Wette*. See also Hayes and Prussner, *Old Testament Theology*, 98–100 and Gignilliat, *Old Testament Criticism*, 37–56. The derivatives of de Wette's theory can be found in various scholarly writings. In his commentary, for example, Walter Brueggemann described, "Deuteronomy looks both *backward to rootage* and *forward to crisis*, and interprets at the precise place where *rootage* and *crisis* intersect." See Brueggemann, *Deuteronomy*, 22, emphasis his. Similarly, Patrick D. Miller described Deuteronomy as a "significant hermeneutical endeavor, speaking to new situations in light of the past, new situations that may be very different from previous ones." See Miller, *Deuteronomy*, 4.

ordering the abrogation of polytheistic worship at the various shrines and high places throughout Judah.[12]

The historical correlation made by scholars between the centralization of the cult and Josiah's reforms has overshadowed other research within Deut 12–18, particularly the five legislative themes associated with the centralization mandate: the abrogation of idolatry, tithes, the Passover and the festival calendar, judiciary officials, and the priesthood. To date, source and redaction criticisms continue to dominate the landscape of Pentateuchal studies, especially among European scholars. The efforts of these scholars have a viable place within Pentateuchal and, more specifically, Deuteronomic studies. It is my contention that a literary analysis of these five themes within the Enneateuch (i.e., Genesis–2 Kings) will also provide valuable theological insights.[13]

I believe the tour de force of source and form criticisms, at times, has constrained the overall understanding of the concept of centralization in Deuteronomy and its interrelationship with the Tetrateuch and the so-called DH. This is evidenced by the sheer volume of articles, essays, and monographs dedicated to the historical placement of the Deuteronomic concept of centralization compared to the literary implications of the five legislative themes throughout the so-called DH. The method of literary criticism and its subsidiary components can provide a unique perspective for understanding how the Deuteronomic concept of centralization interrelates with the Tetrateuch and the so-called DH.

In the chapters that follow, I demonstrate how the aforementioned five legislative themes, interwoven within the legal fabric of Deut 12–18, play an important theological and ideological role in the literary history of the Enneateuch.[14] Thus, one question guides my research: With Deuteronomy as the interpretive lens, what theological and ideological insights can be

---

12. For an update-to-date diachronic approach to the connections between "this book of the Torah" in Deuteronomy (e.g., 28:61; 29:20; 30:10, passim) and 2 Kgs 22:8, 11, see Edelman, *Opening the Books of Moses*, 98–99.

13. Enneateuchal theory will be discussed later. Recently, Paul A. Barker made a similar argument related to a synchronic reading of Deuteronomy: "Synchronic readings have provided a richer and more satisfactory theological understanding of Deuteronomy's outlook for Israel's future." See Barker, "Contemporary Theological Interpretation," 84.

14. I delimit my study to these chapters because of the proportionality of the centralization mandate motifs (i.e., twenty) over and against the rest of the book (26:2; 31:11). Moreover, the other two references to centralization are related to elements within chs. 12–18.

gleaned from assessing these five legislative themes within the Enneateuch? In sum, the goal of this study is to understand the theological ramifications of the mandate for the centralization of the cult within the Enneateuch instead of rehashing the critical theories concerning the historical application of the concept. By using Deuteronomy as a literary guide for interpreting the legislative themes, it is possible to gain greater theological and ideological insights to the Deuteronomic centralization mandate within Israel's literary history.

Before embarking on this task, I must highlight some basic assumptions and parameters for the study. I am not concerned with the literary development of the Deuteronomic concept of centralization.[15] Even with a complex literary history, the collective Deuteronomic concept of centralization in Deut 12–18 substantiates Yahweh's demands for obedience, loyalty, and holiness that are introduced in the Tetrateuch and expounded in the so-called DH. Additionally, the unique theological and literary-historical ramifications of the five legislative themes in chs. 12–18 must be interpreted in the broader and more complex salvation-judgment history of the Enneateuch. Several of the themes have been studied from source, form, and redactional points of view within the Pentateuch; however, a literary study of these themes within the larger literary unit of Genesis–2 Kings provides two different perspectives. First, a literary study moves the centralization discussion away from the historical and to the theological and ideological. Second, by moving the five legislative themes to the forefront and the centralization of the cult to the background, a different perspective on Israel's literary history can be achieved.

But what is the perspective? The answer to the question has several layers. Since Deuteronomy is the theological lens of the study, the perspective of Deuteronomy is first and foremost. James Robson suggested that Deuteronomy "be understood and read from the editor's perspective."[16] To do so, Deuteronomy required two directions of reading: "Against the

---

15. The compositional layers of Deut 12 are most debated. Several scholars have proposed their own theory concerning the source dating and division of Deut 12: Rofé, "Centralization of Worship in Deuteronomy," 221–26; Halpern, "Centralization Formula in Deuteronomy," 20–38; Lohfink, "Zur deuteronomischen Zentralisationformel," 147–77; Reuter, *Kultzentralisation*; Levinson, *Deuteronomy and the Hermeneutics*; and Römer, "Cult Centralization," 168–80. Calum M. Carmichael dismissed the source critical analysis of Deut 12. See Carmichael, *The Laws of Deuteronomy*, 36–37.

16. Robson, "Literary Composition of Deuteronomy," 20. Continuing, Robson explained that Moses was the dominant voice in the book; however, Moses was not the narrator of Deuteronomy (here p. 22).

The Legislative Themes of Centralization

rhetorical time frame *in* the book and against the rhetorical time frame *of* the book."[17] Reading against the rhetorical time frame in the book suggests a literal approach to Deuteronomy. In other words, Deuteronomy presents Moses preparing the Israelites to enter the land of Canaan. On the other hand, reading against the rhetorical time frame of the book suggests an exilic contextual reading.[18] Brent A. Strawn approached the issue of perspective in Deuteronomy from a slightly different point of view. He highlighted three levels of reading: (1) "the literary level of Moses in Moab addressing the second generation of Israelites who have left Egypt; (2) a monarchic audience that can be associated with Josiah's time; (3) the exilic audience reflected in chaps. 4 and 28–30, and by the use of Deuteronomy as preface to DtrH."[19]

The differences between Robson and Strawn are obvious. Yet, both men correctly identify the exilic audience as being one of the perspectives in Deuteronomy. For the purpose of this study, I will be approaching Deuteronomy, and the Enneateuch for that matter, from an exilic perspective. This approach to the perspective of the Enneateuch is not new. By adopting the perspective, I will demonstrate how the exilic compliers of the Enneateuch utilized Deut 12–18 theologically and ideologically. Moreover, the study will suggest the narrators of the so-called DH, with Deut 12–18 in mind, chronicled Israel's abhorrent disloyalty in the land of Canaan.[20] As Deuteronomy retrojects on the literary history in the Tetrateuch, the concept of centralization innovates the five legislative themes in the so-called DH. The innovation of centralization binds the Tetrateuch with the so-called DH, forming the literary history known as the Enneateuch.[21]

---

17. Ibid., 24, emphasis his.

18. Ibid., 58.

19. Strawn, "Deuteronomy," 63.

20. I use the terms author(s), narrator, and editor(s) rather than specific references to individuals allegedly responsible for writing the biblical material. The use of these titles eliminates any unwarranted discussions concerning authorship. In places, I do reference Moses as the speaker in Exodus–Deuteronomy due to his significant role in those books.

21. Describing the literary history of the Enneateuch, Diane Edelman explained, "Yet, from the well-intentioned beginnings depicted in the Pentateuch, a story of constant 'backslidings' by the people and their leaders unfolds in subsequent books (Joshua–Kings), in which Yahweh is abandoned over and over in favour of 'other gods,' thereby breaking the terms of the covenant to which their ancestors had agreed." See Edelman, *Opening the Books of Moses*, 128.

Introduction

Enneateuch theory, though not a new avenue of research, has become more attractive for redaction critics.[22] The historical development of the Enneateuch can be traced, at least in modern times, to David Noel Freedman. For almost thirty years, Freedman discussed and developed his theory that Genesis–2 Kings represented a literary continuity. He surmised that the individual books were part of the "authorized history" of the covenanted people of Yahweh. He labeled this authorized history as the "Primary History" (PH) of the HB.[23]

Ehud Ben Zvi advanced the discussion with an article in which he argued that Genesis–2 Kings shared a unique literary relationship, which he labeled the "Primary Historical Narrative" (PHN). From the outset, he recognized his PHN theory was never considered a canonical unit within ancient rabbinical writings, in later Judaism, or in any Christian group.[24] Ben Zvi maintained, however, that several features found throughout the PHN were shaped and "likely (re)read as a multi-book unit bound together by certain markers of cohesion."[25] The most striking argument for a literary unit in the PHN, according to Ben Zvi, came from the straightforward,

---

22. In 1987, David Gunn prognosticated that literary criticism would extend beyond the captivating arguments supporting the narrative segmentation known as the so-called DH and adopt a more expansive narrative block, Genesis–2 Kings. See Gunn, "New Directions," 72.

23. Freedman, "Canon of the OT," 131–32. Elsewhere, Freedman attempted to establish a relevant date for the PH. Much of his argumentation centered on 2 Kings. He argued that the conclusion of 2 Kings described Babylonian exile, and the terminus ante quem for 2 Kings was the subsequent return of the exiles, which is found in the Chronicler's History (CH). Thus, the PH must have been completed prior to the first wave of Israelites returning from exile. Moreover, the CH supports the terminus ante quem hypothesis since the book records the return of the exiles along with specific references to Cyrus and his edict. With the parameters above, the terminus a quo of the PH can be dated approximately to the Babylonian exile and the death of Gedaliah (ca. 587–582 B.C.E.), which theoretically establishes the completion of the PH shortly thereafter. See Freedman "Law and the Prophets," 252–58. Almost three decades elapsed before Freedman produced a monograph dedicated to the unity of the HB. Freedman called the combination of the Torah and the Former Prophets the "First Bible" because collectively they were the core and foundation of the remaining books of the HB. For him, Deuteronomy was literally at the center of the narrative and functioned as the apex of the entire story. See Freedman, *Unity of the Hebrew Bible*, 1–15.

24. Ben Zvi, "Looking at the Primary (Hi)story," 26–27.

25. Ibid., 27. He preferred to use the term (re)read since he postulated that these books simply were not read once, but continually by the people.

sequential narrative that began with creation of the universe (Genesis) and ended with the demise of the monarchic Judah (Kings corpus).[26]

Konrad Schmid, a Swiss scholar, has become one of the most prominent scholars of Enneateuchal theory. Schmid attempted to alleviate the tension many scholars find between the ancient Israelite traditions outlined in Genesis and the exodus-conquest tradition in Exodus–2 Kings. Through a diachronic reading of the biblical texts, Schmid concluded that Genesis–2 Kings consisted of three narratives: Genesis, Exodus–Joshua, and Judges–2 Kings. These three narratives antedate the traditional tripartite division of the HB. Within the three narratives, Schmid identified two independent traditions: the patriarchal tradition and the exodus–conquest tradition.[27] The aforementioned scholars have inspired the Enneateuchal theory discussion with others building on their seminal efforts.[28]

26. Ibid., 26–43, here p. 27. Additionally, Ben Zvi stated, "This [PHN] is not a potpourri of disparate anecdotes, short stories and unrelated books, not only because it shows a clear multi-book temporal frame in which the narrated events are anchored, but also because the events themselves are reported in a logical progression." He suggested that Genesis–2 Kings possibly belonged to a "repertoire" or collection of books that depicted and constructed broad scores of the (re)readers in "primarily sequential, narrative ways" (p. 27).

27. Schmid, *Erzväter und Exodus*, 1–55. Additionally, Schmid was able to establish what he believed to be conceptual interconnections between the two Israelite traditions. Outside the literary break of Genesis and Exodus, the other narrative breaks and historical transitions within the literary unity of the Enneateuch illustrated the redactional sensitivity to link each book with the preceding one. Thus, he believed the traditional views of the Tetrateuch, Pentateuch, Hexateuch, and so-called DH were challenged based on redactional clues found in the Enneateuch. The tension many scholars find between Genesis and the remaining books of the Enneateuch are silenced with the recognition that redactors combined the two original traditions, probably during the latest redactional level—the Persian period. The Hexateuch was structured as *Heilsgeschichte* (salvation-history), which was followed by the *Unheilsgeschichte* (judgment-history) in Judges–2 Kings (pp. 290–91). Elsewhere, Schmid discussed a possible weakness to the Enneateuchal theory. He questioned whether the content of these writings contained a logical flow. The only unifying theme in Genesis–2 Kings, according to Schmid, was the theme of country. He concluded that Genesis–Joshua recorded the Israelites' possession of the land, whereas Judges–2 Kings told about the ruin of the land. See Schmid, "Une grande historiographie," 35–46.

28. According to Reinhard G. Kratz, the narrative history described in Genesis–2 Kings was comprised of individual narratives and narrative cycles from the period before 720 B.C.E. and 587 B.C.E. Over time, these narrative histories grew into the composition of the Enneateuch (Hexateuch–Enneateuch–Pentateuch). Kratz, *Composition of the Narrative Books*, 310; idem, "Growth of the Old Testament," 482–88. Konrad Schmid and Thomas Römer edited a compendium of articles focusing on the various compositional theories of the HB in 2007. In the introductory chapter, Thomas Römer and

Introduction

Although I do adopt the overarching premise of Enneateuchal theory—the collection of traditions during the Persian period—the redactional emphasis generally associated within Enneateuchal studies will not be utilized in the current study. I am more concerned with the canonical imperative (i.e., literary relationships) within the final structure of the Enneateuch and not with the redactional history comprising the work.[29] The idea of canonical imperative implies a "method of reading" each book independently but also in accordance with the logical progression of the unified larger text.[30] For this reason, the literary history of Deuteronomy and the Enneateuch is reason enough to take a second look at the concept of centralization within a larger literary perspective.[31]

METHODOLOGICAL APPROACH

Related to a literary-critical study of the Enneateuch is my assumption that both diachronic and synchronic readings can provide valuable insights into the five legislative themes associated with the concept of centralization in Deuteronomy.[32] By focusing on the literary nature of the Enneateuch, par-

---

Schmid argued that Genesis–2 Kings should be the starting point for the reconstruction of both Israel's and Judah's histories since the materials in these books date to the second and first millennia, unlike the "classic" presentations of Israel's history written during the twentieth century. The reconstruction of this history should focus on the macrostructure of the possession of the land to its ruin. See Römer and Schmid, "Introduction," 1–8.

29. Redactional criticism continues to be dominated by European scholars. Many of the efforts of redaction critics have answered and provided alternatives to questions related to the transmission of the HB.

30. Cf. McConville, *God and Earthly Power*, 10. Along these lines, J. Gordon McConville suggested, "The traditional intra-canonical divisions of Torah, Prophets, and Writings do not tell against the point, since the canonical idea entails that ultimately all the writings in the canon should be read as constituting a unity." In a similar remark, R. Christopher Heard described Genesis–2 Kings as "one story." See Heard, "Narrative Criticism," 42.

31. Although the Enneateuch presents a complete account of the story of Israel from its origins to exile, I recognize the story consists of various traditions and sources, some of which are part of other popular canonical divisions (e.g., the Torah and the Nevi'im). The literary unity of the salvation-judgment history in the Enneateuch, however, overshadows the other canonical divisional blocks. Cf. McConville, *God and Earthly Power*, 9. Along these lines, McConville argued, "The canonical division between Torah or Pentateuch and Historical Books or Former Prophets cuts across certain narrative and theological interconnections between those blocks."

32. In fact, Gunn, a respected literary and biblical critic, described the emergence of

ticularly with an attentive eye toward these themes, I will reveal the literary strata (i.e., diachronic) and thematic developments (i.e., synchronic) that the biblical narrator(s) utilized in conveying Israel's literary history. Along the way, the discussion of sources, textual divisions, and various compositional theories will be included.

I mentioned earlier the overarching approach of this study is literary; however, it will not follow the precise mechanics of traditional literary-critical theory. Although the arguments and final conclusions will be from a literary reading of the final form of the Enneateuch, discussion of biblical texts, when appropriate and applicable, will employ a variety of methodologies including text, source, and form-critical analyses. Unlike many other Enneateuchal studies, my starting point is the canonical perspective rather than the redactional perspective. Inasmuch, canonical criticism, at least in my estimation, does not necessitate a rejection of the historical-critical methods. Furthermore, the appreciation for and application of literary-critical theory does not suggest an "a-historical" reading of the HB.

In short, my methodological approach will integrate diachronic aspects from historical-critical methods, as well as synchronic aspects from literary criticism. It is my contention that the canonical perspective will counterbalance the integration of these two differing approaches to the HB. At the crux of this methodology is the prophetic undertone of selected pericopes in Deuteronomy. The exact location of Deuteronomy within the HB—concluding the Tetrateuch and introducing the so-called DH—mandates the recognition of the book's prophetic undertone of select pericopes. By integrating diachronic and synchronic aspects, the canonical perspective structures and limits the art of interpretation within the pursuit of the literary history of the Israelites.

Naturally, I recognize that scholars have debated the value of a diachronic over and against a synchronic approach. At the essence of the issue are two questions: What type of methodological approach, historical or literary, should become the driving force behind interpretation? And, can historical and literary approaches be reconciled when interpreting the HB? The answer to the first question, as stated above, is an integrated approach that utilizes both diachronic and synchronic approaches. As for the second

---

literary criticism as a "major challenge" to the traditional methods employed by historical-critical scholars. Literary criticism, within the broader confines of biblical studies, cannot be described as instituting a genuine shift from diachronic to synchronic analysis but rather as initiating the dialogue surrounding a "normative reading" of the biblical text. See Gunn, "New Directions," 69.

Introduction

question, I believe the answer is yes, which I hope to substantiate in this study.

EXCURSUS: METHODOLOGICAL CONSIDERATIONS

I have decided to include an excursus on the integrated methodology. Throughout my training, emphasis was given primarily to source, form, and traditio-historical criticisms. Thus, to venture into literary criticism was somewhat challenging. After studying literary critical theory, the emphasis on the metanarrative, for lack of a better term, grasped my interest due in large part to the theological insights that could be gleaned. Yet, I was still struck with a conundrum: How do I integrate the critical methodologies I adhered so closely to with this new literary approach? In what follows, I outline the musings of many other scholars who have struggled with this complex issue.

Almost fifth years ago a slight shift began within biblical studies. At first the seismic shift was barely noticed; however, as the shift continued to grow a methodological movement emerged, "text-immanent exegesis." The movement focused on the meaning of biblical texts within the shape of the canon rather than dissecting the text in an attempt to uncover and recover the earlier stages behind the finalized text.[33] At the root of this movement were the "new" literary critics. The task of interpretation and exposition, however, is replete with difficult questions and textual conundrums. Recognizing this, Meir Sternberg explained,

> Every literary work opens a number of gaps that have to be filled in by the reader through the construction of hypotheses, in the light of which the various components of the work are accounted for, linked, and brought into pattern. Different gaps or systems of gaps may, however, vary in several important respects: some can, for instance, be filled in almost automatically, while others require conscious and laborious consideration; some can be filled in fully and definitely, others only partially and tentatively; some by a single, others by several (different, conflicting, or even mutually exclusive), hypotheses.[34]

---

33. John Barton coined the phrase "text-immanent exegesis" and further explained that structuralism and canonical criticism were birthed out of this new methodological paradigm. See Barton, *Reading the Old Testament*, 2.

34. Sternberg, *Expositional Modes*, 50.

The Legislative Themes of Centralization

The above quote, in essence, describes the literary work of the Enneateuch. Though this block of materials exists as an interrelated literary history—whether a story containing linear-historical themes or Yahwistic theological disclosure—the literary work contains both written and oral traditions composed by various authors and editors spanning centuries. Historical-critical scholars using a diachronic methodology have identified, isolated, and filled in many of the "gaps," to use Sternberg's designation, with hypotheses. The hypotheses proffered by historical-critical scholars became the focal point of Brevard Childs's canonical criticism. Through multiple works, Childs not only introduced a new paradigm for studying the HB, he incited a dialogue between proponents of diachronic and synchronic readings of the biblical text.

Canonical Criticism

The force driving Childs's devotion to his "canonical context" was the strained relation between the historical-critical study of the Bible and the nature in which the theological riches from the Bible were understood in the various communities of faith. For Childs, the historical-critical studies ignored the theological impetus of the Bible in regard to the communities of faith. Leveling criticism against advocates of the historical-critical study of the Bible was at the forefront of Childs's canonical context. He had three specific reservations concerning the historical-critical study of Scripture. First, he argued that the historical-critical introductions to Scripture ignore the necessity for analyzing canonical literature for use in synagogues and churches. Second, historical-critical introductions do not recognize the Israelite literature and the process involved in its formation and structure. Third, the introductions discount the relationship between the literature and the community that cherished the work. In response, Childs believed a combination of the "canon" and "criticism" allowed for a holistic understanding of the HB in "true historical" and "theological dimensions."[35]

Naturally, Childs identified the various phases of canonization within the corpus but qualified its use for the finalization of the "limits of scripture." By his definition, the canonization of Scripture must include a hermeneutical process that incorporated both history and theology. As a result, Childs vehemently opposed the literary process used in the historical-critical method. To illustrate the historical importance of his proposal,

35. Childs, *Introduction to the Old Testament*, 3–58; idem, *Old Testament Theology*.

Childs analyzed five essentials shared between the canon and criticism. First, Childs addressed the descriptive nature of canonical analysis, which he classified as "Exegesis in a Canonical Context." He maintained that the canonical analysis should focus only on the final form of the text. Second, Childs contrasted his canonical approach to other approaches. He argued that the canonical approach shared similarities with the new literary critical method since advocates of both sought to keep the integrity of the text as a focal point. Third, Childs examined the importance of the final form of the text because it provided the perfect framework for hermeneutical analysis. Fourth, he discussed the canonical process and the shaping of Scripture. The canonization process not only validated the literary process but also aided in its development. Once closed, the canon became the *Sitz im Leben* for the Jewish community. Fifth, after comparing the canonical approach to other methodologies, he analyzed Scripture and tradition.[36]

Diachronic and Synchronic Readings

In *Moses and the Deuteronomist*, Polzin astutely asked, "Should one's approach be primarily historical or literary, diachronic or synchronic?"[37] The basic understanding of diachronic refers to the depth and dimensions of the biblical texts. As an interpretive method, scholars utilize a diachronic study in an attempt to uncover and assess the various layers of composition. A synchronic reading of biblical texts is described accurately in terms of a horizontal dimension, one that interprets the biblical texts on one layer in

---

36. Ibid., 59–106. Many articles have been devoted to the review and critique of Childs's canonical approach. James Barr, however, leveled the harshest and most complete critique of Childs's canonical context. See Barr, "Childs' Introduction to the Old Testament," 12–23; idem, *Concept of Biblical Theology*, 387–438.

37. Polzin, *Moses and the Deuteronomist*, 1. Polzin reduced the diachronic/synchronic assumptions into two assertions. First, a historical-critical assessment and understanding of the biblical text is "necessary for an *adequate* scholarly understanding." Second, a literary assessment of the biblical text is "necessary for even a *preliminary* scholarly understanding" (pp. 3–5, emphasis his). From these two assertions, Polzin proffered a third assertion: "Both literary and historical criticism of the Bible uncover hermeneutical principles within the text that appear to be at fundamental odds with prevailing views on the nature of historical and literary scholarship, views based upon the supposed similarity of both disciplines to the natural sciences" (p. 7). For a similar treatment, see idem, *Biblical Structuralism*, 16–18. Additionally, M. A. O'Brien assessed Deuteronomic research, particularly the historical-critical contributions. See O'Brien, "Book of Deuteronomy," 95–128.

The Legislative Themes of Centralization

its present or final form.³⁸ On the surface, the two manners in which scholars study the HB, diachronic and synchronic, appear at odds. A diachronic reading focuses primarily on reconstructing the layers and sources of history, whereas a synchronic reading is concerned with literary elements.

Barr argued that a synchronic reading, like a diachronic one, could be a historical enterprise, particularly when the question of "time" is asked. If a synchronic reading examines the biblical text "all at one time," what is the length of this time and what is its purpose? Within a synchronic reading of the biblical text, time represents at least a thousand years, a conservative estimate regarding the length in which the HB was produced, redacted, and finalized. The HB is a composite made up of various sources that individually must be distinguished. The process of distinguishing sources from one another is, in essence, a reaffirmation of the traditional historical-critical approach. Synchrony, then, is achieved by separating the various sources into "synchronic states" within the larger corpus of the HB.³⁹ The tenuous relationship between diachronic and synchronic readings of biblical texts has forced scholars to draw battle lines in the sand; however, Barr has summarized and offered an alternative to the current state of affairs regarding this relationship:

> Some think that synchronic exegesis should concentrate on the text itself and ignore questions of the historical background, what may have been thought previously, what circumstances may have occasioned the creation of the text, and even in extreme cases what may have been the purpose and thinking of the writer in creating the text. The text itself, and not the background or mode of its origin, should be central to exegesis. Second, and perhaps more prominent, is the question of putatively composite texts, where it is suggested that two or more sources have previously existed and have been combined with greater or less skill to form the existing text. In this case the idea of synchronic exegesis is that only the final text matters and that the existence of previous versions is irrelevant. The apparent difficulties and inconsistencies, the presence of which has led to the identification of previous versions, are in fact not difficulties or inconsistencies but are highly subtle evidences of the writer's skill and literary talent, qualities which

---

38. See Berlin, *Poetics and Interpretation*, 111; Cotterell and Turner, *Linguistics and Biblical Interpretation*, 25; and Boorer, "Importance of a Diachronic Approach," 195.

39. Barr, "The Synchronic, the Diachronic and the Historical?" 1–3.

the plodding minds of critical scholars were too lacking in insight to detect.[40]

The two above types of interpretation emphasize the very question(s) relating to composite texts, yet it is completely normal, if not logical, to move from a "historical paradigm" to a "literary one."[41]

The idea that a historical paradigm leads to a literary one implies that a diachronic and synchronic reading of biblical texts can be done in conjunction. The two forms of reading the biblical text are not isolated from each other. Diachronic is not simply historically oriented—it is a literary study, but not in the terms of the "new" literary criticism. On the other hand, a synchronic reading is not a-historical just because it is concerned primarily with the final text. Individually speaking, each form breaks down because exegesis and literary theory cannot be separated entirely. In fact, an "interdeterminate mixture" of the two is needed, but due to fears and presuppositions, many biblical scholars are in one of the camps rather than both.[42]

Literary Criticism and Diachronic/Synchronic Readings

Rolf Rendtorff entered the fray with his discussion concerning the consequences of dating texts. He argued for an equilibrium approach that combines the "new" with the "old." Rendtorff recognized the usefulness of dating a text when a deeper understanding was the primary objective, not when the art of dating "becomes an end in itself." He would prefer to interpret the text in its "given form" while still maintaining some relationship with the *Literarkritik* that dominated the landscape of biblical studies for decades. In essence, he suggested that the old diachronic aspects of the *Literarkritik* and its derivatives must be combined with the synchronic

---

40. Ibid., 8–9.

41. Ibid., 9.

42. In 1993, David J. A. Clines realized that an "interdeterminate mixture" consisting of a diachronic/synchronic approach was needed when examining the biblical text. He tested his theory at the joint meeting of Het Oudtestamentisch Werkgezelschap and the Society for Old Testament Study in Kampen, Netherlands. Clines subjected attendees to various exercises including word associations. Clines concluded that the attendees shared an "interdeterminate mixture" of methodology, though non-cognizant. See Clines, "Beyond Synchronic/Diachronic," 52–71.

The Legislative Themes of Centralization

aspects of the "new" literary criticism.[43] Along similar trains of thought, Jon D. Levenson argued, "The price of recovering the *historical* context of the sacred books has been the erosion of the largest *literary* contexts that undergird the traditions that claim to be based upon them."[44] To combine old diachronic aspects with synchronic aspects means attention must be given to the prophetic undertones of select pericopes. In other words, the diachronic assessments and dating of selected pericopes must give way to the given form (=final form).

In reference to the current study, I recognize the important contributions of diachronic analysis. Yet, without an integrated method (i.e., diachronic and synchronic), these contributions continue to be part of a larger, cyclical research pattern. What do I mean by this statement? Over the last fifty years, the JEDP theory popularized by Julius Wellhausen has morphed into a variety of adaptations. In recent years, several American scholars have reenergized the Wellhausen model by introducing a nuanced Pentateuchal source theory. On the other hand, other American scholars, as well as many European scholars, continue to emphasize the importance of redactional criticism, particularly with regard to the Pentateuch and Yehud. The latter positions are repackaging the supplementary and fragmentary hypotheses advocated in the eighteenth to twentieth centuries. The contributions from both positions are scholarly, thought provoking, and, more importantly, viable explanations to many Pentateuchal issues.

As I survey the field of modern Pentateuch studies, two questions continue to challenge me: What will Pentateuchal criticism look like fifty years from now? How will scholars perceive our contributions? Naturally, most of us will not live long enough to discover the answer to either question. But, if the next fifty years is anything like the previous fifty, the paradigm will shift once again (and maybe several times). All the enlightening contributions over the last twenty years will have served as a means to an end that is no longer the standard view. I know that my position sounds pessimistic and dismissive, but it really is not meant to sound that way. In my opinion, anytime we focus on interpreting the HB through one lens (i.e., diachronic or synchronic), we are missing the larger picture. If we cannot find a way

---

43. Rendtorff, "Paradigm Is Changing," 50–53.

44. Levenson, *Hebrew Bible*, 4, emphasis his. Clines and Exum explained that the old German literary criticism termed *Literarkritik* has very little in common with the "new" literary criticism of the HB. The primary difference between the two is that the "new" literary criticism is not a historical discipline but rather a literary one. See Clines and Exum, "New Literary Criticism," 11.

Introduction

to integrate the diachronic and synchronic methods, or diachronic with some other method, we will continue to shift the focus within Pentateuchal studies and, in a sense, recreate the wheel every few decades. However, if scholars can begin to integrate these allegedly incongruous methods, a more stable platform can exist within Pentateuchal studies.

To me, Sternberg identified this perplexing issue. He noted the various methodological approaches to studying the HB, each of which is generally distinguished by subject matter (e.g., theological, historical, linguistic, genetic, and literary). The individual approaches fall under two broader categories: source-oriented and discourse-oriented inquiries. The difference between the two categories is in the type of questions the proponents ask. In short, the source-oriented inquiry is concerned with the *Sitz im Leben* of the biblical world. From a theological perspective, the source-oriented inquiry is an attempt to piece together a coherent portrait of the ancient Israelite religion. Historians are concerned with uncovering what happened to the ancient Israelite religion. Linguists examine the Hebrew language system in an effort to understand the Bible. The geneticists focus on the "real-life processes" that ultimately shaped the biblical text: documents and traditions, oral and written materials, authors and schools, redaction techniques, etc.[45] On the other hand, the primary goal of discourse-oriented inquiry is not to understand in totality the "realities behind the text" but rather "the text itself as a pattern of meaning and effect."[46] The discourse-oriented inquiry is the primary methodology of literary critics and a synchronic method for analyzing biblical narratives.

There are two differences between my position and that of Sternberg. First, Sternberg differentiated and isolated the two methods whereas I propose the two be integrated. Second, Sternberg's emphasis on the discourse-oriented inquiry does not generally identify biblical law as being a "discourse-oriented inquiry." Deuteronomy, probably more than any other Pentateuchal book, can be described as didactic, which makes the book ideological.[47] Sternberg described how "didactic genre moves beyond

---

45. Sternberg, *Poetics of Biblical Narrative*, 14–15.

46. Ibid., 15. Sternberg emphasized that a discourse-oriented inquiry dealt with the significance of the language (i.e., metaphor, epigram, dialogue, and cycle) in a specific context rather than a broader one.

47. Sternberg defined didacticism as "ideological writing" and "the dividing line is precisely where ethics and aesthetics meet to generate the *art* of persuasion." See Sternberg, *The Poetics of Biblical Narrative*, 483, emphasis his. Robert Alter described the Book of Deuteronomy as "the most sustained deployment of rhetoric in the Bible." Alter

The Legislative Themes of Centralization

commitment to self immolation: it not only advances a doctrine but also ruthlessly subordinates the whole discourse—the plot, the characters, the arena, the language, their ordering and interlinkage—to the exigencies of indoctrination."[48] Thus the indoctrination, to use Sternberg's designation or ideology of Deuteronomy is persuasive, in that, the reader is motivated to listen and obey.[49] As a result, the motivation to listen and obey carries with it a sense of evaluation. Thus, Deuteronomy's ideological nature should be understood also as evaluative.[50]

Two scholars seem to share my sentiments regarding the relationship between law and narrative. In a relatively small essay, Otto Kaiser argued that biblical law was the "center" of the HB. Through a theological and existential analysis of the law, Kaiser concluded that the only way the Israelites could experience or participate in the "promised salvation" was by obeying the law.[51] Second, Bernard Levinson questioned the growing trend of comprehending the HB through narrative (contra Sternberg). Although he recognized the importance of narrative criticism, he suggested that focusing primarily on narrative and excluding other literary genres was erroneous. For Levinson, the exclusion of the law codes from literary criticism was a glaring omission of Israelite revelation. In short, he countered the work of Sternberg and other narrative critics by arguing for the centrality of the law codes in the HB. He argued that the HB law codes must be "made central to a theoretical conception of revelation" and must be "made central to the literary study of the Bible."[52] In his eyes, the legal texts were not inferior to narrative texts but rather "reflected unique textuality" and pointed to "techniques of authorship that should be of most interest to literary theorists."[53]

---

argued that the rhetoric of Deuteronomy was absent in the central core (12–26). Thus, the rhetoric of Deuteronomy was used to "underwrite the authority" of the legal portions. See Alter, *Five Books of Moses*, 869.

48. Sternberg, *Poetics of Biblical Narrative*, 37.

49. Strawn, "Deuteronomy," 64.

50. Along these lines, Polzin noted, "It comprises that system of viewing the world according to which the work is conceptually unified. It is the 'ultimate semantic authority' of a work." See Polzin, *Moses and the Deuteronomist*, 44.

51. Kaiser, "Law as Center," 93–103.

52. Levinson, "Right Chorale," 131.

53. Ibid. In addition, he added, "If biblical law indeed constitutes a stumbling block to a literary approach, the law is nonetheless essential to a theory of revelation and of the communicative aims of Israelite authors. . . . The study of biblical law is also essential specifically to the *literary* study of the Bible" (p. 146, emphasis his). Additionally, David Daube suggested a reverse analytical trajectory, that is, using biblical law to illuminate

Introduction

METHOD AND CENTRALIZATION

Kaiser and Levinson aptly noted how the study of the biblical law codes should include an assessment of poetics (i.e., literary criticism) and hermeneutics. With the excursus above, I have shown how other scholars have identified the traditional dichotomy between diachronic and synchronic methodologies. However, it is my contention, and others, that by combining diachronic and synchronic analysis "a theory of revelation" can be substantiated.[54] Similarly, Levinson argued that diachronic and synchronic analysis could not be bifurcated in application.[55] He argued that diachronic and synchronic analysis provided structure and significance to the biblical text: "Viewing the text diachronically in many instances reveals the dynamics of the formation of Israelite literature and the particular literary creativity of biblical authors and editors."[56]

Before beginning my study, several points of reference must be made. First, the law codes of the HB are central to the exposition of revelatory content, as well as the comprehension of its literature. Whereas anonymity characterizes Hebrew narratives, the law codes are characterized by the convention of voice—"the divine or prophetic attribution of law." This convention of voice in the law codes underscores the necessity for recovering the "concept of authority in ancient Israel."[57] By in large, the law codes in the HB have been overlooked by literary critics due in large part to the perception that the texts should be read as legislative works rather than literary

---

the biblical narrative. See Daube, *Studies in Biblical Law*, 1–73. On the other hand, Tod Linafelt explained that the legal texts "demand and reward the close reading that one might associate with poetry and narrative," but he readily described the law codes in the Pentateuch as discursive rather than literary. See Linafelt, "Prolegomena to Meaning," 68.

54. Levinson, "Right Chorale," 131.

55. Ibid., 135. He went on to argue that restricting diachronic analysis of the HB risked "detextualizing" the Bible. Instead, he argued that the elements that narrative critics obscured were the very ones that they should have the most interest in studying (i.e., law codes). This point made by Levinson is foundational for the current study. In essence, I will bridge the gap between two methodological camps that traditionally have not seen eye to eye. Ultimately, this bridging of methodologies within the Deuteronomic law code will provide a new hermeneutical lens for interpreting chs. 12–18.

56. Ibid., 135–36.

57. Ibid., 146–48. For Levinson, the biblical concept of revelation was legal revelation because Yahweh was attributed as the author of the law codes in the HB, unlike the contrasting cuneiform legal texts that had a royal speaker (i.e., Hammurabi's Code). In the HB, the authorship of all the law was Yahweh either directly or through his "prophetic intermediary."

The Legislative Themes of Centralization

ones.[58] Second, the interrelatedness of narrative and law is emphasized by literary conventions and motifs. Some biblical narratives "present themselves as telling a legal story" and, for this reason, the two types of literary genres must not be separated but studied critically together.[59] Third, with regard to Deuteronomy, numerous literary scholars omit any substantial assessment of the text, whereas historical-critical scholars gravitate more toward the historical and redactional implications of the book.

In essence, this study will build upon a diachronic (source-oriented) and synchronic (discourse-oriented) analysis of the five legislative themes and their relationship to the concept of centralization. By doing so, I will provide another perspective on the literary structure, linguistical components, theology, and ideology of Deuteronomy. The study will reveal how literary criticism can shed light on the concept of centralization within the broader literary landscape of the Enneateuch. Also, the study of the concept of centralization in Deut 12–18 will place the legislative materials in these chapters within the unifying and overarching theme of the Enneateuch. Focusing on the relationship between Deuteronomy and the so-called DH, Polzin provided a poignant evaluation: "We can see that the over-all composition of Deuteronomy is one in which we read how Moses is described as declaring and interpreting the word of God as a panoramic preview of how the Deuteronomic narrator will describe and interpret the word of Moses in Joshua–2 Kings."[60] Later, he concluded that Deuteronomy provided readers with a "bird's-eye view of the entire history of Israel shortly to be recounted in detail in Joshua–2 Kings."[61] The editors of the so-called DH recognized the rhetorical nature of the Deuteronomic concept of centralization. The centralization mandate created a comparative discourse through which the so-called DH must be read. Thus, the canonical shaping of the Enneateuch, especially the demise of the kingdom in the Kings corpus, strengthens the rhetorical value of centralization in Deuteronomy. From this canonical perspective, Deuteronomy functions prophetically.

Thus, the task for carrying out this study begins in ch. 2 with a brief review of the scholarly literature concerning the Deuteronomic concept of centralization of the cult. In chs. 3–7, I examine the five legislative themes in Deut 12–18 within the broader literary history of the Enneateuch. Included

58. Ibid., 147.
59. See Barmash, "Narrative Quandary," 5.
60. Polzin, *Moses and the Deuteronomist*, 48.
61. Ibid., 72.

in each chapter is a synchronic analysis of each theme. The synchronic reading of the material does not and should not negate the importance of studying the diachronic strata and traditions within the Enneateuch. What it does provide is an alternative form of reading Israel's PH, mainly through the synchronic lens of the Deuteronomic concept of centralization. For this reason, the diachronic arguments will not always carry over into the synchronic reading.

In ch. 8, an assessment of the themes is given from the Enneateuchal perspective, along with some literary-critical thoughts concerning the theological and ideological structure of the Enneateuch. This step will focus primarily on a synchronic reading of the five legislative themes throughout the Enneateuch in an effort to uncover the extent to which the Deuteronomic concept of centralization conjoins the Tetrateuch and the so-called DH through ideology and theology. In sum, my research will provide a plausible exilic understanding of the Deuteronomic concept of centralization. In the remaining chapters, I will suggest that the five legislative themes of centralization will not be maintained within the divided monarchy. As a result, my research will show how the centralization mandate is an important part of the utopian world of Deuteronomy, particularly in the eyes of the exilic audience.

2

Approaching the Concept of Centralization

THE ROLE OF DEUTERONOMY has been examined in relation to the Pentateuch, the Hexateuch, the Deuteronomistic History, and now the Enneateuch.[1] The purpose of Deuteronomy and its compositional development are a point of contention among many scholars.[2] In short, the purpose of the book is related to the date and province of its composition: Is the book

---

1. Several summaries of the derivation and expansion of Pentateuchal criticism have appeared over the years. For example, see Nicholson, *Pentateuch in the Twentieth Century*, 3–28 and Van Seters, "Law (Torah)," 3–52. The Hexateuch theory can be traced to the works of Wellhausen and Gerhard von Rad. See Wellhausen, *Composition des Hexateuchs*; idem, *Prolegomena*; and Rad, "Form-Critical Problem," 1–78; idem, *OTT*, 1:129–35. Jean-Louis Ska provided a helpful discussion on the development of Hexateuchal theory prior to von Rad. See Ska, *Reading the Pentateuch*, 4; cf. Auld, *Joshua, Moses and the Land*, 1–5. In 1943, Noth challenged the state of HB studies with his now-famous, *Deuteronomistic History*. Since his seminal argument, the post-Nothian Deuteronomistic History theory has taken on various nomenclatures, which have been discussed and critiqued in great detail. See Alexander, *Origin and Development*; Römer and De Pury, "Deuteronomistic Historiography," 24–141; and Römer, *So-Called Deuteronomistic History*. The historical development of the Enneateuch was discussed in ch. 1. In recent years, more Enneateuchal theorists have provided viable contributions. Aurelius, *Zukunft Jenseits Des Gerichts*; Römer and Schmid, *Les dernières rédactions du Pentateuque*; Braulik, "'Die Weisung und das Gebot' im Enneateuch," 115–40; Dozeman, "Context of the Enneateuch," 175–89; Schmid, "Prolegomena zur Enneateuchfrage," 1–14; and Dozeman et al., *Pentateuch, Hexateuch, or Enneateuch?*

2. For an excellent, yet concise, summation of scholarly approaches to Deuteronomy, see Robson, "Literary Composition of Deuteronomy," 19–59.

pre-monarchal, monarchal, exilic, or postexilic?[3] For many, the compositional date, and to some degree the purpose, is related to the concept of centralization. For purposes of clarity and brevity, I will mainly focus on approaches to the centralization mandate within Deuteronomy.

In ch. 1, I briefly discussed the significance of de Wette on the field of biblical studies. He was first modern scholar to identify the lawbook in 2 Kgs 22:8 as an *urdeuteronomium*.[4] His correlation of an *urdeuteronomium* with Josiah's reform certainly impacted Wellhausen's approach to the HB. Like de Wette, the weight and influence of Wellhausen continues to influence Deuteronomic studies. For Wellhausen, Deuteronomy, at its foundation, was built upon the Book of the Covenant (Exod 20:22—23:19) but preceded the exilic Priestly Code. Although the Book of the Covenant and Deuteronomy differed somewhat, the issue of centralization and the innovations of reform led Wellhausen to differentiate even further between the two sources. The innovations of reform, specifically the "polemical and reforming attitude," introduced in Deut 12 corresponded with the "attacks" against the במות by the reforming party in Jerusalem. Whereas the Book of the Covenant reflected the "pre-prophetic period" of the Israelite cult, Deuteronomy became the "legal expression" of Israel's "second period of struggle and transition." In Deuteronomy, centralized worship was an assumption, but this concept did not come to fruition until the Priestly Code.[5] For this reason, Wellhausen explained that in Deuteronomy "the unity of the cultus is *commanded*; in the Priestly Code it is *presupposed*."[6]

Like the Book of the Covenant, the ideals of Deuteronomy were quite different from the Priestly Code. Deuteronomy was in the "midst of movement and conflict" and declaring with clarity a reforming intention away from the "what we do here this day" tradition. On the other hand, the Priestly writings had the aim of Deuteronomy in mind—centralized worship—yet, it was free from the struggle and conflict rooted in the Deuteronomic discourse. Only Deuteronomy recognized the onerous and even spiraling condition of the nation that was anxious to embrace a "strict monotheism." Thus, Deuteronomy was written to combat these tensions

---

3. Several succinct descriptions of the scholarly research in Deuteronomy have appeared over the years. For example, see Preuss, *Deuteronomium*; Collier, "Problem of Deuteronomy," 215–33; Römer, "Book of Deuteronomy," 178-212; O'Brien, "Book of Deuteronomy," 95–128; and Robson, "Literary Composition of Deuteronomy," 19–59.

4. See ch. 1, n. 11.

5. Wellhausen, *Prolegomena*, 32–35.

6. Ibid., 35, emphasis his.

The Legislative Themes of Centralization

facing the people of Judah, albeit through the investiture of the historical character Moses.[7]

In the wake of de Wette and Wellhausen, Samuel R. Driver continued the progression of solidifying Deuteronomy as one of the most important books in the HB. The influence of his monumental commentary, although dated by today's standards, still reverberates through scholarly circles. For Driver, Deuteronomy embodied "spiritual lessons and experiences" over many generations, not simply a single lifetime.[8] Even though the foundation of Deuteronomy was the laws from JE, the book presented the material as Deuteronomic discourses through a combination of historical, legislative, and *paraenetic* elements. For Driver, the *paraenetic* was the most important of the three since it inculcated "fundamental religious and moral principles." Due to the entrapment of idolatry, the message of Deuteronomy proclaimed an unabated gratitude and obedience to Yahweh.[9] The centrality of the law code was given pride of place, yet these laws represented more than mere legal statutes. Within and through these legal statutes, the writer expressed an ethical and religious spirit.[10]

Deuteronomy, according to Driver, "combines the spirit of the prophet and the spirit of the legislator: it is a *prophetical law-book*, a law-book in which civil and ceremonial statutes become the expression of a great spiritual and moral ideal, which is designed to comprehend and govern the entire life of the community."[11] The significance of the book, however, must not be separated from its place within the history of Israel. For Driver, the book was written in the seventh century B.C.E. during the reign of Manasseh and the centralization of worship by Josiah was a polemic against syncretism and idolatrous practices (2 Kgs 21:1–9).[12] Moreover, he interpreted the centralization of the cult as a "corollary of the monotheistic idea" attempting to differentiate Yahwism from other ANE conceptions of worship. Furthermore, centralization intended to stifle any syncretistic confusion of Yahweh and the other ANE deities. Thus, the unification of worship

---

7. Ibid., 35–37.
8. Driver, *Deuteronomy*, xiii.
9. Ibid., viii–xix.
10. Ibid., xxvi.
11. Ibid., xxvi–xxvii, emphasis his.
12. Ibid., xxvii.

at the chosen place of Yahweh was a "providential stage in the purification of the popular idea of God."[13]

At the turn of the twentieth century two questions continued to dominate the landscape concerning the concept of centralization of the cult. Does the Deuteronomic mandate for centralization symbolize a progression of central sanctuary locales during Israel's history?[14] Or, does the mandate specifically refer to the temple of Jerusalem? This debate, however, has been overshadowed by the pervasive discussion on the origin of the centralization of the cult motif in Deuteronomy, due in large part to the influential works of de Wette, Wellhausen, and Driver. Generally speaking, the basic arguments fit within three broad categories.[15] The first argument parallels the central shrine described in Deuteronomy with the overall characteristic of the amphictyonic center.[16] A second argument places the

---

13. Ibid., xxix. Many scholars have recognized the centralization of the cult mandate in Deuteronomy as a uniquely monotheistic element. Concerning this idea, Frank Crüsemann explained, "Cult centralization is the shape which Deuteronomy gives to the first commandment. To be sure, cult unity is never based in the unity of God. Nevertheless, we cannot doubt that there is a correlation. The only question is *how* we should think about it.... The one YHWH is to be associated with a single shrine." See Crüsemann, *The Torah*, 222, emphasis his. The Deuteronomic concept of centralization, according to Richard Nelson, "combines a characteristically utopian flavor with pragmatic considerations." The concept of centralization, then, was a "radical cure" for the rampant idolatry by the Israelites. By emphasizing the centrality of worship, Deuteronomy safeguarded the "Yahweh alone" concept in the first commandment. See Nelson, *Deuteronomy*, 146–47.

14. Several scholars have advocated the evolution of central sanctuary locales but have dramatically different conclusions regarding the book itself. See Oestreicher, *Das deuteronomische Grundgesetz*; Welch, *Code of Deuteronomy*; Wenham, "Deuteronomy and the Central Sanctuary," 103–18; McConville, *Law and Theology*, 29–35; idem, "Time, Place and the Deuteronomic Altar-Law," 89–139; Niehaus, "Central Sanctuary," 3–30; Pitkänen, *Central Sanctuary*; and Vogt, *Deuteronomic Theology*, 42–51; idem, "Centralization and Decentralization," 118–38.

15. Due to the diminishing number of scholars who advocate a Mosaic dating of Deuteronomy, the basic tenets will be overlooked. This decision, however, should not overshadow some of the scholarly contributions regarding the concept of centralization. Most Mosaic advocates of Deuteronomy believe the book was "one of anticipation," meaning Yahweh would choose a location at a later date. Jeffrey Niehaus was critical of the argument equating the centralization mandate with the Josianic reforms: "The fact that Deuteronomy 12:5 was not perfectly fulfilled before Solomon's temple, or even after, does not require the conclusion that it was written as part of a reform effort in Josiah's day, any more than Israel's persistent syncretism, from the wilderness wanderings onward, necessitates a seventh century date from Deuteronomy's polemic against idolatry." See Niehaus, "Central Sanctuary," 17.

16. For example, see Wijngaards, *Dramatization of Salvific History*, 23ff.

concept during the reign of Hezekiah since he was the first to attempt the centralization of worship in Jerusalem.[17] The final argument maintains that the concept of centralization was a product of the seventh century B.C.E. related directly to the Josianic reforms and eradication of idolatry from all the extant high places.[18]

These three categories are concerned with the historical timetable of centralization; however, more important to the task at hand is the theological implications attributed to the Deuteronomic concept of centralization.

CENTRALIZATION WITH THE ACADEMY

Since de Wette, Wellhausen, and Driver there has been no shortage of theories related to Deuteronomic concept of centralization. The scholarly adumbrations below are some of the most influential and/or controversial. The discussion, however, should not be considered exhaustive. The diversity among these proposals substantiates the importance of the Deuteronomic concept of centralization, as well as its historical allusiveness. For this reason, I divide the discussion into manageable subheads: the centralization as the center of Deuteronomy, centralization as a method for reform, centralization as a succession of altars, centralization and Deuteronomic name theology, and centralization as a revolution/innovation.

---

17. See Rowley, "The Prophet Jeremiah," 164; idem, "Hezekiah's Reform," 395–431; Nicholson, "Centralization of the Cult," 380–89; idem, *Deuteronomy and Tradition*; Rofé, "Centralization of Worship in Deuteronomy," 221–26; Lohfink, "Deuteronomy," 231; and Braulik, "Joy of the Feast," 29–33.

18. For example, see Albertz, *History of Israelite Religion*, 1:195–231. Ska provided a similar synopsis. He argued the centralization of the cult was in response to Assyrian invasions, both in Israel and Judah. Thus, Deuteronomy "'unifies' by asserting that Israel constitutes one people with one God and one temple." The unification of Israel, however, did not take place until the time of Josiah, given Assyria's decline in power during this period. See Ska, *Reading the Pentateuch*, 188–89. Additionally, Menahem Haran argued Deuteronomy was at the core of the Josianic reforms whereas the Priestly source heavily influenced the reforms of Hezekiah. See Haran, *Temples and Temple Service*, 132–48. Although Jack Lundbom believed Deut 1–28 was fundamental in the reforms of Hezekiah, he dismissed the notion that Deuteronomy was the law book discovered in 2 Kgs 22–23. Due to the similarities between the Song of Moses in Deut 32 and 2 Kgs 22:16–20, he concluded that the law book in the Josianic narrative was none other than the Song of Moses. See Lundbom, "Lawbook of the Josianic Reform," 293–302; idem, *Deuteronomy*, 16, 442–47. On the other hand, McConville rejected the connection between Deuteronomy and Joshia's programme of reform. See McConville, *Deuteronomy*, 30–33, 216–17.

Centralization as the Center of Deuteronomy

Ingrid Hjelm offered a different interpretation than that of Driver. For her the primary goal of the Deuteronomic concept of centralization was not the location of cult worship on Gerizim or in Jerusalem. The purpose of these paradigmatic phrases extended beyond a thematic sublevel within Deuteronomy in that collectively they constructed the overall purpose of book. Thus, the centralization of cult in Deuteronomy heightened the authority of the temple and priesthood, and protected the institution of the priests and the Levites. This provisional component, then, made the centralization of the cult a "device of cult control" and primarily served the king's interests.[19]

Centralization as a Method for Reform

Several scholars take a benign treatment of the Deuteronomic concept of centralization. That is to say, these scholars interpret the concept as a movement of historical reformation. For example, Ernest Nicholson favored a "two-campaign theory," consisting of the Hezekiah narrative, the surrendering and submitting to Sennacherib (2 Kgs 18:13–16), and Sennacherib's historical account of the events. Moreover, he suggested that Hezekiah centralized the cult during the intermediate period when Assyria was fighting the Egyptians. Thus, the "two-campaign theory" provided balance for interpreting the centralization of the cult since it formed a historical relationship with the reign of Hezekiah.[20] In the Kings corpus, however, the centralization of the cult, along with the eradication of idolatry and destruction of the high places throughout the land, became the defining judgment for each king, not just Hezekiah.[21]

Yoshihide Suzuki argued that Josiah had the Deuteronomic law code written in an attempt to reorganize the monarchical administration. Using Mosaic instruction not only aided in the codification of the law code, but it also established the "legal standard of the name of Yahweh." Moreover, the Mosaic pseudonym of the law code countered an "antireformation group" in Jerusalem. The benign centralization motif, therefore, was constructed

---

19. Hjelm, "Cult Centralization," 298–309. Ingrid Hjelm constructed her "device of cult control" theory around Josephus's writings about Onias, Ptolemy, and Queen Cleopatra (*Ant* 13:65–68).

20. Nicholson, "Centralization of the Cult," 380–89.

21. Nicholson, *Deuteronomy and Tradition*, 28.

The Legislative Themes of Centralization

as a "strategy of reformation" that would aid in the construction of a new national structure substantiated not by tradition but Mosaic Yahwism.[22]

Centralization as a Succession of Altars

Gordon J. Wenham adapted John Wijngaards's theory that Deuteronomy was written sometime during the united monarchy and that the concept of centralization in the book actually represented a series of sanctuaries in ancient Israel. He readily admitted that Jerusalem functioned as a religious center during the monarchic period, even though much of its prestige derived from the erection of the temple during the reign of Solomon. Wenham also recognized that the first king to centralize all worship in Jerusalem was Hezekiah, but in the end, his policies never truly materialized. Through the efforts of Josiah, the temple functioned as the lone sanctuary in Judah. Like Hezekiah, however, the reforms of Josiah did not continue after his unfortunate death since high places reemerged throughout the land. According to Wenham, during the exile the centralized worship of Yahweh became a reality. Though the concept of centralization was strictly a policy of Hezekiah and Josiah, the origin of the Deuteronomic concept predated both kings. Naturally, both kings, through their reforms, attempted to centralize the worship of Yahweh to one sanctuary, which limited all worship in the land. The designation to sacrifice on Mount Ebal (Deut 27), however, made any attempt to relate Deuteronomy to the Josianic reforms implausible. Since Mount Ebal was listed specifically, the natural argument appeared to favor a northern provenance for Deuteronomy. If true, then, the book was a product of the official royal court or a sectarian group.[23]

In an attempt to counterbalance de Wette and the largely Wellhausenian consensus within Pentateuchal studies, Pekka Pitkänen provided a detailed exegetical investigation of the relationship between the Pentateuchal altar laws in the Priestly writings and Deuteronomy (Exod 20:22–26; Lev 17; Deut 12; 16:21–22). The purpose for his study was an attempt to understand and, at some level, reveal the dependency between these texts concerning the central sanctuary and Deuteronomic concept of centralization. Beyond the confines of the Pentateuchal altar laws, Pitkänen investigated other biblical texts deemed applicable to the larger issue of centralized worship. Succinctly, then, Deuteronomy and its focus on the centralization of

22. Suzuki, "'Place Which Yahweh,'" 338–52.
23. Wenham, "Deuteronomy and the Central Sanctuary," 103–18.

the cult suggested a textual dependency on the Priestly writings and the Book of the Covenant. To support his conclusion, he compared the textual presentations of the Passover (Exod 12–13; Deut 16:1–8) and surmised that the Priestly material identified the importance of the central sanctuary but never demanded centralization, whereas Deuteronomy portrayed centralization as ideal. In other words, the Priestly material must be understood as "acentralized" when compared to the "centralized" Deuteronomy. From this perspective in literary dependency, he placed Deuteronomy as the latest literary component of the Pentateuch.[24] By way of conclusion, he explained, "Local altars are not places of Yahweh's dwelling, and are thus conceptually subordinate to the central sanctuary. However, Yahweh promises to 'come' to worshipers at local altars which have been built at an appropriate place."[25]

Centralization and Deuteronomic Name Theology

The Deuteronomic name theology derives its title from the Qal infinitive phrase "to put his name there" (לשום את-שמו שם) and the Piel infinitive phrase "make his name dwell there" (לשכן שמו שם). Variants of the name theology idiom occur eight times in Deuteronomy, all of which accompany a centralization motif (12:5, 11, 21; 14:24; 16:2, 6, 11; 26:2). The contribution by von Rad concerning the centralization of the cult and the Deuteronomic name theology was interrelated with his theory concerning the origins of the book. Von Rad did not think every occurrence of the centralization motif was revolutionary for its time. In fact, he contended that several of the laws in Deuteronomy seemed to allude to the demand for the centralization of the cult. To substantiate his claim, he questioned the revolutionary characteristics generally attributed to the laws requiring centralization. Judges and its emphasis on the ark at Shiloh functioned as a cultic center, one in which the tribes of Israel visited during pilgrimage festivals. Furthermore, Judges did not prescribe sacrifices, save those offerings at the place "chosen by Yahweh" (i.e., firstlings and tithes). In short, the author of Deuteronomy was faced with secularization stemming from the decay portrayed during the time of the judges. Deuteronomy as a whole, in particular the mandate for centralization, was an improvement of the

---

24. Pitkänen, *Central Sanctuary*, 1–24, 95–109.
25. Ibid., 271. Similarly, Robert R. Wilson argued the centralizing of the sanctuary clearly "involves the reform of an earlier system" of local worship. The reforms extend to the clergy at local shrines. See Wilson, "Deuteronomy, Ethnicity, and Reform," 117.

religious life of the people. The concept of centralization aided in the secular lifestyles of the people while also maintaining urgency to keep Yahweh in their sight (i.e., the Passover transformation).[26]

In addition, the author of Deuteronomy challenged the archaic form of Yahweh dwelling in the midst of the Israelites. Von Rad dismissed the suggestion that the centralization of the cult formed the theological center of Deuteronomy. His rationale stemmed from the limited number of centralization motifs in Deut 12–18.[27] On the other hand, he recognized the new paradigm intertwined in the mandate for centralization. He understood the "dwelling" of Yahweh's name at the centralized place of worship to being "existent in its own right." This new focus attacked the old idea that Yahweh's presence was at the place of worship. In the new paradigm, the dwelling of Yahweh's name in the central sanctuary represented a spatial separation between his presence and his name.[28] Along these lines, von Rad suggested the Deuteronomic *theologumenon* of Yahweh's name contained a polemic element or theological corrective. Yahweh was no longer present but rather his name was at the shrine. The presence of Yahweh's name functioned as a guarantee of salvation. In short, the Deuteronomic concept of centralization replaced the archaic idea of Yahweh's presence and indwelling with a "theologically sublimated idea." From this perspective, von Rad interpreted the idiomatic centralization motif as the essential component in developing the name theology.[29]

In 1969, McBride examined the linguistic intricacies of the centralization motifs and determined that the Deuteronomic name theology was a "clear example of a biblical tradition whose origins and context simply cannot be understood on the basis of the internal biblical evidence alone."[30] Thus, he maintained the only efficient methodology for understanding the Deuteronomic name theology was through a linguistical and philological analysis of the Deuteronomic and ANE texts. His research led him to proclaim, "Creation by naming attains its most sophisticated expression in the so-called *logos* and *fiat* theologies of the ancient Near East where the vitality of the divine 'word' is but an extension or abstraction of what we have seen

---

26. Rad, *Deuteronomy*, 16–17.
27. Ibid., 88–89.
28. Rad, *OTT* 1:184.
29. Idem, *Studies in Deuteronomy*, 38–40.
30. McBride, "Deuteronomic Name Theology," 4.

to be true of 'name.'"³¹ Building upon this understanding, McBride began with the interpretive crux of Deuteronomic name theology, the motifs לשכן שמו שם and לשום את-שמו שם, both of which are unattested in the HB, save Deuteronomy.³² These motifs represented a "hybrid or synthetic construction" that fulfilled the purpose of the individuals who attempted to reunite all of Israel through the "reform program," which emphasized the worship of Yahweh at a central shrine (i.e., Jerusalem).³³

For McConville, the name theology of Deuteronomy was an expression of the "Deuteronomic theme of conquest and possession of the land" that did not have cultic origins but rather a legal one. Obviously, this view is opposed diametrically to the cultic interpretation offered by von Rad. The "name" and "glory" of Yahweh, according to McConville, were complementary elements in Deuteronomy, used together since both have separate functions. The revelation of Yahweh through his name expressed the feelings of "normal worship," whereas his glory expressed the "dramatic manifestations of God."³⁴ Moreover, McConville argued, "It is by no means obvious ... that the Deuteronomic name theology signifies a deliberate assertion of divine transcendence over against conceptions which located him crudely in the sanctuary."³⁵ Additionally, the divine name in Deuteronomy did not preserve the transcendence of Yahweh but rather it affirmed two parts of his character: his transcendence and presence. Inasmuch, then, the phrase "before the Lord" in Deuteronomy must not be interpreted beyond its basic meaning—Yahweh could be encountered at the sanctuary. Thus, McConville maintained the basic meaning of "before the Lord" was the "purpose of meeting God at the 'place' which he will choose." This interpretation, then, supplanted the demythologizing view of Deuteronomy with a sacral view.³⁶

The place of Yahweh incorporated in the Deuteronomic centralization motifs actually affirmed his divine presence among the Israelites, but the chosen place would not bind Yahweh forever. The place motif also contained an element of openness since the specific identification of the place was omitted. For McConville, this omission of the specific place must be

31. Ibid., 74.
32. Ibid., 77.
33. Ibid., 197–210.
34. McConville, "God's 'Name' and God's 'Glory,'" 149–63.
35. McConville, "Time, Place and the Deuteronomic Altar-Law," 113.
36. Ibid., 121.

understood as an ideology of "Yahweh's relationship with his people in a covenantal history."³⁷ In sum, McConville interpreted the "chosen place" motifs in Deuteronomy as affirmations of Yahweh's presence among the Israelites, containing two tendencies that at least on the surface appear paradoxical. Yahweh was not associated with a single, specific place, yet his presence was affirmed in "places." This paradox can be understood only in terms of transcendence and immanence. Deuteronomy 4, according to McConville, strongly suggested the immanence of Yahweh among the Israelites. At Horeb, the people encountered the nearness of Yahweh, forging a bond between covenantal law and the divine call to faithfulness. Even with his immanence or covenantal presence among the people, Yahweh's divine freedom was retained. This retention of freedom by Yahweh exemplified a "function of his transcendence."³⁸ Thus, the paradox of transcendence and immanence was understood best as a covenantal relationship between Yahweh and Israel, a people in need of a "location in space and time; yet, Yahweh is not bound by any necessity to that people, nor to any one place."³⁹

In her book *The Deuteronomistic History and the Name Theology*, Sandra L. Richter examined the name motif לשכן שמו שם in Deuteronomy and its reflexes in the DH.⁴⁰ The premise of her argument was threefold. First, the DH went through double redaction, evidenced by the historical and thematic unity of Deuteronomy through the Kings corpus. Second, the Dtr placed an unbalanced emphasis on the righteousness of Josiah and the sins of Manasseh (2 Kgs 21–22). Third, the themes within the law code and the *paraenetic* form of Deuteronomy were continued throughout Israel's

---

37. Ibid., 122.

38. Ibid., 133–37. Ian Wilson offered a similar argument. He believed that the attempts by some biblical scholars to examine and compare the name theology in Deuteronomy with the ANE material overlooked the biblical concept of divine presence. See Wilson, "Divine Presence in Deuteronomy," 403–6; idem, *Out of the Midst*. Wilson concluded, "The claim . . . that the Deuteronomic cult envisages YHWH only in heaven is thus open to serious question, and the existence of a thoroughgoing Name Theology in Deuteronomy become increasingly unlikely. It is clear that the significance of the Name at the 'chosen place' will require further investigation" (p. 406).

39. McConville, "Time, Place and the Deuteronomic Altar-Law," 137.

40. Richter, *Deuteronomistic History*. Recently, Richter defended her original thesis. See Richter, "Placing the Name," 64–78. Several scholars have been critical of Richter's work. For example, see Van Seters, "The Formula *leshakken shemo sham*," 1–18; Otto, "Altorientalische Kontexte," 237–48; and Morrow, "'To Set the Name,'" 365–83.

Approaching the Concept of Centralization

history. In other words, she maintained that the Dtr utilized the ancient Deuteronomic law code as the "prolegomenon to his epic."[41]

The expansion of the ancient version of Deuteronomy (4:44—28:68) by David (2 Samuel 7) and later Solomon (1 Kgs 8:1–9:9) has drawn the interest of some scholars. Within the broader literary unit of the DH, the Dtr never spoke of Yahweh's presence in the physical temple. The temple was the location where Yahweh's name dwelled. The designation of Yahweh's name being present in the temple in the DH was synonymous with his essence.[42] Grouped with the centralization motifs were two theological themes—the name of Yahweh and the presence of Yahweh. In Deuteronomy, the noun שׁם was used several times as a substitution for Yahweh.[43] The centralization motifs were in "essence a circumlocution intended specifically to correct the older concept that Yahweh literally dwelt in the temple, and to replace it with the idea that Yahweh owned the temple."[44]

In the DH, the Deuteronomic לשׁכן motif (לשׁכן שׁמו שׁם) was replaced by the לשׂום motif (לשׂום את-שׁמו שׁם). The DH motif was used in conjunction with Yahweh's affirmation of Solomon's temple becoming his "chosen place" (1 Kgs 9:3). The same motif was used to proclaim the fate of the chosen city following Yahweh's judgment against Solomon (1 Kgs 11:36) and the reign of Rehoboam in the southern kingdom (1 Kgs 14:21).[45] The Deuteronomic centralization idiom proclaimed the future location of the central sanctuary, which was "depicted as the pulse-point of Israel's relationship with Yahweh in that it is the only place in which Israel may seek its suzerain, the only place to which tribute must be brought, and the special place at which the redemptive acts of Israel's conquering champion should be celebrated."[46]

---

41. Ibid., 1–6.

42. Ibid., 6–8.

43. Ibid., 11; cf. Rad, *Studies in Deuteronomy*, 40.

44. Ibid., 24.

45. Ibid., 48.

46. Ibid., 57. Additionally, Richter has argued that the first location designated by the Deuteronomic concept of centralization was Mount Ebal. She substantiated her argument on the parallels between inscribed Akkadian stele and the Deuteronomic directive to "inscribe and display the words and heroic acts of Yahweh" on a stele (27:5–8). The name theology in Deuteronomy also builds upon this principle. The Israelites were commanded to remove the Canaanite inscriptions from Yahwistic cultic sites and replace them with an inscription bearing Yahweh's name (e.g., Deut 11; 27). See Richter, "Place of the Name," 342–66.

The Legislative Themes of Centralization

Centralization as a Revolution/Innovation

In modern times, possibly no one has impacted the study of Deuteronomy as much as Moshe Weinfeld. His scholarly contribution helped shape the theological landscape and his legacy will continue to influence future generations. His keen attention to detail and his intimate study of Deuteronomy challenged the theories of his predecessors and, more importantly, radically changed the theological horizon of Deuteronomic and Deuteronomistic studies. Through a plethora of outlets, Weinfeld cogently and consistently described the purpose of Deuteronomy as an attempt "to curtail" and "circumscribe" the Israelite cult rather than expand or elaborate its power.[47] According to Weinfeld, Deuteronomy was the work of the scribal circles within the royal court at Jerusalem. The book embodied a turning point in the development of Israel's faith, quintessentially a "theological revolution."[48] The revolutionary characteristics of Deuteronomy extended into the three foundations of Israel's religion: faith, cult, and law. It was through the rubric of theological revolution that Deuteronomy took shape. In many ways, the laws and statutes went through the "process of rationalization."[49]

For Weinfeld, the centralization of the cult and the laws connected to the Deuteronomic mandate provided the key to understanding the origins of the book. First, he questioned the theory popularized by von Rad that the Levites wrote Deuteronomy. He contended that von Rad's theory was insufficient since the office of the Levites was depreciated to the point of *personae miserables* as a result of the laws mandating the centralization of the cult. Thus, the Levitical priests, following the centralization of the cult, were placed in the same social class as the poor, the resident alien, the

---

47. Weinfeld, *Deuteronomic School*, 190; idem, *Deuteronomy 1–11*, 37; idem, "Deuteronomy's Theological Revolution," 44. Similarly, Nelson argued that the centralization mandate was created to eliminate apostasy. See Nelson, *Deuteronomy*, 146–49.

48. Ibid., 191–243; idem, *Deuteronomy 1–11*, 37–44; idem, "Deuteronomy's Theological Revolution," 38, 44. Other scholars have adopted Weinfeld's classification of Deuteronomy as being a theological revolution. See Clements, "Book of Deuteronomy," 2:275; idem, *Deuteronomy*; Mayes, *Deuteronomy*, 57–60; and Tigay, *Deuteronomy*, xvii–xviii; Recently, Peter Vogt continued his critique of Weinfeld's revolutionary programme of reform. He has argued, "[T]he textual data point to seeing something in Deuteronomy that is very different from the programme of centralization and secularization, Deuteronomy instead centralizes sacrifice to the central sanctuary to highlight Yahweh's supremacy in being able to determine where and how he is worshiped while decentralizing other aspects of worship, extending it through the land." See Vogt, "Centralization and Decentralization," 118–38, here 137; idem, *Deuteronomic Theology*, 42–46.

49. Weinfeld, "Deuteronomy," 257.

orphan, and the widow.⁵⁰ Weinfeld argued that the centralization mandate did not come into existence until after the temple was built during Solomon's reign. Furthermore, he supported this theory by examining the differences between sacrifices at various high places in David's time (1 Kgs 3:2) and the mandate for centralization following the erection of the temple.⁵¹

Similar to von Rad, Weinfeld believed Deuteronomy was an oration following the pattern of a sermon. The main difference, however, was Weinfeld's interpretation of the "Torah of Yahweh" in Jer 8:8, which he believed was Deuteronomy. He readily admitted that the identity of the scribes responsible for writing Deuteronomy could not be legitimized. Still, he proffered the theory that the Shaphan scribal family wrote Deuteronomy. Moreover, he believed the scribes responsible for recording the "book of the law" presented the prescriptions in a "new form," which in turn made the laws culturally relevant for the new age.⁵²

The centralization laws, thus, represented this new paradigm within the adapting culture particularly with regard to the executive, judicial, and military procedures. Although the reforms dictated by the centralization of the cult influenced many societal layers, the religious adaptations contained the most nationalistic aims. Weinfeld argued that the scribes used the centralization laws to express religious aims initiated by Hezekiah and Josiah. Both kings of Judah desired to extirpate foreign cults. The abrogation of foreign cults, although started by Hezekiah, became a reality following the social and religious reforms carried out by Josiah.⁵³ Ultimately, Weinfeld argued that Deuteronomy combined elements from ANE treaties, the ancient Israelite covenant, and a law code to form a constitution that became

---

50. Ibid., 55.

51. Ibid., 154.

52. Ibid., 157–59; cf. Weinfeld, "Deuteronomy's Theological Revolution," 38. For a similar argument, see Jepsen, *Die Quellen des Königsbuches*, 94–95. Sigmund Mowinckel popularized the theory that the book of Jeremiah contained various traditions or sources: "A," "B," and "C." The "A" tradition was mainly a prophetic oracle that dated to preexilic prophetic books (including the majority of poetry in Jeremiah). The "B" source was mainly biographical prose written as a narrative account with Jeremiah being referenced in third person. Finally, the "C" source consisted mainly of prose discourses incorporating an extensive rhetorical style. Usually the "C" literature was structured within an autobiographical framework. See Mowinckel, *Zur Komposition des Buches Jeremia*. Weinfeld attributed the "C" source in Jeremiah to the Shaphan scribal circle since the prophet Jeremiah was rescued by Ahikam the son of Shaphan the scribe (Jer 26:24). See Weinfeld, *Deuteronomic School*, 159.

53. Ibid., 166; idem, "Deuteronomy's Theological Revolution," 38.

The Legislative Themes of Centralization

a theological revolution.[54] For Weinfeld, the central sanctuary predicted in Deuteronomy was a house of prayer rather than a cult center. This new paradigm, particularly chs. 12–18, minimized the cult while signifying a religious turning point or reform.[55] With the centralization of the cult to a single sanctuary, many traditional functions permissible at local sanctuaries were divorced from their original purposes, leaving them secular.[56] Even amidst the various arguments and theories concerning the Deuteronomic concept of centralization, most scholars agree that this tenet of the book introduced a "new religious orientation" or innovation.[57] The centralization of the cult was a "sweeping innovation in the history of the Israelite cultus" with consequences that were "more revolutionary in nature" since the old system of concepts collapsed due to their perception being "sacrosanct."[58]

Norbert Lohfink also viewed the whole book of Deuteronomy as a program of centralization; however, he recognized much of the book was ancient in origin but dated the redaction of Deuteronomy to the postexilic period. More important was his understanding of the centralization ideology, which developed through interaction with other ancient works and assimilated ideas.[59] Lohfink noted, "The greatest innovation that Deuteronomy produced was the demand to centralize the cult at the place which Yahweh chose."[60] In short, Lohfink viewed Deuteronomy as an attempt to reinterpret and "systematize" ancient traditions. The systematization of ancient traditions was not an evolutionary development of Israelite religious views but rather a response to the decaying worldview.[61]

Bernard Levinson wrote one of the most influential works concerning Deuteronomy in the last 20 years. He viewed the book as a "radical revision" of the Book of the Covenant. Through legal innovation, the authors of Deuteronomy implemented extensive transformations in the areas of religion, law, and social structure. These sophisticated authors reinterpreted not only

---

54. Ibid., 168.

55. Ibid., 213.

56. Ibid., 233. See pp. 233–43 for a complete list of permissible functions at local sanctuaries.

57. Weinfeld described the concept of centralization as a "new religious orientation." See Weinfeld, "Deuteronomy," 258.

58. Weinfeld, *Deuteronomic School*, 190.

59. Lohfink, "Deuteronomy," 229.

60. Ibid., 231.

61. Lohfink, "Culture Shock and Theology," 2–22.

the texts from Israel but also cuneiform texts. Through their writings, these authors confronted the problems associated with the history of religion, which according to Levinson was the "justification of innovation."[62] Thus, he explained, "Deuteronomy was already a complex hermeneutical work from the beginning; it was the composition of authors who consciously reused and reinterpreted earlier texts to propound and justify their program of cultic and legal reform, even—or particularly—when those texts conflicted with the authors' agenda."[63] The authors' agenda was the deliberate reworking of legal texts "in light of the innovation of centralization."[64]

Paramount to Levinson's theory of legal innovation in Deuteronomy was the centralization of worship. The authors of Deuteronomy radically changed the sacrificial worship of Yahweh from multiple altar sites (e.g., Shechem, Bethel, Shiloh, Ramah, and Mount Carmel) to one centralized location and temple. In addition, the authors of Deuteronomy revised the cultic rituals and institutions at the local cultic level. In sum, the Deuteronomic authors confronted and revised the legal texts that legitimized local shrines throughout the land. Behind the Deuteronomic requirement of centralization in Deut 12:4–28 stood the altar law from the Book of the Covenant (Exod 20:24). The Deuteronomic prescription of sacrifices to a centralized sphere extended beyond cultic rituals and into the transformation of public institutions and societal roles. Furthermore, the centralized sphere decreased the royal throne and power in favor of the temple. The centralization innovation differed from earlier prescribed empirical institutions both historically and literarily.[65]

---

62. Levinson, *Deuteronomy and the Hermeneutics*, 3–4. Timo Veijola offered a similar treatment of Deuteronomy. He argued the *urdeuteronomium* was a product of the Josianic period and the centralization of the cult was a reworking of the Book of the Covenant. This reworking was an attempt at social reform by a "national religious reform movement." See Veijola, *Das fünfte Buch Mose*, 1–3. Other scholars have discussed the reforms in relation to sociopolitical reforms. For example, Clements noted, "The demand for cult centralization was simply one aspect of a policy aimed at securing a unified, coherent and centrally administered state." See Clements, *Deuteronomy*, 87. Likewise, Römer viewed the centralization of the cult, an exilic concept, as the centralization of economics and politics (Deut 13–18). More importantly, the centralization of the cult in the Kings corpus became the standard in which all northern kings could not achieve. See Römer, *So-Called Deuteronomistic History*, 3, 10.

63. Ibid., 4.

64. Ibid., 4–6.

65. Ibid., 4–10.

The Legislative Themes of Centralization

For Levinson, the literary history described in the law code of Deuteronomy was associated primarily with Josiah's centralization and purification of the cult (2 Kgs 22–23). The abolishment and denunciation of other local shrines described in 2 Kgs 22–23 were related explicitly to the innovation of cultic centralization in Deuteronomy.[66] In an attempt to implement religious and societal changes, the Deuteronomic authors reinterpreted and rewrote portions of the Book of the Covenant, and in doing so they created a "new vision of the religious and public polity."[67] Driving the authors' hermeneutical innovation was the cultural transformation of Israel's tithes and firstlings, the festival calendar, and Passover with the centralization of the cult being at the center of the legal innovation.[68] Levinson noted,

> The authors of Deuteronomy employed the Covenant Code . . . not merely as a textual source but as a resource, in order to purchase the legitimacy and authority that their reform agenda otherwise lacked. The reuse of the older material lent their innovations the guise of continuity with the past and consistency with traditional law. The authors of Deuteronomy cast their departure from tradition as its reaffirmation, their transformation and abrogation of conventional religious law as the original intent of that law.[69]

According to Levinson, Deut 12 was a composite of redundancy consisting of six centralization motifs interwoven within four legal units (vv. 2–7, 8–12, 13–19, and 20–28). The final redaction highlighted a chiastic structure (A-B-C-B'-A'), forming a composite arrangement of original independent paragraphs. In Deut 12, the authors utilized exegesis as a method for sanctioning a transformation of legal, cultic, and literary history. This innovative exegesis went against the social and religious status quo by allowing sacrifices to be offered at local altars and sanctuaries. In other words, Levinson believed the authors of Deuteronomy presented an innovation of cultic centralization that was in direct contrast and conflict with earlier authoritative texts. To offset the tension between the earlier traditions concerning multiple altars and sanctuaries, the Deuteronomic authors included justification and defense for their innovation.[70]

---

66. Ibid., 9–10.
67. Ibid., 16.
68. Ibid., 13–22.
69. Ibid., 21. The Covenant Code and the Book of the Covenant are synonymous.
70. Ibid., 23–28.

Approaching the Concept of Centralization

Thus, Deut 12 did not just sanction the centralization of the cult but also justified the authors' rationale. Describing this pivotal development in the history of Israelite religion, Levinson explained,

> The innovation of cultic centralization entailed, moreover, a direct conflict with existing prestigious or authoritative texts that circulated within the scribal schools, even if they were not yet publicly known, and that contemplated precisely the opposite of centralization. In order for the Deuteronomic agenda to succeed, therefore, the authors and editors of the legal corpus had to find some way to justify their innovation. They had not only empirically to proscribe the local altars and sanctuaries, to which the people turned for cultic access to their God, but also to qualify the validity of the older texts whose content they contradicted and that might have jeopardized the success of their innovative agenda. In order to do so, the authors of Deuteronomy paradoxically turned to those very texts and coerced them to call for centralization.[71]

As a whole, then, Deut 12 was a "redactional anthology" that repeatedly commanded, as well as justified, the innovation of centralization. Chapter 12 provided the first glimpse of the deconstructed and recast syntax of the old altar law from the Book of the Covenant, which reappeared as a distinctive innovation.

Although the older altar law was reworked, the "ostensible validity" of the older law remained intact in Deuteronomy. Naturally, the revision of older legal material must be substantiated for widespread acceptance to take place. For this reason, the Deuteronomic authors usurped the fiction of Moses as the "voice of authoritative antiquity." By reworking key terms with exegetical remarks, the authors of Deuteronomy transformed the Exodus altar law (Exod 20:24) and ultimately prohibited the earlier sanctioned law. In doing so, the authors secularized the language and literary history found in Exod 20:24. Both cultic and secular sacrifices described in earlier literature could be offered at local altars and sanctuaries; however, in Deuteronomy, these sacrifices were prohibited and revolutionized into a mandate of centralized cultic action (Deut 12:14).[72]

---

71. Ibid., 28.
72. Ibid., 28–34, 46–52.

The Legislative Themes of Centralization

ASSESSMENT

The interpretation of the Deuteronomic concept of centralization is anything but clear. Before moving forward, I must make some general remarks concerning the centralization mandate. It seems to me that Weinfeld was correct when he suggested Deuteronomy functioned as a constitution. The constitutional power of Deuteronomy most likely rested solely in the hands of the redactors in the exilic period. The power of Deuteronomy, especially the centralization mandate, certainly represents a theological revolution, but one must question its theological thrust given the uncertainty of redactional layers. Furthermore, I am not sure Weinfeld's reform programme was engineered by secularization and demythologization. In many ways, I believe the meaning behind the centralization mandate lies somewhere between a modified combination of Weinfeld, Lohfink, and Levinson.

Through an exilic lens, Deuteronomy certainly appears to reposition, reinterpret, and systematize ancient traditions. Moreover, an exilic reading of Deuteronomy adds a prophetic voice to the centralization of the cult (cf. Driver). When viewed holistically within the Enneateuch, Deuteronomy, and specifically the centralization mandate, becomes a utopian desire for what Israel's faith and culture should look like in the united and divided monarchies.[73] In the so-called DH, the reforming efforts of two kings play an important role for reading Deuteronomy through an exilic lens. By way of oversimplification, Hezekiah's attempts at reforming and possibly centralizing Judah never come to fruition during the Assyrian period (2 Kgs 18–20). Josiah, on the other hand, successfully centralized the cult and eradicated idolatry from the kingdom (2 Kgs 22–23). Unfortunately, the centralizing reforms of Josiah were short lived due to his untimely death. With the death of Josiah, the people of Israel abandoned his reforming efforts and returned to their previous ways (cf. 2 Kgs 24–25). Given the literary history of Israel in Joshua–2 Kings, we can assume that an exilic reading of Deuteronomy, and especially the centralization mandate in chs. 12–18, was interpreted as an unsustainable—if not unattainable—utopian desire.

Moving forward, I will provide evidence that the exilic audience probably interpreted the centralization mandate as a utopian desire. This desire, and the failures of the previous generations, might actually be the inspiration for the reforms during the postexilic period. To build on this

---

73. Nelson made a similar argument and coined the phrase "utopian flavor." My view is slightly different from his. See Nelson, *Deuteronomy*, 146.

assumption, I will examine five legislative themes associated with centralization mandate (chs. 3–7). Much of the material discussed, particularly the diachronic contributions, is not new; however, when interpreted holistically through the lens of centralization and within the narrative framework of the Enneateuch a theological reading emerges. In sum, with the following chapters I will reveal how the exilic, prophetic voice of the centralization mandate is used to highlight "the decaying worldview" of the divided monarchy (as Lohfink described it). And, I will show how the utopian world of Deuteronomy becomes the barometer for the demise of the kingdom in the eyes of the exilic readers.

3

The Abrogation of Idolatry

THE PROSPECTIVE PROCLAMATION AGAINST pagan altars, graven images, and the continual mandate for holiness and worship in the Pentateuch fortify the socio-religious foundation of the so-called DH. With the Abrahamic covenant, Yahweh establishes a relationship not only with the patriarchs but also with the future generations of Israelites. The demand for holiness is solidified with the Decalogue (Exod 20:2–17; cf. Deut 5:6–21) and the subsequent law codes in the Pentateuch. The monotheistic relationship mandated by Yahweh is tested by the polytheistic influences of the Egyptians and the inhabitants in the land of Canaan.

DIACHRONIC AND EXEGETICAL ANALYSIS[1]

The Yahwistic directive to purge the pagan influences of the Egyptians during Israel's wilderness experience and future ratification of idolatries in the land of Canaan is an important theme in the Pentateuch.[2] The theme of

---

1. I divide chs. 3–7 into two broad categories: (1) diachronic and exegetical analysis; and (2) a synchronic reading of each legislative theme. Within the diachronic and exegetical category, I examine relevant texts associated with the specific theme. In some cases I analyze the diachronic contributions of a text more so than the exegetical aspects. At other times, I do not mention the diachronic contributions. The decision is based on the importance of each text.

2. For a relatively concise treatment of idolatry in the Pentateuch, see McKenzie, *Idolatry in the Pentateuch*. Tracy McKenzie identified just over 25 examples of idolatry in the Pentateuch: Exod 20:3–5; 22:19; 34:12–17; Lev 17:7; Num 25:1–3; Deut 4:14–35;

The Abrogation of Idolatry

abrogating idolatry in the Pentateuch continues in the so-called DH. Thus, in this chapter, I will examine specific texts that discuss and construct the abrogation of idolatry theme within the Enneateuch. Attention will be given to significant texts dealing with idolatry. That being said, several texts reiterate Yahweh's demand for holiness through the abrogation of idolatrous practices: intercourse with an animal (Exod 22:19; Deut 27:21), utter the names of other gods (Exod 23:13), interact with inhabitants in Canaan (Deut 20:17–18), and worship foreign gods (Lev 17:7; Deut 8:19–20). In addition, there are several Deuteronomic references demanding that the Israelites stand firm and not have their hearts turned from Yahweh (Deut 11:16, 28; 29:17–18; 30:17). If the Israelites cannot remain faithful to Yahweh, then they will experience exile (Deut 28:15–68; v. 36 especially speaks to this threat). Although these examples are within the confines of the abrogation of idolatry theme, I do not find it necessary to examine each of these texts since most of them are descriptive in nature. Emphasis will be given to more significant texts that address the topic more specifically.[3]

Exodus 15:22–27

Within the legal fabric of the Pentateuch, several key words and idiomatic phrases are used to signify legislative data. One such phrase is the combination of "statute" (חק) and "ordinance" (משפט). The first occurrence of the idiomatic axiom (חק ומשפט) is found in the water of Marah pericope in Exod 15:22–27, which follows the parting of the Sea of Reeds (ch. 14) and the song of Moses (15:1–18) pericopes.[4] In the water of Marah pericope, the Israelites travel three days without water in the wilderness of Shur. Once the people reach Marah, they realize the water is bitter and undrink-

---

5:6–10; 7:2–5, 16, 25–26; 11:16, 28; 12:2–3, 30–31; 13:1–15; 16:21–22; 17:2–3; 18:9–14; 20:17–18; 27:5; 28:36; 29:17–18; 30:17; 31:16–20, 29; and 32:16–21. See pp. 115–16. Due to the nature of my study, I will not be examining each of these texts since several reiterate or restate a more common text.

3. Exod 20:3–5; 23:20–25; 32:7–20; 34:11–16; Lev 18:1–4; 20:22–26; Num 25:1–3; 33:50–56; Deut 4; 5:6–10; 6; 7; 9:12–21; 12:1–5; 13; 16; 18; 31:16–20; 32:16–21; Josh 24; Judg 1–2; 3:7—16:31; 1–2 Samuel; 1 Kgs 13; 14:21–23; 18–19; 2 Kgs 9:1—10:31; and 2 Kgs 17.

4. The parenthetic phrase חק ומשפט occurs twenty-one times in the Enneateuch. Particular attention should be paid to the multiple occurrences in Deuteronomy: Exod 15:25; Lev 26:46; Deut 4:1, 5, 8, 14, 45; 5:1, 31; 6:1, 20; 7:11; 11:32; 12:1; 26:16, 17; Josh 24:25; 1 Sam 30:25; 1 Kgs 8:58; 9:4; 2 Kgs 17:37.

The Legislative Themes of Centralization

able. Naturally, the Israelites become disgruntled with Moses, which results in Yahweh intervening on the people's behalf by turning the bitter water sweet (vv. 22–25a).

Subsequent to the water becoming sweet, Yahweh makes "a statute and an ordinance" (חק ומשפט) for the people (15:25b). Unfortunately, the actual legal material associated with the statute and ordinance in v. 25 is unclear, if not lost indefinitely.[5] The consequences for abrogating the statute and ordinance are described in v. 26, a text rich in Deuteronomic language. First, a substantiation is made with the issuing of the statue and ordinance along with a casuistic law: "If you surely listen to the voice of Yahweh your God" (אם־שמוע תשמע לקול יהוה אלהיך), then Yahweh will not afflict the people with the diseases placed upon the Egyptians.[6] Second, the inclusion of the phrase "do what is right in his eyes" (הישר בעיניו תעשה) between the protasis and the apodosis parallels the deplorable social and religious climate in the book of Judges (cf. Judg 17:6; 21:25).

Due to these similarities, several scholars have suggested the phrase indicates a late Deuteronomistic revision.[7] On the other hand, other scholars have suggested the inclusion of חק ומשפט along with the vocabulary and syntax of v. 26 does not necessitate a Deuteronomistic redactional argument.[8] The arguments against vv. 25b–26 not being Deuteronomistic do not take into account the limited frequency of חק ומשפט in the Tetrateuch (cf. Exod 15:25b; Lev 26:46), whereas in Deuteronomy the axiom occurs fourteen times and another five times in the so-called DH. Thus, the textual evidence suggests that vv. 25b–26 is a late addition and should be interpreted in light of the Deuteronomic polemic against pagan altars, pillars, Asherim, and worship.[9]

---

5. Nahum M. Sarna surmised the phrase was a parenthetic note that reflected some law(s) given to the people at this location (i.e., Marah). See Sarna, *Exodus*, 85.

6. The phrase אם־שמוע תשמע לקול יהוה אלהיך is paralleled in Deut 15:5 and 28:1. Modified forms of the phrase are used repeatedly in Deuteronomy (13:19; 15:5, 26:14; 27:10; 28:1, 2, 15, 45, 62; 30:10) and other Deuteronomistic books (2 Kgs 18:12; Jer 3:25; 7:28; 26:13; 42:6, 13, 21).

7. Noth argued the inclusion of חק ומשפט was a Deuteronomistic addition along with v. 26. See Noth, *Exodus*, 129. Similarly, John I. Durham noted the Deuteronomistic characteristics of Exod 15:25b–26, but he also suggested the covenantal language of the verses overshadows the Deuteronomistic component. See Durham, *Exodus*, 214.

8. See Childs, *Book of Exodus*, 266–67 and Van Seters, *Life of Moses*, 175–76. Lohfink provided a comparison of the similarities of the Dtr and other sources. See Lohfink, "Ich bin Jahwe," 29–41.

9. In addition to חק ומשפט in v. 25, other Deuteronomistic words are found in v. 26,

Exodus 20:3–5 (cf. Deut 5:6–10)[10]

The first two commandments of the Decalogue provide one of the most concise declarations against idolatry in the HB. The Decalogue is introduced by a prefatory sentence or historical prologue (Exod 20:2; Deut 5:6), which emphasizes the "reality of God in relation to the world and to humankind."[11] The historical prologue aids in establishing a relationship between the first two commandments, as well as the entire Decalogue.[12] With a safe passage from Egyptian bondage to Mount Sinai, Yahweh is now demanding complete obedience (Exod 20:3) and faithfulness through the renunciation and destruction of idols like those in the previous land (v. 5).

In addition to the historical prologue, the grammar and syntax of the first two commandments establishes a thematic link between the two. First, the inclusion of "other gods" in the first commandment—"You shall not have other gods before me" (Exod 20:3; Deut 5:7)—directly corresponds to the phrase "bow down or worship them" in the second commandment (Exod 20:5; Deut 5:9). Second, the use of the pronoun "them" in v. 5 also references back to the "other gods" in v. 3.[13] From a theological perspective,

---

חקי and למצותי. The combination of the words "statutes" and "commandments" are found also in Deut 4:40; 27:10; 28:15, 45; 30:10, 16; 1 Kgs 3:14; 8:61. Weinfeld provided a thorough list of Deuteronomic and Deuteronomistic phraseology. See Weinfeld, *Deuteronomic School*, 320–65.

10. Due to the scope of my research, the nuances of the Decalogue in Exod 20 and Deut 5 will not be discussed. Dean McBride summarized the prevailing assessment of this relationship succinctly: "The classic Decalogue was in large measure a literary synthesis whose versions were designed to serve particular theological interests." See McBride, "Essence of Orthodoxy," 135; cf. Lohfink, "Decalogue in Deuteronomy," 248–64.

11. Harrelson, *Ten Commandments*, 51. Exodus 20:2 reads: "I am the Lord your God, who brought you out of the land of Egypt, out of the house of bondage."

12. See Levinson, "Right Chorale," 146–48. William Propp provided a helpful source analysis of the entire Decalogue (Exod 20:1–17), see Propp, *Exodus 19–40*, 145–46. The source allocation of the Decalogue is debated among scholars. For example, Frank Moore Cross argued the Decalogue (Exod 20:1–17), in its present form, was Priestly; however, like the Deuteronomic Decalogue, the Priestly version has been reworked from "an old document" among the "Epic sources." See Cross, *Canaanite Myth*, 312. Von Rad also argued that some of the commandments were actually older than the Decalogue. See Rad, *OTT*, 1:190. Dale Patrick maintained that the Decalogue in Exodus was the work of the Elohist, see Patrick, *Old Testament Law*, 18. Albertz argued the present form of the Decalogue (Exod 20:1–17) was an exilic version. See Albertz, *History of Israelite Religion*, 55.

13. Childs, *Book of Exodus*, 403–4; cf. Patrick, *Old Testament Law*, 46; and Miller, *Ten Commandments*, 14.

The Legislative Themes of Centralization

the first commandment is a clear renunciation of idolatrous practices. Moreover, this initial commandment demands that the Israelites recognize Yahweh as sovereign and, consequentially, "other gods" should have no place or power in their lives. Jeffrey Tigay cogently captured the theological thrust of this commandment: "In practical terms the commandment means that Israelites may have no relationship of any kind with other gods: they may not build altars, sanctuaries, or images to them, make offering to them, consult them, prophesy or take oaths in their names, or even mention their names."[14]

Related to theological profundity of the first commandment is the interpretation of the phrase על-פני ("before me," Exod 20:3; Deut 5:7). Six interpretive possibilities exist for על-פני in v. 3: no other gods "next to me," "except me," "over me," "in front of me," "opposite me," "before my face," and "in defiance of me."[15] Whatever interpretation is adopted—spatial or preferential—the premise behind the no "other gods" directive is the avoidance of the rivaling ANE gods.[16] In short, Yahweh is a jealous God and will not tolerate Israel's worship of a rival god (Exod 20:5; Deut 5:9).[17]

The second commandment furthered the impact of the no other gods directive: "You shall not make for yourselves an idol" (Exod 20:5; cf. 34:17; Lev 19:4; 26:1; Deut 5:8a; 26:1).[18] This commandment radically symbol-

---

14. Tigay, *Deuteronomy*, 64.

15. *HALOT*, 2:944. For a similar treatment, see Miller, *Ten Commandments*, 20.

16. On the issues of spatial or preferential, see Roberts, "Exodus 20:1–6," 60–62 and Heiser, "Monotheism, Polytheism," 24–26. John Walton and Baruch Levine both argued for a spatial interpretation; however, each came to slightly differing conclusions. See Walton, "Decalogue Structure," 98 and Levine, "Cultic Scene," 283–99.

17. Scholars have debated whether the first commandment emphasized monotheism (Albright, *From the Stone Age*, 297 and Rooker, *Ten Commandments*, 27) or a demand of exclusive worship of Yahweh. Over the years, the latter view has garnished more scholarly support. See Keszler, "Die Literarische," 9; Cassuto, *Commentary on Exodus*, 235–41; Childs, *Book of Exodus*, 402–4; Durham, *Exodus*, 284–85; Greenberg, "Decalogue Tradition," 83–120; Patrick, *Old Testament Law*, 42–44; Harrelson, *Ten Commandments*, 53–54; Tigay, *Deuteronomy*, 63–64; Miller, *Ten Commandments*, 26–27; Propp, *Exodus 19–40*, 167; Hess, *Israelite Religions*, 163; Heiser, "Monotheism, Polytheism," 24–25; Levine, "Cultic Scene," 283–99; Walton, "Decalogue Structure," 98–99; Block, *Deuteronomy*, 162; and Lundbom, *Deuteronomy*, 279.

18. Regarding the relationship between the two commandments, Walter Harrelson noted, "If the first commandment is the comprehensive one, the touchtone for all biblical religion, the second commandment is clearly the most striking and distinctive, with the possible exception of the fourth (the Sabbath commandment)." See Harrelson, *Ten Commandments*, 61.

izes Israel's break with other ANE cultures and religiosity, especially the Canaanites.[19] Central to this commandment is Yahweh's insistence that "no" representation of Him and/or images of foreign gods is permissible.[20] The first commandment can be described as Yahweh's expression of divine possession while the second focuses on the manufacturing of pagan images or idols. Theologically speaking, the command might suggest a prohibition against objects of Yahweh's likeness; however, the description of Yahweh as "jealous" (Exod 20:5; cf. Deut 5:9) makes this option less likely. The manufacturing of images/idols of "other gods" would make Yahweh jealous. Additionally, the inclusion of "bow to them and worship them" emphasizes plurality.[21] Together, the first two commandments dually emphasized Yahweh's claim and election of Israel. As result, these two commands describe the obedience that Yahweh demands. If the Israelites bow to other gods, they would be committing an act of "double-mindedness," which would divide their allegiance to Yahweh.[22]

Exodus 23:20–25

The next significant text regarding the abrogation of idolatry is found in the conclusion of the Book of the Covenant. In ch. 23, Yahweh promises to send a messenger (מלאך) before the people to protect and guide them to the place that Yahweh "determined" (אל-המקום אשר הכנתי). In addition, Yahweh commands (השמר) the people to listen to the voice of the messenger and not to rebel against him. The verse is concluded with a unique element—the messenger, not Yahweh, is responsible for not pardoning the people's transgressions. The authority granted to the messenger is related to the name (שמי) of Yahweh being within him (v. 21). Ironically, in the following verse, Yahweh explains that if the people obey, then the Lord will become hostile (איבתי) to their enemies. The actions of Yahweh are somewhat unexpected since the messenger of Yahweh judges the transgressions of the Israelites, whereas Yahweh is the judge of the inhabitants in the land. Though the enemies are not defined specifically in vv. 20–22, the logical progression would suggest the inhabitants in the land of Canaan listed in

---

19. See Noth, *Exodus*, 162–63; cf. Childs, *Book of Exodus*, 405–6; and Harrelson, *Ten Commandments*, 61–64.

20. Durham, *Exodus*, 286–87 and Miller, *Ten Commandments*, 48.

21. Hamilton, *Exodus*, 329–30.

22. Harrelson, *Ten Commandments*, 54–57, 61–64.

The Legislative Themes of Centralization

v. 23 will become enemies and adversaries to the Israelites (i.e., Amorites, Hittites, Perizzites, Canaanites, Hivites, and Jebusites). The messenger will not precede the Israelites into the foreign land, but the inhabitants will be effaced (הכחדתי) from the land.[23]

The divine proclamation of the removal or destruction of the inhabitants from the land, however, does not align itself chronologically with v. 23. In the next verse, Yahweh commands the Israelites not to worship (-לא תשתחוה) or serve the pagan deities of the land. From a chronological standpoint, if the messenger of Yahweh is to precede the people and remove the inhabitants, how could the Israelites fall victim to the idolatrous ways of the foreign nations? Moreover, why are the Israelites commanded to overthrow (הרס תהרסם) the inhabitants and surely break (שבר תשבר) their pillars? Verse 25 might provide insight into the chronological sequence. This verse builds upon the narrator's use of the *hištap̄ʿel* verb תשתחוה in v. 24 to construct further the unifying dictum of 20:3–6. The use of the *hištap̄ʿel* verb in v. 24 directly links vv. 20–25 with other important texts, particularly the first two commandments (20:3–6) and the covenant renewal (34:14). Collectively, an attempt is being made to prepare the Israelites to enter the land of Canaan. In doing so, a vibrant portrait emerges contrasting Yahwistic monotheism and idolatry.

Exodus 32:7–20 (cf. Deut 9:12–21)

Related to the material in chs. 23 and 24, Yahweh pronounces a similar message in the golden calf narrative in Exod 32. While Moses is on Mount Sinai, the people of Israel make a molten calf and declare their allegiance to

---

23. The first reference to the land of Canaan, particularly with regard to the inhabitants, is located in the burning bush pericope (Exod 3:8). In this text, Yahweh tells Moses that he will bring him into a good and broad land, one that flows with milk and honey. The land, however, is inhabited by Canaanites, Hittites, Amorites, Perizzites, Hivites, and Jebusites. The most glaring omission from the text in ch. 3 is the command to "drive out" the pagan inhabitants from the land (v. 17). In Exod 33:1–3, Yahweh tells Moses to depart for the land promised to Abraham, Isaac, and Jacob, yet in this text the same inhabitants of the land of Canaan are referenced in a slightly different order (Canaanites, *Amorites, Hittites*, Perizzites, Hivites, and Jebusites). This time Yahweh explains that he will "drive out" the inhabitants from the land (v. 2). Both references to the inhabitants of the land of Canaan in 3:8 and 33:1–3, along with the golden calf narrative in ch. 32, form the theological backdrop of the covenant renewal in ch. 34. Of particular note, the listed order of the inhabitants in the land of Canaan in 34:11 is different from 3:8 and 33:2 (*Amorites*, Canaanites, Hittites, Perizzites, Hivites, and Jebusites).

The Abrogation of Idolatry

pagan deities (v. 4). Several prevalent theories have been proposed regarding the nature of the Israelites' violation against the covenant. First, the golden calf breaches the commandment prohibiting graven images (Exod 20:4–6; Deut 5:8–10).[24] Second, the calf is a fertility symbol that precipitated sexual deviancy. Third, the calf represents a "war-emblem" or celebration of divine victory.[25] Fourth, Aaron attempts to create an idol that mimics Yahweh's fame and power.[26] Fifth, Exod 32 is later and used to as deterrent against an iconic "veneration of Yahweh."[27] Sixth, the text "presupposes" the idolatrous acts of Jeroboam at Bethel and Dan (1 Kgs 12).[28]

The diverse theories concerning the rationale for making the golden calf only cloud the story in the chapter. For this reason, I am not inclined to accept a specific theory. One thing is certain, the golden calf Aaron made was a breach of commandments 1 and 2. As a result of his actions and the people's idolatrous acts, Aaron builds an altar to worship the pagan gods. The actions of the people cause Yahweh's anger to intensify to the point of consuming the people for their sin. Moses intercedes on behalf of the people, and Yahweh relents. With the wrath of Yahweh somewhat abated, Moses' anger continues to the point of destroying the tablets containing the words of Yahweh.[29] More importantly, Moses proclaims the necessity of atonement for the people's sin (vv. 1–30), which is why some scholars view chs. 32–34 as a literary unit.

---

24. Cf. Patrick, *Rhetoric of Revelation*, 62.

25. Janzen, "Character of the Calf," 597–607.

26. Master, "Exodus 32," 592.

27. Edelman, *Opening the Books of Moses*, 170.

28. Aberbach and Smolar, "Aaron, Jeroboam, and the Golden Calves," 129–40; Clements, *Exodus*, 206; Noth, *History of Pentateuchal Traditions*, 143; Hyatt, *Exodus*, 301–4; and Cassuto, *Commentary on the Book of Exodus*, 408.

29. Dale Ralph Davis suggested that Yahweh withdrew the sentence of immediate extinction (32:14), but the individuals guilty of idolatry would receive retribution later. See Davis, "Rebellion, Presence, and Covenant," 76. Deuteronomy 9:12–21 provides a similar, albeit shorter, account of the golden calf narrative in Exod 32. Since the Deuteronomic text revisits the Exodus account, I will not be examining that text in detail. Of note, McKenzie provides a case study of the innerbiblical relationship between Exod 32:7–20 and Deut 9:12–21. See McKenzie, *Idolatry in the Pentateuch*. Christopher T. Begg maintained that Deut 9:12–21 represented "a (Deuteronomistic) reworking" of Exod 32:7–20. See Begg, "Destruction of the Golden Calf," 469–79.

The Legislative Themes of Centralization

Exodus 34:11–16

The renewal of the covenant outlined in Exod 34:11–16 continues the growing polemic against idolatry in the Tetrateuch and, more specifically, shares a unique relationship with Deut 12:1–4. First, the narrative reiterates the inhabitants within the land of Canaan with some variation in the order: Amorites, Canaanites, Hittites, Perizzites, Hivites, and Jebusites (v. 11). Next, Yahweh commands the people to "be attentive" (השמר)[30] and avoid making a covenant with the inhabitants of the land because they will become a "snare" (למוקש) in the midst of the people (v. 12). Building upon this command, Yahweh directs the people to "tear down their altars" (מזבחתם תתצון), "break their pillars" (מצבתם תשברון), and "cut down their Asherim" (אשריו תכרתון). Thus, the divine directive in Exod 34:11–16 is a literary precursor to the Deuteronomic command (Deut 12:1–4).

Lev 18:1–4

Exodus concludes with the Israelites still at Mount Sinai, yet a Yahwistic hegemony is solidified through the divine revelation of the Decalogue and the Book of the Covenant. Leviticus continues the theological impetus of Exodus by emphasizing holiness and worship. In fact, portions of the Holiness Code (Lev 17–26) continue to build upon the polemical ideology introduced in Exodus.[31] Thus, Lev 18:1–4 provides a retrospective and prospective declaration regarding the abrogation of idolatry and pagan worship. The message of Yahweh to Moses is introduced with the formulaic phrase "I am Yahweh your God" (אני יהוה אלהיכם). Next, Moses reminds the people to avoid the worship ideals that were present in Egypt, as well as the worship practices of the individuals in the land of Canaan. In somewhat of a comparison, Yahweh explains that the statutes of the people in Canaan should not be followed but rather the Israelites should keep his ordinances and statutes. Verse 4 closes with the same formulaic phrase that introduces the pericope (אני יהוה אלהיכם). The following verse reiterates the basic

---

30. See *HALOT* 2:1584.

31. The Holiness Code is one of three major law codes in the Pentateuch. The literary structure of the Holiness Code, however, is not as coherent as the other two Pentateuchal law codes. Unlike the *paraeneses* of Deuteronomy, the literary structure of the Holiness Code has been described as juxtaposed clusters of laws and exhortations around singular subjects or phrases. See Eissfeldt, *The Old Testament*, 234; Patrick, *Old Testament Law*, 152; Hartley, *Leviticus*, 249; and Childs, *Old Testament Theology*, 158.

The Abrogation of Idolatry

teaching of v. 4 but includes one addition—the promise that keeping the statutes and ordinances of Yahweh will result in life. The remaining portion of Lev 18 outlines the stipulations for abominable sexual relations. Verse 22, however, is related to idolatry in that the Israelites are commanded not to sacrifice their children to the Ammonite god Molech (cf. 1 Kgs 11:7).

Leviticus 20:22–26

A similar polemical argument to Lev 18:1–4 is presented in Lev 20:22–26.[32] The sentence structure of 20:22 is dissimilar to 18:4, although the majority of the words are the same. A stark difference is found in the proclamation for keeping the statutes and ordinances: "You will not be vomited out of the land in which I bring you to live" (v. 22).[33] Verse 22 is actually a verbatim quote of 18:28a, save the "metathesis of subject and object."[34] The use of קיא ("to vomit") is not found in any other book of the Enneateuch but occurs in Leviticus three times (18:25, 28; 20:25). Additionally, the phrases "and you shall not walk in statutes of the nation that I am sending out from before you" (ולא תלכו בחקת הגוי אשר-אני משלח מפניכם, v. 23) and "I will give to you to inherit" (אני אתננה לכם לרשת, v. 24) are emphasized further in Deuteronomy and Joshua.[35]

Number 25:1–5

Numbers 25:1–5 is preceded by the Balaam cycle (Num 22–24). In this cycle, Balak procured the diviner Balaam to curse Israel as they passed through the land of Moab. In an ironic turn of events, Balaam blessed the Israelites rather than cursing them. The Balaam cycle concludes with a blessing of Jacob's descendant and a pronouncement of destruction upon

---

32. Mary Douglas described chs. 18 and 20 as symmetrical sets of prohibitions that bracketed ch. 19, the apex of Leviticus. Together, chs. 18 and 20 addressed the "sexual irregularities as known in foreign cults," whereas ch. 19 emphasized justice and love within the community of Yahweh. See Douglas, "Justice as the Cornerstone," 341–50.

33. ולא-תקיא אתכם הארץ אשר אני מביא אתכם שמה לשבת בה.

34. Milgrom, *Leviticus 17–22*, 1759.

35. The only use of נתן and ירש together as an idiomatic phrase outside of a Deuteronomistic book is found in Lev 20:24. More importantly, the combination of these words is found in Deuteronomy (1:39; 5:31; 11:31; 15:4; 17:14; 19:2, 14; 21:1; 25:19; 26:1), Joshua (Josh 1:11; 21:43), and Jeremiah (Jer 30:3).

The Legislative Themes of Centralization

Moab, Edom, and Seir (Num 24:15-24). Immediately after the Balaam cycle, the people of Israel dwell in Shittim and begin to commit apostasy through the influence of the daughters of Moab (Num 25:1).[36] The acts of apostasy included sacrifices and worshiping the gods of the Moabites (v. 2). In v. 3, the Israel's are described as being "yoked" to Baal of Peor. In these verses, emphasis is given to the apostasy with Moabite women (vv. 1-2) and Baal of Peor (vv. 3-5; cf. Deut 4:1-8). Thus, a dichotomy might exist between vv. 1-2 and vv. 3-5. The possible dichotomy is strengthened by the subjects of the idolatrous acts: the people and Moabite women in vv. 1-2 and Israel and Baal of Peor in vv. 3-5.[37] Traditionally, the worship of the Baal of Peor included some form of sensual rites.[38] Moreover, Baal of Peor was probably the "Canaanite god of fertility" and worshipers "hoped to contribute to his bringing new life out of death."[39] Thus, the phrase "the people began to play the harlot to the daughters of Moab" (ויחל העם לזנות אל-בנות מואב) underscores the demise of Israel's morals, both sexually and spiritually. The punishment for their idolatrous intermarriages was death at the hands of the judges of Israel (v. 5).[40]

---

36. Recently, Joseph Blenkinsopp suggested that Num 25:15 was literarily positioned at the end of the "wilderness itinerary," but in reality the setting suggested the Israelites dwelling in Moab rather than wandering through the land. See Blenkinsopp, "Baal of Peor Episode," 93.

37. Budd, *Numbers*, 275-76. Additionally, these verses have been attributed to JE. The possible dichotomous stories may suggest other issues. That being said, the unity of vv. 1-5 is still a viable option. See also Gray, *Numbers*, 380-82. George Gray also contended that vv. 1-2 were the work of J whereas vv. 3-5 were attributed to E.

38. Baal of Peor was one of the prominent deities in the Moabite, Midianite, and Ammonite pantheon. See Slayton, "Baal-Peor," 1:553.

39. Spronk, "Baal of Peor," 147. Additionally, Ps 106:28 identifies "eating sacrifices of the dead" with Baal of Peor. Philip Budd does not completely agree with Spronk's argument. See Budd, *Numbers*, 279.

40. See Kim, "Finalization of Num 25,1-5," 263-64. The primary objective of Young Kim's article was to examine the Priestly redaction of Num 25:1-5. Through his assessment, he concluded that the narrative aligned itself with other postexilic writings that were anti-intermarriages. Levine argued that Num 25:1-5 was the work of northern Israelites during the ninth or eighth centuries who retrojected the deterioration of the religious climate of their day into the wilderness period. For a slightly different approach to the idolatrous intermarriages the Israelites, see Levine, *Numbers 21-36*, 294-96.

Numbers 33:50–56

Numbers records the Israelites' sojourn from Mount Sinai to Kadesh-Barnea and finally to the plains of Moab. The struggles experienced by the Israelites while in the wilderness tax their relationship with Yahweh and Moses. Like the texts discussed above, Num 33:50–56 continues the prospective theme of entering the land of Canaan, but the text includes the driving out of all the inhabitants of the land. Once the Israelites are securely in the land, they are to destroy all the figured stones, molten images, and high places. Upon the removal of these items, the Israelites will take possession of the land. The land will then be divided among the tribes. Any residents of the land of Canaan not driven out by the people will become like pricks in the eyes and thorns in the side (לשׂכים בעיניכם ולצנינם בצדיכם). Numbers 33:50–56 shares some thematic similarities with Deut 12:1–4, yet the syntax and verbs are not parallel. The glaring omission within the theological impetus of Num 33:50–56 is the absence of the centralization motif (cf. Deut 12:5).

Deuteronomy 4 and 6

Deuteronomy contains several important declarations regarding the expunging of the inhabitants and particularly their pagan rituals from the land of Canaan. Most of the polemical remarks toward pagan rituals are incorporated within the opening Deuteronomic phrase in 4:1: "Now, Israel listen to the statutes and to the commandments." Although this portion of Deuteronomy is recognized by some as the literary work of the Dtr, the phrase does introduce the coming polemical elements found throughout the remainder of the book. Of note, vv. 15–31 serve as a warning against idolatry, particularly, the prohibition against a carved image (vv. 15–19; cf. Exod 20:4–6; Deut 5:8–10). Unlike the second commandment, vv. 15–19 identify unacceptable images: any male or female figure, any animal, any bird, any creeping animal, or any fish.[41] Additionally, the prohibition warns that such images can cause the Israelites to stumble resulting in the worshiping of the images (v. 19). The penalty for such grievous actions is introduced with Yahweh persecuting Israel in a court setting (vv. 25–26a). The penalty for their breach of the covenant would be destruction and dispersion (vv. 26b–28).

---

41. This list resembles the creation account in Gen 1.

The Legislative Themes of Centralization

The Shema (6:4–5) serves as the acme of Deuteronomy and must be viewed as the backdrop for the polemic against pagan idols and worship in 6:13–15. The polemical undertones of vv. 13–15 are introduced by the declaration to "fear" (ירא) Yahweh. The polemical nature of vv. 13–15 builds upon the first three commandments in 5:3–7 and the Shema (6:4–5). If any individual contravenes the laws outlined in 6:13–15, then the anger (חרה) of Yahweh will be kindled, and the result will be death. From a literary perspective, the use of verbs ירא and חרה are used metonymically to compare righteous and sinful hearts. Moreover, failure to obey the laws in 6:13–15 would be the antithesis of Yahweh's primary command, "Love the Lord your God with all your heart, soul, and might" (6:5).

Deuteronomy 7

The demand for holiness continues to build in intensity with the election of Israel in Deut 7. Moses prepares the people to enter the land of Canaan and explains that Yahweh will clear away (נשל) the nations, though this process will require the military action of the people (vv. 1–2; cf. Exod 18:20–25).[42] The people are told "to utterly destroy" (הכיתם החרם תחרים; cf. Deut 20:17–18) the inhabitants and make no covenant with them or show them mercy. Furthermore, intermarrying with the inhabitants of the land will lead to corruption of the monotheistic demands of Yahweh (vv. 3–4).[43] More specifically, the underlying purpose of vv. 1–5 is the election of Israel. Moses substantiates his demands of purging the idolatrous inhabitants from the land with the simple dictum that the Israelites are a holy people whom Yahweh chose. Obedience to Yahweh's laws and commandments will continue a vibrant relationship between the supreme deity and his covenanted people (vv. 6–11). At a conceptual level, the polemical elements in vv. 1–5 form a relationship with 12:1–5. Both texts contain the same verbal roots (גדע, שבר, נתץ, and שרף); however, the two contain slightly different

---

42. Note in Deut 7:1 the inclusion of the Girgashites into the list of nations: Hittites, Girgashites, Amorites, Canaanites, Perizzites, Hivites, and Jebusites. The Girgashites are found also in the list of nations in Josh 3:10, 24:11, and Neh 9:8, though the order differs in each.

43. Along these lines, Edelman made an excellent point: "Deuteronomy forbids cultural contact with the 'nations of Canaan' and commands them to be exterminated; the danger is not so much that Israel would lose its genealogical distinctiveness by intermarriage, but rather lose its divinely given culture." See Edelman, *Opening the Books of Moses*, 116.

conjugations of verbs. In 7:5, the structure of the verbal conjugations is Qal imperfect (נתץ), Piel imperfect (שבר), Piel imperfect (גדע), Qal imperfect (שׂרף), which can be denoted simply as an a-b-b-a pattern, whereas Deut 12:3 is an a-b-a-a-a pattern.

Deuteronomy 12:1–5

The literary structure of Deut 12 contains the land motif and two additional purposes. First, v. 1 introduces the Deuteronomic law code. The phrase "statutes and ordinances" (החקים והמשפטים) serves as the preliminary declaration that the Israelites must follow the laws to inherit the land promised by Yahweh. The constant changing between second-person singular and second-person plural, called the *numeruswechsel*,[44] is meant to hold the attention of the addressee and represents how each individual is part of the community.[45] The *numeruswechsel* is intertwined with four independent laws, each of which emphasizes the centralization of the cult (12:2–7, 8–12, 13–19, 20–28). A conclusion emphasizes the concern for purity (12:15, 21).[46]

The first law (vv. 2–7) parallels the polemical elements in 7:1–5. The fundamental difference between 7:1–5 and 12:1–5 is rather basic. In the former text, the polemical language is necessitated by the election of the people, whereas the latter text introduces the theological concept of centralization, which will eliminate apostasy.[47] The Deuteronomic motif "the place which Yahweh your Lord will choose" (המקום אשר-יבחר יהוה אלהיכם) introduces the concept of centralization and emphasizes Yahweh's supremacy for choosing the land for not only inhabitance but also the location for his name and corporate worship (12:5). The place *chosen* by Yahweh is the antithesis of the *place* where the Canaanites worshiped.

---

44. Syntactically, Deuteronomy is composed of several rhetorical techniques that enlighten readers to the book's purpose. One example is the rhetorical shift from second-person singular to second-person plural, which is called the *numeruswechsel*. Duane Christensen examined the *numeruswechsel* on the basis of metrical structure within the MT. He admitted that mainline biblical scholars have ignored the influence of the metrical structure in Deuteronomy. See Christensen, "*Numeruswechsel* in Deuteronomy 12," 394–402.

45. Römer, "Le Deuteronome," 72–73.

46. See Levinson, *Deuteronomy and the Hermeneutics*, 24.

47. See McConville, *Deuteronomy*, 229; cf. Nelson, *Deuteronomy*, 149.

The Legislative Themes of Centralization

In 12:1–5, Moses addresses a plural audience and commands the Yahwistic cult to unite against the Canaanite plurality of altars.[48] The verbal pattern in v. 3, however, does not replicate completely that of 7:5, particularly the conjugation of parallel verbs and the literary arrangement. For example, three of the verbs in 12:3 are Piel perfects (נתץ, שבר, גדע), whereas the verb "to burn" (שרפ) is a Qal imperfect. From a structural standpoint, v. 3 reverses the order of the last two verbs (שרפ, גדע) and inserts the phrase "destroy their name from that place." Thus, the verbal pattern of v. 3 is a-b-a-a-a compared to the a-b-b-a pattern in 7:5.

In addition, v. 3 loosely parallels the commands in Exod 34:13; however, in v. 3 the verb "to tear down" (נתצתם) is a Piel perfect second-person masculine plural, the verb "to break" (שברתם) is a Piel perfect second-person masculine plural, and the verb "to cut down" is replaced with the verb "to burn" (תשרפון). Due to the similarities in vocabulary and the theology, Exod 34:11–16 and Deut 12:1–4 are related since the texts magnify the narrator's polemical ideology against the pagan nations inhabiting Canaan. Both texts not only describe the idolatrous practices by the inhabitants of Canaan but, more importantly, the narrator subtly presents the pagan gods as futile and untenable in a theomachy with Yahweh (cf. Judg 6:31–32; 1 Kgs 18:20–39).[49] In sum, the polemical language is rich with satire between the unsurpassable Yahweh and the pagan deities created by the hands of men.

Deuteronomy 13

Deuteronomy 13 begins with Moses commanding the people not to add or subtract from the law. Thus, v. 1 is not a concluding exhortation but rather an opening statement[50] that emphatically reaffirms the Israelites' primary duty of obedience.[51] The chapter consists of three laws, each of which represents a defining case that sequentially juxtaposes cultural values of individuals with the complete devotion to Yahweh. Collectively, the three laws deal with various forms of apostasy.[52] In many ways, the stories about apostasy function as case studies of the previous mandate to abrogate idolatry

---

48. See Levinson, *Deuteronomy and the Hermeneutics*, 24.
49. Cf. Block, "Joy of Worship," 141.
50. Merrill, *Deuteronomy*, 229.
51. Driver, *Deuteronomy*, 152; cf. Craigie, *Book of Deuteronomy*, 222.
52. Levinson, "Recovering the Lost Original Meaning," 601.

The Abrogation of Idolatry

(12:1–5). The strict form of monotheism in ch. 12, then, is expanded into specific examples, or cases in ch. 13.

The first case relates to a prophet or an interpreter of a dream (vv. 2–6). Moses commands the people to ignore the false teachings and proclamations of these false prophets and dreamers. The false prophet could potentially lead the people down a path of idolatry (נלכה אחרי אלהים אחרים). The misleading words of the prophet function as a cohortative, since his words are used to encourage the Israelites into action contrary to the word of Yahweh.[53] The misguiding words of the prophet and dreamer are a form in which Yahweh tests the faithfulness and obedience of his covenant people (v. 3). In short, Yahweh wants to discover whether his chosen people truly love him (v. 4). The syntax of v. 4 heightens the loyalty and love of the Israelites.[54] At the crux of this test is the command to kill the prophet of dreams who preaches against Yahweh. Moses commands the people to kill the transgressor since Yahweh is responsible for delivering his people from Egyptian bondage (vv. 5–6). Thus, the prophet is equated with the evil of the Egyptians.[55]

Similarly, the second case (vv. 7–12) describes a family member or close friend who commits an act of apostasy by destroying the covenant relationship with Yahweh. If the individual guilty of apostasy entices others to worship "other gods" (אלהים אחרים), then his punishment is death (vv. 9–10).[56] The final case addresses the successful conversion to apostasy

---

53. *IBHS* 573.
54. See Nelson, *Deuteronomy*, 163.
55. McConville, *Deuteronomy*, 234.
56. Syntactically, the phrase לא-תכסה עליו in v. 9 has challenged biblical scholars. Levinson, however, provided a convincing argument concerning its interpretation. He argued the traditional translation of לא-תכסה עליו ("nor shall you conceal him") does not adequately reflect the force of the Hebrew idiom consisting of the Piel כסה and the preposition על. According to Levinson, the previous four verbs in v. 9 concerned "the subjective response of the law's addressee." The final verb תכסה ("to conceal") appears out of place when viewed through the larger lens, since the two previous verbs emphasized the internal feelings of pity and compassion for a beloved. The series of five negative imperatives forbade any sympathy for anyone who was guilty of apostasy. Furthermore, the people were forbidden to allow personal feelings to interfere with the gravity of apostasy, particularly on the account of love. In v. 10, the infinitive absolute הרג ("to slay") commanded the addressee to take action immediately and execute the one guilty of apostasy. For this reason, לא-תכסה עליו in v. 9 cannot mean "to cover over someone." When viewed holistically, the five-verb sequence in v. 9 "represented a rhetorical *tour de force.*" The first two verbs represented noncompliance, while the next two forbade the people from having pity or compassion. With the final prohibition לא-תכסה עליו,

57

of an entire town (vv. 13–18). If the inhabitants of towns refuse to submit and follow Yahweh, then they are to be destroyed and slaughtered with the sword. Before taking such actions, however, the people are commanded to inquire, probe, and investigate the situation (ודרשת וחקרת ושאלת היטב). The Hiphil infinitive absolute היטב literally means "good" or "well," but within the context of v. 15, the verb functions as an adverbial accusative of manner to the verb "to inquire" (שאלת).[57] If the individual is found guilty after the investigation, then he is sentenced to "judgment of annihilation" (החרם).[58] In short, the case laws in ch. 13 highlight the concept that Yahweh is the theocratic king of Israel and the worship of other gods is considered high treason.[59]

Deuteronomy 16 and 18

Relatively concise statements against idolatry are found in Deut 16 and 18. Chapter 16 concludes with another emphasis on abolishing any forms of pagan worship, particularly the planting of Asherah trees near the altar of Yahweh. In Deuteronomy and the so-called DH, Asherah poles and sacred pillars are synonymous with idolatry (1 Kgs 14:23; 2 Kgs 17:10; 18:4; 23:14). The placement of an Asherah pole or pillar next to the sanctuary is an abomination to the worship of Yahweh. Manasseh allows these idolatrous acts to take place during his reign, and in turn he becomes known as the most blatant apostate (2 Kgs 21:7).[60]

After discussing the provisions for the priests (Deut 18:1–8), the Deuteronomic law code shifts the focus back to idolatry (vv. 9–14). These laws reiterate the command not to adhere to the pagan practices of the people in Canaan, particularly their sacrifices of offspring, the practice of divination, and other abominable acts. In Deuteronomy, the term "abomination" (תועבת) occurs seventeen times and is the favorite term used to express

---

Moses deliberately expanded the force of the previous two verbs by intensifying its force; therefore, the more appropriate meaning of לא-תכסה עליו would be "nor shall you condone him" but "you must surely slay him with your hand" (כי הרג תהרגנו ידך, v. 10). See Levinson, "Recovering the Lost Original Meaning," 601–20.

57. *IBHS* 40.

58. Eugene Merrill explained that in the context of Deuteronomy, חרם was the judgment reserved for the "recalcitrant pagans" in the land of Canaan. See Merrill, *Deuteronomy*, 233.

59. Tigay, *Deuteronomy*, 128.

60. Cf. McConville, *Deuteronomy*, 289.

"all that is repulsive to Yahweh."[61] Furthermore, Yahweh commands the Israelites to "take possession" (מוריש) of the land. The message conveys, however, a deeper meaning. The Israelites are expected to "drive out" the evil Canaanites from their midst, and in doing so the people of Israel will be blameless before Yahweh (v. 13).

Deuteronomy 31:16–22

At the end of Moses' life, Joshua is commissioned to lead the Israelites into the land of Canaan. As this transition of leadership approaches, Yahweh declares that following the death of his servant Moses the people will worship the foreign gods of the land they will inhabit. These idolatrous acts will breach the covenant of Yahweh and, as a result, the anger of Yahweh will be kindled and his presence will be removed (vv. 16–18). To teach the people of Israel about their idolatry, Yahweh commands Moses to write a song that commemorates the breach of the covenant (vv. 19–22).

Deuteronomy 32

Deuteronomy 32 has a long history of scholarly interpretations. Much of the scholarly attention regards the song's setting and date. Since the primary focus of this chapter is on the theme idolatry, I will not interact with the plethora of works related to the compositional date and context of the song. This should not, however, diminish the importance of such inquiries.[62] In short, I am more concerned with the message of idolatry in the song than on the scholarly reconstructions of its context and background.

The chapter is traditionally known as the "Song of Moses," but a more appropriate name could be the "Song of Yahweh."[63] Even though the song is couched as the message of Moses, the primary focus is on the relationship

---

61. Merrill, *Deuteronomy*, 270.

62. Several works summarize and critique the various interpretations of Deut 32. Lundbom has recently provided a concise history of research into the Song of Moses. See Lundbom, *Deuteronomy*, 852–56. Although arguing for the redaction of Deut 32 during the reign of Josiah, Mark Leuchter examined and compared a variety of scholarly theories related to the song. See Leuchter, "Song of Moses," 295–317. Somewhat dated, Paul Sanders has provided the most through overview of the Song of Moses. See Sanders, *Provenance of Deuteronomy 32*, 1–98.

63. Block, *Deuteronomy*, 746.

The Legislative Themes of Centralization

between Yahweh and Israel. Within the context of Deuteronomy, the song "describes the consequences of Israel's anticipated betrayal of God."[64] Thus, the designation of "Song of Yahweh" makes sense particularly given the structure of the song. The structure (=stanzas) emphasizes the severity of Israel's idolatry and Yahweh's mercy: lawsuit language (vv. 1–3); the comparison of Yahweh's faithfulness and Israel's faithlessness (vv. 4–9); an explanation of Yahweh's compassion (vv. 10–14); Israel's apostasy (vv. 15–18); the judgment of Yahweh (vv. 19–25); Yahweh's reconsideration of judgment (vv. 26–35); and Yahweh's vindication through saving Israel (vv. 36–43).[65] The introduction to the song shares some similarities to a lawsuit.[66] The lawsuit language introduces the overarching theme within the song: the comparison of Yahweh's faithfulness and Israel's idolatry. Turning to the message of the song, I will only focus on the texts related to the theme idolatry.

In v. 5, Yahweh abruptly declares Israel as no longer being his children due to their corruption and idolatry. The idolatry of Israel is counter to the "greatness" of Yahweh in v. 3.[67] Additionally, the declaration that Israel is no longer Yahweh's children is reminiscent of Hos 1:9. In vv. 15–18, Israel is given the name "Jeshurun," which means "upright." The irony of the name is found in description of Jeshurun as being fat. The idolatrous acts of the Israelites kindled the jealousy and anger of Yahweh (vv. 16, 21–22; cf. Exod 20:5; Deut 5:9) because they sacrificed to gods, old and new (vv. 17 and 21). As a result, Yahweh spurned the people and hid his face (v. 18). The image and language of Yahweh in vv. 19–43 is that of Divine Warrior: "kindled fire" (v. 22), "sword" (vv. 25, 41), and "arrows" (v. 42).[68] In vv. 19–43, Yahweh decides to punish Israel by withdrawing his sovereign protection and

---

64. Tigay, *Deuteronomy*, 298.

65. The above structure of the song is adopted from McConville, *Deuteronomy*, 451.

66. See Wright, "Lawsuit of God," 26–67; cf. Mayes, *Deuteronomy*, 380–81; Miller, *Deuteronomy*, 266; Nelson, *Deuteronomy*, 369; and McConville, *Deuteronomy*, 451. Acknowledging the overwhelming support of the covenant lawsuit interpretation of Deut 32, Tigay still found the argument unconvincing when applied to then entire chapter. See Tigay, *Deuteronomy*, 509–10. Matthew Thiessen critiqued Wright's article, "Lawsuit of God," and challenged his argument that Deut 32 was a covenant lawsuit. Instead, Thiessen suggested that Deut 32 was a "text of liturgical worship." See Thiessen, "Form and Function," 401–24, here 407.

67. See Nelson, *Deuteronomy*, 371.

68. Ibid., 369. See his discussion on pp. 373–79.

The Abrogation of Idolatry

bringing war and natural disasters upon the people (vv. 21–25).[69] In an amazing turn of events, the imminent wrath and destruction depicted in vv. 19–24 is abated and replaced with a "robust self-asseveration"—Yahweh alone is God (v. 43).[70] Thus, at the conclusion of the song (v. 44), Yahweh gives a theological meaning to Israel—experience disaster and hope for restoration.[71]

Joshua 24

The Deuteronomic covenant ceremony at Shechem in ch. 27 is related to Deut 11:26–32, and together the texts form an inclusio around the Deuteronomic law code. With that in mind, the covenant ceremony at Shechem in Josh 24 must be interpreted in light of Deut 12–26. Moses uses the ceremony formally to outline the curses and blessings, as well as provide closing remarks to his second sermon. In the final chapters of Deuteronomy, Moses commissions Joshua to lead the people (31:7–8, 23–29; see also Josh 5–9) and then dies following his song (Deut 32). The covenantal sequence at the end of Deuteronomy (chs. 32–34) is significant for the book of Joshua since it provides the backdrop of chs. 1–5. The subsequent events in Joshua record the military advancements and actions of the Israelites (chs. 6–12). Following the military expeditions of the people, the biblical narrator explains in detail the allotment of the land to the tribes of Israel. Joshua, similar to Deuteronomy, ends with a covenantal ceremony at Shechem.[72] In ch. 24, Joshua gathers all the tribes to Shechem, particularly the elders, leaders, judges, and officers.[73] The significance and tradition of ch. 24 has been described as the "parliament" at Shechem,[74] a later redaction of the *Landtag von Sichen* ("legal assembly of Shechem") by the Dtr,[75] a recurring

---

69. Tigay, *Deuteronomy*, 307.
70. Lundbom, *Deuteronomy*, 907.
71. Nelson, *Deuteronomy*, 369.
72. Eduard Nielsen wrote a comprehensive study of Shechem throughout Israel's history, which included analysis of Josh 24. See Nielsen, *Shechem*, 86–141.
73. William T. Koopmans provided a thorough analysis of the various theories concerning the diachronical composition of Josh 24 and its relationship with the theological concept of covenant. See Koopmans, *Joshua 24 as Poetic Narrative*.
74. Rad, "Form-Critical Problem," 36–37.
75. Noth, *Das Buch Josua*, 105–9.

festival,[76] an example of a covenantal treaty,[77] the work of a scribe utilizing Pentateuchal traditions to create a "pure literary work,"[78] and a source-critical summation of Israel's history stretching from Abraham (Gen 12) to Joshua (Josh 24).[79] Though several of the above theories are viable, the literary unity associated with Shechem must not be diminished. After sojourning from the land of Ur to the land of Canaan, Abram enters the land near Shechem. Yahweh appears to Abram while in Shechem at the oak of Moreh. At this sacred location, Yahweh promises Abram's descendants the land (Gen 12:7). Thus, the covenant renewal at Shechem (Josh 24) is related to the divine promise between Abram and Yahweh.

An examination of ch. 24, however, will provide a more comprehensive understanding of Yahweh's mandate to remain holy and purge the evil from the land. Following a historical synopsis chronicling the Israelites' derivational path, Joshua speaks authoritatively to the people (v. 14), similar to the historical credo in Deut 26:5–9.[80] The forcefulness of the message is underscored by the imperatives throughout the verse. First, Joshua demands the people to "fear Yahweh" (יראו את-יהוה)[81] and serve him (עבדו) with

---

76. Advocates for the recurring festival argument maintain the law was read aloud and stipulations reiterated each year. See Sellin, *Gilgal*, 1–60; idem, *Geschichte des Israelitisch-jüdischen Volkes*, 1:28, 96–98; Kraus, *Gottesdienst in Israel*, 47; and Rad, "Form-Critical Problem," 42–46.

77. For example, see Mendenhall, "Ancient Oriental and Biblical Law," 50–76; idem, "Covenant Forms," 50–76.

78. Moshe Anbar was the first scholar to suggest that Josh 24 was the work of a scribe who formulated "a pure literary work" (*une pure oeuvre littéraire*) from the primary Pentateuchal traditions. See Anbar, *Josué et l'alliance de Sichem*. Other prominent scholars have adopted Anbar's conclusions. See Schmid, *Erzväter und Exodus*, 209–30 and Na'aman, "Law of the Altar," 141–43.

79. Christophe Nihan argued that Josh 24 should be viewed as a "post-Deuteronomistic" and "post-Priestly" creation that solidified "various traditions of origins" into a concise summation of Israel's past history, which might suggest the author of the text was attempting to create a Hexateuch. See Nihan, "Torah between Samaria and Judah," 196–97.

80. Von Rad included Josh 24:2–13 into his list of historical credos (Deut 6:20–24; 26:5–9) that functioned as the most archaic record of Yahweh's saving acts. These credos introduced Yahweh as the God who brought Israel out of Egypt and were used widely as confessional formulae. See Rad, "Form-Critical Problem," 3–8; idem, *OTT* 1:121–28, 1:296–98; idem, *Deuteronomy*, 156–59; idem, *God at Work in Israel*, 140–41.

81. Though the concept of fearing Yahweh spreads the breadth of Israelite history, an argument can be made that the concept of יראו את-יהוה is Deuteronomistic. The combination of these words or the general concept that utilizes the words יהוה and ירא is found 137 times in the HB with seven being in the Tetrateuch (Exod 9:20, 30; 14:31; Lev 19:14,

The Abrogation of Idolatry

faithfulness.[82] Next, he commands the people to "turn aside" (הסירו) from the gods[83] of their fathers and serve Yahweh (עבדו את-יהוה). The retrospective emphasis on idolatry possibly revisits the worship rituals at Shechem.[84] In v. 15, Joshua again uses the verb עבד five times. The ultimatum is given to the people to serve Yahweh or the gods of their fathers. This ultimatum is followed with Joshua proclaiming his allegiance to Yahweh. Moreover, Joshua's proclamation resonates within the centrality of the Shema (Deut 6:4–5) in the presence of Israel's leaders. The positive response by the people in vv. 16–18 is related directly to the historical account in vv. 1–13. Again, Joshua warns the people that Yahweh is a jealous God and requires total commitment, including the abrogation of worshiping other gods. The people reiterate their willingness to follow Yahweh (vv. 19–24). Following the outward proclamation to serve Yahweh, Joshua makes a covenant with the people, which includes statutes and ordinances that he records in the book of the law of Yahweh (vv. 25–28).[85]

Judges 1–2

The Shechemite covenant in Josh 24 is one of the theological apexes in the Israelites' relationship with Yahweh. The transition from Joshua to Judges introduces a new theological disjunction—life without a spiritual and communal leader. In fact, the book of Judges opens with the imperfect *waw*-consecutive (ויהי) and the "temporal speculation" concerning the death of Joshua. Together, these literary connectors relate the events in Judges with the preceding developments described in Joshua.[86]

30, 32; 26:2), ten in Deuteronomy (Deut 3:22; 6:2, 24; 10:12; 14:23; 17:19; 20:1; 28:58; 31:12, 13), and fourteen in the so-called DH (Josh 2:24; 22:25; 24:14; 1 Sam 12:14, 24; 2 Sam 6:9; 1 Kgs 18:3, 12; 2 Kgs 4:1; 17:25, 28, 32, 34, 41).

82. The combination of the imperatives יראו את-יהוה and עבדו encapsulates and centers the focus on transferring loyalty to Yahweh. See Boling, *Joshua*, 537.

83. The LXX reads "foreign gods."

84. Boling, *Joshua*, 537.

85. Charles H. Giblin provided an intriguing argument for the structural pattern of Josh 24. He maintained the structure of the chapter contained a "sevenfold dialogue," which followed the seven *wayyiqtol* forms of אמר and alternated between Joshua and the people (vv. 2a, 14a, 16a, 19a, 21a, 22a, 22d, 23a, 24a). Coincidentally, Josh 24 also included seven imperatives in vv. 14–23. See Giblin, "Structural Patterns," 50–69.

86. Many scholars have noted this connection. See Eslinger, *Into the Hands*," 55; cf. Boling, *Judges*, 53; Niditch, *Judges*, 32; and Webb, *Book of Judges*, 92–93.

The Legislative Themes of Centralization

At the macro level, the link between Joshua and Judges can be classified as a "cause and effect relationship." Both books open with a similar syntactical problem (ויהי אחרי מות), yet the respondent to the situation is quite different. Following the death of Moses, Yahweh is the respondent that who provides the solution, which is emphasized by two imperatives. Joshua is commanded "to rise" and "crossover" (קוּם עֲבֹד) the Jordan River and to lead the people into the land of Canaan (Josh 1:2). Yet in the Judges account, the people of Israel are the respondents to the problem surrounding the death of Joshua. The people inquire of the Lord, and the solution is given through the casting of lots. With the shift in respondent and the striking difference in solutions, a simple question must be asked: Why does Yahweh not provide a successor for Joshua like he did for Moses? The narrator, however, allows this dilemma to mount with tension until Judg 2. By allowing the dilemma to linger, the narrator is increasing the interest, involvement, and familiarity with the current situation.[87]

In addition to the literary features of Judg 1, the narrator explains the military oversight or failures of the conquest described in Joshua. With the incumbent failures of the tribes to expunge the inhabitants from their presence, along with the death of Joshua (Josh 24:29–30; Judg 1:1; 2:6–9), the moral demise of the tribal league begins to crystallize. In doing so, the narrator makes a temporal shift in the narrative in Judg 2:6. By introducing a shift in time, the narrator briefly describes the moment in Josh 24:28 when the people are dismissed from Shechem, and the narrator uses the event as a "panoramic temporal overview" in Judges.[88] The panoramic temporal overview is summarized in an archetypal manner: "And a generation arose after them that did not know Yahweh, and the people did not know the work that he had done for Israel" (2:10).

In 2:11, the narrator further highlights the gravity of the current setting. With no apparent successor to Joshua, "the people of Israel do what is evil in the eyes of Yahweh and serve the Baals" (2:11).[89] The idiomatic phrase

---

87. Ibid., 55–61.

88. Polzin, *Moses and the Deuteronomist*, 150–51. See also Latvus, *God, Anger and Ideology*, 36.

89. ויעשו בני־ישראל את־הרע בעיני יהוה ויעבדו את־הבעלים. The Deuteronomistic nature of the idiomatic phrase is found in various forms throughout the so-called DH and other Deuteronomistic writings: Deut 4:25; 9:18; 17:2; 31:29; Judg 2:11; 3:7, 12; 4:1; 6:1; 10:6; 13:1; 1 Sam 15:19; 1 Kgs 11:6; 14:22; 15:26, 34; 16:19, 25, 30; 21:20, 25; 22:53; 2 Kgs 3:2; 8:18, 27; 13:2, 11; 14:24; 15:9, 18, 24, 28; 17:2, 17; 21:2, 6, 16, 20; 23:32, 37; 24:9, 19;

The Abrogation of Idolatry

is the antithesis to the aforementioned Shechemite covenant that demands serving Yahweh (עבדו את־יהוה). In fact, the idiomatic phrase illustrates the depravity of the people chasing after pagan gods and introduces the narrative cycles of the six major judges: Othniel (3:7–11), Ehud (3:12–30), Deborah (4:1—5:31), Gideon (6:1—8:35), Jephthah (10:6—12:7), and Samson (13:1—16:31).[90] The narrator includes the phrase at the beginning of each judge cycle as an allusion to the theological pungency in 2:10–11.[91] Diachronically, the phrase becomes the precursor to the theological paradigm "every man did what was right in his own eyes" (איש הישר בעיניו יעשה 21:25 17:6). As a result of the people's worship of Baal and Ashtaroth, Yahweh turns his vengeance against them and raises up judges to help deliver them from oppressing nations (2:12–15). During this turbulent time, the people play the harlot (זנו) and seek after other gods rather than walking in the way of their forefathers and the commandments outlined by Yahweh (vv. 16–17). The severity of the spiritual declivity reaches a climax insofar as the Israelites intermarry the inhabitants of the land of Canaan, an act which is deemed anathema earlier in their history (cf. Judg 3:5–7; Deut 7:1–2; 12:1–4; 20:17).[92]

Judges 3:7—16:31

The intermarrying between the Israelites and the inhabitants of the land forms the *Sitz im Leben* for the judges' cycle in 3:7—16:31. Interwoven in the judges' cycle are stories about oppressing nations that hinder and subjugate the Israelites due in large part to the people's idolatrous ways. Yahweh hears the cries of the people and provides charismatic leaders (i.e., judges) to break the bondage of servitude. In each judge cycle, Yahweh allows a surrounding nation to oppress a tribe of Israel for breaching the covenant. The people cry out to Yahweh seeking deliverance from their oppressors. Though Yahweh uses these human agents to deliver his oppressed people,

---

Jer 7:30; 52:2.

90. In his commentary, Robert Boling argued the concept of "evil" was a religious offense with sociopolitical consequences that directly related Judges with Deuteronomy (4:25; 9:18; 17:2; 22:19). See Boling, *Judges*, 74.

91. Eslinger, *Into the Hands of the Living God*, 193.

92. The narrator obviously is making a connection between the Israelites and the inhabitants of the land: Canaanites, Hittites, Amorites, Perizzites, Hivites, and Jebusites.

65

The Legislative Themes of Centralization

relatively few examples exist in conjunction with the Deuteronomic law of abolishing idolatry.[93]

Gideon is the only judge, at least temporarily (cf. 8:27), who appears sensitive to the Pentateuchal statutes and ordinances. The Lord commands him to pull down the altar to Baal (נתץ מזבח הבעל) with his father's bull and cut down the Asherah.[94] The demands upon Gideon are pivotal to the narrative since Yahweh is proclaimed as the true God.[95] Next, Gideon is commanded to take a second bull from his father and offer it as a burnt offering (6:25–26). In an effort to conceal his actions, Gideon waits until the night to follow the command of the Lord. The next morning the inhabitants of the town become indignant over the actions of Gideon. As a result, the people desire the life of Gideon, yet he stands defiant in his cause and questions the spiritual dependency of the people (8:27–32). Interestingly, the Ophrahites are in dialogue with Gideon and not Baal. Such actions only underscore that Baal cannot defend himself, and the followers of the idol must avenge the sacrilege committed by Gideon.[96] The faithfulness of Gideon is short lived unfortunately. After turning down the notion of becoming king, Gideon resolves himself to making an ephod from the jewelry of his supporters. Subsequent to the death of Gideon, the people turn and once again play the harlot by making Baal-berith their god. More importantly, the people do not remember Yahweh as their God (8:27–33). This act of idolatry conceptually echoes the message of 2:10.

The essence of the theological message in Judges is summarized in the phrase "every man did what was right in his own eyes" (איש הישר בעיניו יעשה). After the closing of the judge cycles, the narrator incorporates this new theological paradigm, which counters the words of Joshua at Shechem (cf. Josh 24:15). That the Israelites have no king and every person does what is right in his own eyes augments the downward-spiraling spiritual and civil setting in Israel (17:6; 18:1; 19:1; 21:25).[97] The narrator places this

---

93. Cf. Judg 2:11–19; 3:7–11; 10:6–16. Kari Latvus suggested these texts were related due to common vocabulary, phraseology, and structure. See Latvus, *God, Anger and Ideology*, 42–43.

94. The combination of מזבח and נתץ in a phrase occurs only fifteen times in the HB. The phrase connotes the theological mandate to destroy the altars of the Canaanites (Exod 34:13; Deut 7:5; 12:3). See Bluedorn, *Yahweh versus Baalism*, 98.

95. Ibid., 90.

96. See also Deut 12:1–4 and 1 Kgs 18:20–39.

97. Recently, Barry Webb adopted the same "downward-spiraling" view. See Webb, *Book of Judges*, 34, 139–45.

The Abrogation of Idolatry

literary device at the end of the book as a retrospective summary of the demoralization during the period of the judges and as a prospective hope in the establishment of the monarchy.[98]

1–2 Samuel

The introductory chapters of the Samuel corpus share the same sociopolitical and religious climate as the end of Judges. Spiritual infidelity spills over from the social arena in Judges to the cultic centers in the Samuel corpus (2:22–25). In addition, spiritual complacency is found in the temple at Shiloh (3:1b). These narrative markers introduce the Samuel narrative and form the backbone for the narrator's forthcoming account of the united monarchy (1 Sam 8—2 Sam 24). Just as Joshua ends on a positive note, Judges opens and later closes at a theological low point. Hope can be restored through the establishment of a monarchy. For this reason, the narrator emphasizes the characters within the broader story and simply ignores the idolatrous actions of the previous generations. In fact, Joshua and the Samuel corpus contain theological norms, as do the books of Judges and the Kings corpus. The theological high watermark of the Samuel corpus is the establishment of the Davidic monarchy. Thus, idolatry is not a focal point in the Samuel corpus outside the story of Eli's sons (1 Sam 2:12–17).

1 Kings 11:1—12:33

Although Saul and David had low points in their reigns, neither man could attain the stature of idolatry that is narrated in the Kings corpus. In 1 Kgs 1–11, the narrator uses irony when depicting the reign of Solomon.[99] At the height of Solomon's glory, the narrator interjects the blatant apostasy by the king due to his unscrupulous desires (11:1–13, 31–33). The result of Solomon's apostasy is the divided monarchy with only the tribes of Judah

---

98. Cf. Polzin, *Moses and the Deuteronomist*, 204. He questioned whether the end of Judges represented the Deuteronomic narrator's attempt to convey optimism about the coming monarchy in the subsequent DH.

99. Gary Knoppers, on the other hand, argued the Dtr used the opulence, power, and international trade of Solomon as "signs of divine favor" in the so-called DH. Thus, he rejected any notion that 1 Kgs 1–11 was an ironic portrayal of the king. See Knoppers, *Two Nations under God*, 1:77–134; idem, "The Deuteronomist," 337–44; idem, "Deuteronomy and the Deuteronomistic History," 409–12.

The Legislative Themes of Centralization

and Benjamin remaining within the Davidic dynasty (v. 13). Following the demoralizing portrayal of Solomon, the narrator introduces the adversaries to the monarchy (11:14-27). Among the adversaries is Jeroboam. The narrator inserts Jeroboam into the narrative between the reign of Solomon and the reign of his son Rehoboam. This literary technique not only shifts the story away from Solomon but also introduces the future of the northern kingdom. The literary purpose of the Jeroboam narrative (11:26—12:33) can be placed within two broad categories: a positive view of Jeroboam and his reign[100] or a "sign of derision and of chastisement" for Israel due to Solomon's aberration from the Davidic ideal.[101] The latter view seems to be the most acceptable proposition when 1 Kgs 11:26—12:23 is interpreted in light of 12:25-33 and the historical annals of 2 Kings.

The narrative begins with Yahweh sending the prophet Ahijah to Jeroboam with the promise of ten tribes (11:13, 31). The sin of Solomon and the insatiable desire for power by his son Rehoboam destroy the very fabric of the Davidic monarchy. Thus, Yahweh intervenes and promises to transfer the blessing of the nation to Jeroboam. The harsh treatment of Solomon's house is substantiated in v. 33. Solomon is guilty of worshiping the pagan gods of his wives (i.e., Ashtoreth, Chemosh, and Milcom). The verse closes with an anti-Deuteronomistic theology, as well as the proclamation of Solomon as the antithesis of his father David: "He did not walk in my ways and did not do what was right in my eyes and keeping my statutes and ordinances."[102] For Solomon, Jeroboam becomes his spiritual and political demise. The ten tribes represent Yahweh's faithfulness to Israel, particularly through Jeroboam, whereas Judah remains with the house of Solomon because of David's faithfulness a generation earlier (vv. 34–36).

The incumbent Solomon desires to kill Jeroboam; yet Jeroboam is able to flee to Egypt and avoid the ominous desires of the king (11:40). While Jeroboam is in Egypt, Rehoboam continues to exceed the practices of his father Solomon (12:1-19). It is not until the return of Jeroboam from Egypt

---

100. Knoppers believed the Dtr intended to portray Jeroboam and his reign in a positive light. He argued, "Although he will later vilify Jeroboam, the Dtr does not impugn the character of Jeroboam in 1 Kgs 11:26—12:20. On the contrary, 1 Kgs 11:26—12:20 presents Jeroboam as YHWH's designated king to govern the incipient kingdom of Israel. This new monarch . . . was awarded the same God-given opportunities to succeed as David enjoyed before him." See Knoppers, *Two Nations under God*, 1:170–71.

101. See Schenker, "Jeroboam and the Division," 226–27.

102. The narrator intentionally uses the Deuteronomistic phrase to revile Solomon and promise blessing to an obedient Jeroboam. See 1 Kgs 11:33, 38.

The Abrogation of Idolatry

that the people of Israel desire a new king of Israel (12:20), whom Yahweh protects from the fury of Rehoboam (12:21–24). The narrator uses the protection of Jeroboam as an ironic twist in the developing narrative.

In 12:25–33, the promise to Jeroboam (11:13, 31) becomes a reality. The king of Israel faces the challenge of creating a "state where none existed." The appointment of a capital, administrative structures, and official cult make sense given the blank slate.[103] After receiving protection from Yahweh, Jeroboam builds a capital in Shechem and erects altars at Bethel and Dan (vv. 25, 29). His rationale for building the altars is to protect his reign and keep the people from returning to the "house of David" (v. 26). The establishing of the cult was by far Jeroboam's most significant act. By creating competition to the Jerusalem temple, Jeroboam provided an alternative to Davidic loyalists. The erecting of shrines at Bethel and Dan—sites located at the extremes of the territory—allowed Israelites convenience over arduous pilgrimage.[104] This is done to stymie the people's peregrination back and forth to the temple in Jerusalem (v. 26). Unfortunately, the erection of altars at Bethel and Dan are "distortions of an established orthopraxis" in Jerusalem (vv. 28–29). After taking counsel, Jeroboam builds two golden calves that are placed at Bethel and Dan. The golden calves are praised as the gods that delivered the Israelites out of the land of Egypt.[105] The Jeroboam cult immediately "revived and perpetuated" the apostasy of Aaron (cf. Exod 32).[106] Though the temples at Bethel and Dan are built to keep the people from traveling back to Jerusalem, the temples themselves are indirectly complements to the Yahwistic temple in Jerusalem. The only use of the name "Yahweh" in the entire pericope is in v. 27—a

---

103. Bright, *History of Israel*, 236–37.

104. Ibid., 237. Bethel was a national shrine until the destruction of Israel.

105. Knoppers, "Aaron's Calf and Jeroboam's Calves," 95. It has been suggested that in Northern Israel Yahweh was associated with the bull. Yahweh may have been depicted as riding the back of the bull or the bull represented the deity. See Edelman, *Opening the Books of Moses*, 130. On a different note, Juha Pekkala challenged the scholarly consensus regarding 1 Kgs 12:26–31. He suggested a later editor inserted the golden bulls into the narrative. In the oldest version of the 1 Kgs 12:26–31, Jeroboam opposed Jerusalem as the sole place of sacrifice. It was the addition of the golden calves by the later editor that introduced the idolatrous portrait of Jeroboam. Thus, all kings that followed in the sins of Jeroboam were idolaters. See Pakkala, "Deuteronomy and 1–2 Kings," 142.

106. Has Christoph Schmitt highlighted the literary relationship between the so-called DH (1 Kgs 12) and the Pentateuch (Exod 32). See Schmitt, "Erzählung von Goldenen Kalb," 235–50.

The Legislative Themes of Centralization

reference to the "house of Yahweh" in Jerusalem.[107] The irreverent and idolatrous act not only undermines the historical works of Yahweh, but it also indicts Jeroboam. Moreover, his designation of the golden calves as the god(s) of the exodus, in essence, modifies the historical tradition of the original exodus (v. 28; cf. Deut 26:5–9) and connotes the cult as "idolatrous and dyotheistic, if not polytheistic."[108] Thus, the inauguration of the golden calves at the behest of Jeroboam "became a sin" (לחטאת) to the people (12:26–30).[109] In addition to the sins at Bethel and Dan, Jeroboam appoints priests from "all the people" (i.e., non-Levites) and allows them to serve in houses at multiple high places.

The actions of Jeroboam breach several laws in Deut 12–18. First, he builds altars at Bethel and Dan to compete with the temple in Jerusalem, ignoring the Deuteronomic mandate to centralize the worship of Yahweh (Deut 12). Second, the installation of golden calves mimics the idolatrous practices of worshiping Baal by the inhabitants of the land prior to the Israelite occupation (Deut 5:5–8; 12:1–4). Third, the cultic calendar is permuted when Jeroboam "devises" (בדא) in his heart an alternative to the Feast of Booths (Exod 23:16; 34:22; Lev 23:33–43). This newly appointed feast takes place at Bethel on the fifteenth day of the eighth month rather than in the seventh month in Jerusalem (vv. 32–33). Again, the actions taken by Jeroboam are in direct violation of Deuteronomic law that requires the

---

107. Knoppers, "Aaron's Calf and Jeroboam's Calves," 95–100. Knoppers argued the purpose behind Jeroboam's cult was to reorganize and preserve the cult rather than to create a "new ex nihilo" cult.

108. Ibid., 101.

109. In their article, Moses Aberbach and Leivy Smolar presented thirteen "points of identity" between Exod 32 and 1 Kgs 12:25–33. Concerning these points of identity, they argued, "To dismiss them as a series of coincidences is manifestly impossible" (p. 134). When viewed side-by-side, the two accounts might resemble authorial intentionality to formulate the identity of the two principle characters. The authors provided two possibilities of solving the tension between the two accounts. First, Jeroboam intentionally imitated the actions of Aaron and based his actions on existing northern traditions. Second, the Exodus account was a later account written by the Zadokite priesthood of Jerusalem that discredited and defamed the northern kingdom and the bull cult. See Aberbach and Smolar, "Aaron, Jeroboam, and the Golden Calves," 129–40. Whereas Aberbach and Smolar focused on the similarities between the two texts, Knoppers recognized the similarities between Exod 32 and 1 Kgs 12:25–33 but maintained the disparities between the two texts were just as important and generally overlooked by scholars. The main difference between Exod 32 and 1 Kgs 12:25–33 was the descriptions of Aaron's calf and Jeroboam's calves. The establishment of Jeroboam's calves as the state religion of the northern kingdom "constitutes a leitmotiv in Kings." See Knoppers, "Aaron's Calf and Jeroboam's Calves," 94, 103.

The Abrogation of Idolatry

celebrating and offering of sacrifices during the Feast of Booth at the "place which Yahweh will choose" (Deut 16:13–16).

1 Kings 13

The severity of the situation permeated by Jeroboam is antithetical to the covenantal promise initiated by Ahijah the prophet in 1 Kgs 11:29–40. The impending judgment passed upon Jeroboam (1 Kgs 13) is linked directly to the conditional clause in 1 Kgs 11:38 (והיה אם-תשמע). Ahijah explains to Jeroboam that if he will listen and keep the statutes and commandments like David, then Yahweh will build him a "trustworthy house" (בניתי לך בית- נאמן).¹¹⁰ At the very least, Jeroboam will receive similar covenantal blessings that were bestowed upon David, and the Davidic blessing might be transferred to his house. Unfortunately, the power placed upon him by the people and the pressure to secure his own reputation lead to his moral and spiritual demise.

Rather than following the covenantal promise issued by Ahijah, Jeroboam prefers to establish his own kingdom rooted in his insatiable thirst for power and willingness to adhere to the idolatries of the inhabitants. As a result, ch. 13 records the emergence of a prophet who turns against the reign of Jeroboam. The prophet pronounces the word of Yahweh at the pagan altar in Bethel. His prophetic message announces the future coming of King Josiah, a descendant of David, who will sacrifice the pagan priests upon the altars before tearing them down (vv. 1–4). Naturally, the words of the prophet do not resonate with Jeroboam, which results in the narrator using the explicit declaration of evil (חטאות ירבעם) to describe the ensuing kings of the northern kingdom.¹¹¹

---

110. The importance of this divine promise is heightened by the other occurrences in the HB. In the first parallel proclamation, Yahweh explains that the sons of Eli have debased their father's house. Death is the penalty for their heinous acts before the Lord; however, Yahweh promises Eli that he will "raise up" a faithful priest (cf. Zadok, 2 Sam 8:17; 15:24; 1 Kgs 1:8; 2:35) and build him a "trusting house." The second occurrence comes during the dialogue between David and Abigail. Following the death of her husband Nabal, Abigail, in somewhat of a prophetical manner, proclaims that Yahweh will build David a "trusting house" because of his faith in the Lord (1 Sam 25:28).

111. Cf. 1 Kgs 14:16; 15:30; 16:31; 2 Kgs 10:31; 13:2, 11; 14:24; 15:9, 18, 24, 28; 17:22. The characterization of transgressions by the kings in the northern kingdom is antithetical to the sanguine description of the Davidic good kings in Judah. Due to the benign nature of the descriptions and to the scope of the book, each idolatrous king will not be discussed.

The Legislative Themes of Centralization

The sins of Jeroboam become the characteristic watermark for the remaining kings of Israel. Unlike Judah, a good king never rules from the throne in the northern kingdom.[112] The narrator's intentional use of irony casts Jeroboam in direct contrast with keeping the law of Yahweh. The good kings in Judah "did what was right in the eyes of Yahweh."[113] Of the eight good kings, only three receive additional praise from the narrator by attaining the unique status of living in accordance of their forefather David—Asa, Hezekiah, and Josiah.[114]

1 Kings 14:21–23

Subsequent to the Jeroboam story, the narrator returns to Rehoboam and the house of Solomon (14:21–23). Under the auspices of Rehoboam's reign, the tribe of Judah does evil in the sight of the Lord, which exceeds the transgressions of the previous generations (v. 22). Jerusalem, during the united monarchy, is devoted to Yahweh. Though Solomon apostatizes due to his blinding, earthly desires, the temple in Jerusalem remains devoted to Yahweh. The tribe of Judah under the reign of Rehoboam, however, builds high places, pillars, and Asherim. The narrator equates the incriminating acts of the Judahites with the abominable acts of the inhabitants of the land prior to the Israelite occupation (v. 23). The narrator's depiction of the Judahites is syntactically synonymous with the laws mandating the destruction of the idolatrous practices by the inhabitants of the land of Canaan (Deut 12–13).[115]

---

112. The narrator does not pass negative judgment (חטאות ירבעם) on two northern kings, Tibni (1 Kgs 16:21–22) and Shallum (2 Kgs 15:10–15).

113. The narrator uses various forms of the Deuteronomistic phrase עשה הישר בעיני יהוה (Deut 12:25; 13:19; 21:9) to describe the "good kings": Asa (1 Kgs 15:11), Jehoshaphat (1 Kgs 22:43), Jehoash (2 Kgs 12:2), Amaziah (2 Kgs 14:3), Uzziah (2 Kgs 15:3), Jotham (2 Kgs 15:34), Hezekiah (18:3), and Josiah (2 Kgs 22:2).

114. Asa did what was right in the eyes of Yahweh as David his father (1 Kgs 15:11). Similarly, Hezekiah did what was right in the eyes of Yahweh, according to all that David his father did (2 Kgs 18:3). The narrator gives pride of place, however, to Josiah. He did what was right in the eyes of Yahweh and "walked in all the pathways of David his father" (וילך בכל-דרך דוד אביו, 2 Kgs 22:2).

115. Notice the similarities in Deut 12:2 and 1 Kgs 14:23: רענן על-הגבעות ותחת כל-עץ (Deut 12:2) and על כל-גבהה ותחת כל-עץ רענן (1 Kgs 14:23). In addition, the Deuteronomistic phrase in 1 Kgs 14:23 parallels the apostasy of the Israelites in 2 Kgs 17:10 and Jer 2:20.

The Abrogation of Idolatry

1 Kings 18–19

Three specific cases of purging idolatry from the midst of the people are found in the Kings corpus. The acts of Elijah are documented well as he demoralizes and ultimately defeats the priests of Baal and Asherah atop the mountain.[116] Sadly, the fervor of Elijah lasts only atop the mountain because once he descends, the threat of Jezebel forces him to flee to the wilderness of Beer-Sheba and later to Mount Horeb (1 Kgs 18–19). The failure by Elijah to remove Ahab and Jezebel from the throne tarnishes Yahweh's miraculous work upon the mountain with the Baal and Asherah prophets. The narrator waits to present the climax in the Elijah narrative. After the Lord reveals himself to Elijah at Horeb, the prophet is commanded to return through the wilderness of Damascus. The actions at Horeb are subsided when the narrator introduces Jehu as king over Israel. Elijah is commanded to anoint Jehu as king, which becomes the apex of the Elijah narrative. The irony of the text is found in that Elijah anoints another man as king while the real king and his queen still remain upon the throne due to the prophet's lack of obedience. The narrative culminates with the anointing of Elisha as the prophet who replaces Elijah (19:15–18).

2 Kings 9:1–10:31

The actions of Elijah on the mountain with the Baal and Asherah prophets overshadow his insufficiencies as a prophet. The introduction of Jehu by the narrator does not come to the forefront until 2 Kgs 9:1—10:31. Elisha anoints and commissions Jehu as king over Israel and directs him to purge the house of Ahab, including his wife Jezebel, for dire acts against the Lord's prophets (9:6–10). To accomplish his military objective, Jehu deceives the sympathizers of Baal into thinking he is more idolatrous than Ahab. His clever ruse helps expunge the Baal worshipers from Israel (10:18–28). Like Elijah, the actions of Jehu are overshadowed by his own personal divergences from Yahweh. Like the other preceding kings of Israel, Jehu does not walk in accordance to the law, and as a result, the narrator immortalizes him with the Deuteronomistic, pejorative description "he did not turn from the sins of Jeroboam" (10:31).

---

116. Due to the structure of the chapter, I will discuss the actions of Elijah and Jehu in this section. The acts of Josiah will be discussed later.

The Legislative Themes of Centralization

2 Kings 17

The punitive measures against idolatry reached a climax with the destruction of Samaria at the hands of the Assyrians (2 Kgs 17). Hoshea, the son of Elah, reigns for nine years over Israel after he assassinates Pekah. The narrator's description of Hoshea is tempered slightly from that of the other Israelite kings. Though he does evil in the eyes of Yahweh, Hoshea's sin does not equal the acts of the preceding kings of Israel. During his reign as king the northern kingdom falls to the Assyrians. From the beginning, Hoshea inherits a poor relationship with the Assyrians. In an attempt to save the land, he submits to the foreign power. With the death of Tiglath-pileser, Shalmaneser V takes over as king of the Assyrians. The transition of power within the Assyrian ranks proves too great a temptation for Hoshea. In an attempt to form a coalition with Egypt, the Israelite king officially withholds tribute and formally rebels against the Assyrians. The result of the Assyrian assault is utter chaos and leads to the devastation of Samaria and the northern kingdom (vv. 1–6).

The destruction and exile of the northern kingdom at the hands of the Assyrians has intrigued scholars due in large part to the narrator's theological and ethical depiction of Israel. From a literary perspective, the narrator appears to explain that the Assyrian exile extends beyond the sins of Hoshea (cf. 17:2). Verses 7–23 represent the narrator's closing act for interpreting the fall of the northern kingdom.[117] The people of Israel are completely responsible for the destruction of Samaria. In fact, the narrator introduces the three incriminating deeds of the Israelites with the proclamation that "the people of Israel sinned against Yahweh their God" (כי-חטאו בני-ישראל ליהוה אלהיהם). The Israelites fear other gods, walk in the customs of the nations that Yahweh already displaced, and walk in the customs of the Israelite kings. Of the three deeds, the first, worshiping foreign gods, serves as the interpretative umbrella for the entire passage (vv. 7–8).[118] Such a claim can be substantiated simply by looking at the demands to abolish idolatry in the land of Canaan (Deut 12–13). In addition, the worship of pagan gods functions antithetically to the Shema (Deut 6:4–5) and the Israelites' historical-credo (Deut 26:4–9).

---

117. Hartmut N. Rösel described 2 Kgs 17:7–23 as displaying arguably the most Deuteronomistic characteristics in the HB. See Rösel, "Why 2 Kings 17," 85.

118. Long, *2 Kings*, 182.

The Abrogation of Idolatry

Scholars have proffered various diachronic interpretations of vv. 7–23. The apostasy described in these verses parallels the deplorable conditions in Judg 2.[119] Second Kings 17 appears to assess the history surrounding the collapse of the Davidic empire (1 Kgs 11–14).[120] The narrator gives an interpretative summation of Jeroboam (1 Kgs 13–14).[121] And, the chapter is actually a summation or reflection of the so-called DH.[122] Each of these suggestions provides valuable insight for interpreting ch. 17; however, the literary structure, syntax, and theology are aligned closer with Deuteronomy than the other aforementioned texts.

In vv. 9–12, the narrator describes the actions of the Israelites as being similar to the customs of the Canaanites in the land (cf. Deut 12–13). Moses commands the people to destroy the all the places of pagan worship, upon high mountains, upon hills, and under every green tree. Additionally, the altars, pillars, Asherim, and graven images must be expunged from the presence of Yahweh (cf. Deut 12:2–4). The destruction of the inhabitants at the hands of the Israelites is to protect Yahweh's chosen people from being ensnared by idolatrous ways (cf. Deut 12:29–31). The narrator then shifts to a court scene with incriminating evidence against the sins of the Israelites being the message of the prophets (vv. 13–18). Yahweh sends prophets and seers demanding the cessation of idolatry and the returning to Yahweh's commandments and statutes. The evidence of Yahweh against the Israelites relates to the promise of future prophets (cf. Deut 18:15–18). The Israelites are to expect Yahweh to use prophets to guide faithfulness.

In response to this, the narrator explains now the people simply ignored the message of the prophets (v. 14). In fact, the narrator compares the Israelites' lack of obedience to the words of the prophets as paramount to the sins of their forefathers in the wilderness—the generation that "rejected" (מאס) the statutes and ordinances of Yahweh (vv. 15–18). The use of מאס as an "expression of human sin" coincides with the characteristics of the biblical prophets rather than the so-called DH portrayal of מאס as

---

119. See Eslinger, *Into the Hands*, 202–19. Several other scholars suggested a link between Judg 2 and 2 Kgs 17 but not to the level of Eslinger. See Rad, *OTT*, 1:335; Noth, *Deuteronomistic History*, 6; and Nelson, *Double Redaction*, 53–65.

120. Weippert, "Die Atiologie des Nordreiches," 346–55, 374–75.

121. Becking, "From Apostasy to Destruction," 288; cf. Long, *2 Kings*, 182.

122. Römer, *So-Called Deuteronomistic History*, 39; idem, "Form-Critical Problem," 240–52. Along these lines, Pakkala suggested the narrative served as the turning point from the "location of the cult to its content." See Pakkala, "Deuteronomy and 1–2 Kings," 143.

The Legislative Themes of Centralization

"divine reaction."[123] The forefathers also forsook Yahweh's commandments and made two molten images of calves. They also worshiped Asherah and served Baal, which the narrator describes as the people selling themselves "to do evil in the eyes of Yahweh" (v. 17; cf. Deut 9:18; Judg 3:12; 41; 10:6; 13:1; 1 Kgs 16:19; 21:20, 25; 2 Kgs 21:6, 16).

The sins of the Israelites result in the expulsion from the presence of Yahweh. The only tribe to remain is Judah, but the narrator quickly indicates that Judah is disobedient also to the Deuteronomic demand of obedience (vv. 19–20). Last, the narrator concludes the demise of the Israelites by paralleling their sins with the grievous sin of Jeroboam (vv. 25–33). In the final hours of the ten tribes of Israel, the narrator outlines the people's willingness to become like the inhabitants of the land (chs. 7–12; cf. Deut 12:1–4), explains that the people's sins exceed their forefathers due to the lack of obedience to the prophets (vv. 13–14; cf. Deut 1–4; 18:15–18), and underscores how the people despise the commandments and statutes (v. 13; cf. Deut 10:13; 28:15, 45; 30:10, 16; 1 Kgs 9:6; 11:34) of Yahweh and worship pagan deities (vv. 13, 16; cf. Deut 13). The narrator concludes the narrative about the northern kingdom by equating the people's sin with their first king—Jeroboam (v. 22).[124] In essence, the narrator introduces the divided monarchy with the story of Jeroboam's sin. What better end to the history of the northern kingdom than to equate the sins of the people with their first king? The stories about the sins of Jeroboam and the Israelites form bookends to the history of the northern kingdom.[125] The divided kingdom is introduced with a narcissistic ruler, and the history of the northern kingdom closes with the very same attitude being adhered to by the people.

2 Kings 21

Manasseh reigned as king over Judah for fifty-five years (v. 1). The narrator describes Manasseh as doing "evil" in the sight of Yahweh due to the king's assimilation of Assyrian practices (v. 2). As a loyal vassal, Manasseh erects

---

123. See Rösel, "Why 2 Kings 17," 88.

124. Ibid., 89.

125. The recurring theme of Jeroboam's sin is representative of what Altar described as narrative analogy: "Where one part of the story provides a commentary on or a foil to another." See Altar, *Art of Biblical Narrative*, 180. Sternberg also provided a thorough treatment of the principle of analogy (i.e., the structure of repetition). See Sternberg, *Poetics of Biblical Narrative*, 365–440.

altars in the Jerusalemite temple to the Assyrian gods (vv. 3–5). These syncretistic practices of Manassah allow "pagan cults and practices to flourish" (v. 6).[126] Coupled with the pagan practices, divination and magic is welcomed in the capital (v. 6). Arguably the lowest point is the return of child sacrifices (v. 6a). The Yahwistic zeal during Hezekiah's reign (2 Kgs 18:3–7; 19:19) is replaced with rampant polytheism not only by Manasseh, but also the people (vv. 3–6, 9). Reflecting on this portrait of spiritual decay, Paul House astutely noted, "It is clear that Manasseh follows all the wrong role models. He imitates the detestable Canaanites, Jeroboam I the builder of high places, Ahab the advocate of Baal worship, Ahaz the proponent of child sacrifice, and Saul the visitor of mediums. It is hard to image a more damning critique."[127] Due to these spiritual shortcomings, the narrator contrasts Manassah's idolatry with David's faithfulness (v. 7). Ultimately, Yahweh declares judgment upon Judah and Jerusalem for the idolatrous ways of Manasseh and the people (vv. 12–15).[128] Following his death, Manassah's son Amon continues the policies of his father (vv. 21–22).

A SYNCHRONIC READING OF THE ABROGATION OF IDOLATRY

The construction of a synchronic reading of the abrogation of idolatry in the Enneateuch is no small task. In many ways, the Pentateuch chronicles the birth of the Israelite people first through the covenant between Yahweh and Abraham (Gen 12–22) and then through the covenant at Mount Sinai (Exod 20:1–17; 20:23—23:19). The so-called DH, on the other hand, records the demise of the covenantal relationship between Yahweh and the Israelites. Interspersed within the literary history of the Enneateuch are complex stories of human failure, deception, and apostasy. The purpose of this section is not to regurgitate the exegetical work above but to provide a

---

126. Bright, *History of Israel*, 311–12. Similarly, Marvin Sweeney described Manasseh as a willing and loyal ally to the Assyrians. See Sweeney, *I & II Kings*, 430.

127. House, *1 and 2 Kings*, 378.

128. Even though the narrator's depiction of Manasseh is harsh, he has been given a variety of titles. Manasseh is viewed as a scapegoat of "Josiah's scribes and an exilic editor." The royal scribes slandered Manasseh as an apostate to bring honor to Josiah. See Halpren, "Jerusalem and the Lineages," 65–66. Additionally, he has been described as the "foil" of Josiah and "Judah's Ahab." See Hobbs, *2 Kings*, 309–11 and Sweeney, *I & II Kings*, 427. One of the most thorough treatments of the Manasseh pericope is by Keulen, *Manasseh through the Eyes of the Deuteronomists*.

The Legislative Themes of Centralization

synchronic reading of the idolatrous derivation of the Israelites as a people to their final destruction.

The obedience of the Israelites is an important theme throughout the Enneateuch. In the Pentateuch, the clearest declaration against idolatry is found in the first two commandments of the Decalogue (Exod 20:3–6; cf. 5:7–10). These two commandments accentuate Yahweh's demand for holiness and faithfulness from the Israelites. In short, these commandments are a divine decree: Yahweh will not share his divine presence with any other gods or permit images/idols of him or other gods. Breaches of these two commandments would circumvent the election of Israel and represent an act of double-mindedness. Thus, the first two commandments, along with the monotheistic declarations in Deut 4–6, are the foundation for the abrogation of idolatry in the Enneateuch, which are expanded upon in the various legal codes.

The governing formal proclamation of statutes and ordinances serves as regulatory measures for procuring obedience from the people (e.g., Exod 15:22–27; 20:23—23:19). The divine plan of expelling the inhabitants from the land of Canaan is introduced first in the Book of the Covenant. At the heart of the juxtaposition between the Israelites and the inhabitants of the land of Canaan is the issue of idolatry (e.g., Exod 34:11–16; Lev 18:1–4; 20:22–26; Num 25:1–5; 33:50–56). The consequence(s) of not complying with the statutes and ordinances of Yahweh usually included some form of judgment. The cornerstone of idolatry in the Pentateuch, like its counterpart in the so-called DH (1 Kgs 12:25–33), is the golden calf narrative in Exod 32. The sins of the people and that of Aaron the high priest are the first corporate abominations against Yahweh. The sins of the people continue in Numbers, where Moses, and at times Aaron, is challenged for leading the people in accordance of Yahweh's providence.

Scholars have long noted the relationship and differences between the Book of the Covenant and Deuteronomy. In many ways, the Deuteronomic polemic against idolatry builds on earlier material (e.g., Exod 18:20–25). The concept of centralization, however, is the defining difference between Deuteronomy and rest of the Tetrateuch. The introductory message of the Deuteronomic law code is a preliminary declaration emphasizing the relationship between the land of Canaan and the covenant between the people and Yahweh (Deut 12:1–5). For this reason, the Israelites are commanded to utterly destroy the inhabitants of the land. Moreover, once in the land of Canaan, Yahweh will choose a central location that will be used strictly for

The Abrogation of Idolatry

worshiping him (v. 5). By centralizing the worship of Yahweh to a single sanctuary, apostasy will be eliminated completely. Before the centralized worship of Yahweh can begin, all remnants of idolatry in the land of Canaan must be eradicated—people, high places, altars, and idols (Deut 7; 12:1–4, 29–32; 13:1–18; 18:9–14). The centralization of the Israelite cult protects the people from apostasy and preserves the social, political, and religious hegemony of Israel (Deut 12:1–5; 17:1–13, 14–20; 18:1–8; 31:16–22).

The Song of Moses in Deut 32 anticipates the Israelites' betrayal of Yahweh through corruption and idolatry. In the song, the idolatrous pagan sacrifices will drive a wedge between Yahweh and Israel (vv. 15–18). The anger of Yahweh will be ignited by his jealousy. The once benevolent hand of Yahweh will be removed and replaced with divine wrath (vv. 19–25); however, divine wrath is abated due to Yahweh's sovereign mercy and love (v. 43). The song is important not only in Deuteronomy but also the Enneateuch. From a synchronic perspective, the song predicts the idolatrous acts of the people in the land of Canaan and their demise.

The so-called DH in many ways becomes antithetical to Deuteronomic mandate to destroy the pagan places of worship and the idolatrous people. Whereas Deuteronomy discusses the generic eradication of idolatry and apostasy from the land of Canaan, the so-called DH provides a vivid account of Israel's defiant self-absorption of the Canaanite abominations. The last semblance of hope is the Shechemite covenant in Josh 24, yet the unavoidable death of Joshua signifies the end of the Mosaic mediator tradition. Each family must determine whether they will remain faithful to Yahweh or succumb to the idolatrous ways of the Canaanites (vv. 1–28). The people's declaration of obedience to Yahweh in vv. 19–24 obviously falters, given the grim introduction in Judg 1–2. The spiraling depravity of the Israelites during the period of the judges is antithetical to the Pentateuchal proscriptions against idolatry, which are evidenced by the indictment "every man did what was right in his own." The apathy toward Yahweh described in Judges carries over into the Samuel corpus, particularly in the lives of Eli the high priest and his two sinful sons. The dedication of Samuel to the shrine at Shiloh is certainly refreshing when compared to the dreary portrait of Israel's spirituality in Judges.

One of the heights of idolatry, not only in the so-called DH but also the Enneateuch, is Jeroboam's sin (1 Kgs 11:1—12:33). His abominable acts against Yahweh become the catalyst for the idolatrous acts in the northern kingdom. The far-reaching effects of Jeroboam's sin culminate with the

The Legislative Themes of Centralization

destruction of the northern kingdom and the capital city Shechem (2 Kgs 17). In the southern kingdom, the idolatrous practices of the people during the reign of King Ahab are met by the wrath of Yahweh through the intervention of the prophet Elijah (1 Kgs 18–19). Abominations reach epic proportions in the southern kingdom when King Manasseh ousts Yahweh from the temple (2 Kgs 21:2–9). The damage inflicted by Manasseh is subsided somewhat during the reign of Josiah, but the decay of people's faith and morals is insurmountable, particularly after the death of Josiah (2 Kgs 22:1—23:30). As a result, the southern kingdom yields to the Babylonian onslaught and destruction of Jerusalem (2 Kgs 24–25).

The above synchronic reading introduces a key component in the literary history of the Enneateuch. Deuteronomy expands the theological thrust of the Tetrateuchal polemic against idolatry. The Deuteronomic concept of centralization underscores the threat of idolatry in the land of Canaan. Theoretically, the centralization of the cult will protect the religious hegemony of Yahweh; however, the books of the so-called DH, particularly Judges and the Kings corpus, provide a different theological portrait of Israel's spirituality. In Judges, the worship of Yahweh is supplanted with the indictment "every man did what was right in his own eyes." In the Kings corpus, the central sanctuary of Yahweh is challenged by Jeroboam and becomes the epicenter of idolatry during the reign of Manasseh. In short, the idolatrous practices in the so-called DH are the antithesis of the Deuteronomic mandate of monotheism and religious hegemony at the central sanctuary.

4

The Israelite Concept of Tithing

THE CONCEPT OF TITHING was a widespread practice in the ANE and not unique to the Israelites.¹ The Hebrew noun מעשׂר literally means "tithe" and occurs only thirty-two times in the HB.² Due to the shortage of textual references, scholars have posited various theories regarding the Israelite concept of tithing. On a macro level, a reconstruction of tithing in ancient Israel is difficult due to the constant adaptation of customs, places, and situations. Furthermore, the use of מעשׂר and עשׂר in the HB can refer to an actual "tenth part" or represent a standardized term that describes a tax or gift.³ Concerning this conundrum, Weinfeld noted, "It seems that the tithe, whose main purpose was the maintenance of the temple and its personnel, was provided by way of an obligatory tax as well as by voluntary donation. It is only Deuteronomy which stripped the tithe of its original purpose and turned it into an obligatory gift to the destitute and the poor."⁴ Thus, Weinfeld is correct in that the HB provides a glimpse of two differ-

---

1. See Averbeck, "מעשׂר," 2:1035–36; cf. North, "עשׂר," 11:404–5.

2. Of the thirty-two occurrences of מעשׂר in the HB, eight references are in the Tetrateuch (Gen 14:20; Lev 27:30, 31, 32; Num 18:21, 24, 26, 28) and six in Deuteronomy (Deut 12:6, 11, 17; 14:23, 28; 26:12). See Averbeck, "מעשׂר," 2:1036.

3. Jagersma, "Tithe in the Old Testament," 117. Similarly, Joseph M. Baumgarten suggested that מעשׂר could mean a literal tenth, but he also conceded that the idea might represent a general term that designated a tax payable to the temple and the clergy ("hieratic tax"). See Baumgarten, "On the Non-Literal Use," 245–51.

4. Weinfeld, "Tithe," 15:1158. Originally, the article was attributed incorrectly to Mark Wischnitzer.

The Legislative Themes of Centralization

ent motivations—voluntary (e.g., Gen 14:20) and obligatory (e.g., 1 Sam 8:11–17). Before I examine the Israel concept of tithing in the Enneateuch, an overview of scholarly contributions will provide a helpful foundation for my analysis.

Since Wellhausen's *Prolegomena to the History of Ancient Israel*, scholars have utilized source criticism as the preferred method for interpreting the concept of tithing. Through source criticism, the textual matrix is reduced to a chronological sequence based on the various Pentateuchal sources.[5] Certainly, the source-critical assessment of tithing does provide a viable explanation for the inconsistencies in the HB.[6] According to Wellhausen, the concept of tithing gradually evolved through Israel's history. The tithe was given originally to Yahweh and eaten at sacred banquets. In fact, Jacob voluntarily dedicated the first tithe to the God of Bethel (Gen 28:22).[7] The narrative, however, actually represented a story projected from a later time.[8] With Deuteronomy, a shift occurred from the old custom of tithing. The tithe was derived from the produce of the land, or a monetary equivalent was brought yearly to the sanctuary and consumed in the presence of Yahweh as a sacrificial meal (Deut 14:22ff). Every third year, the tithe was not brought to the sanctuary; instead, it was offered in the local villages to the desolate individuals of the land, which included the Levites. The third year exemption of the tithe was an "innovation" that was connected to the abolition of the sanctuaries and the opportunistic Dtr, who used "festal mirth for humane ends." The final shift occurred in the Priestly Code when the tithe evolved into a "due" that was collected by the Levites

---

5. Wellhausen exemplified the source-critical interpretation of tithing in the HB. See Wellhausen, *Prolegomena*, 156–59. Several other works rely heavily on a source-critical approach to studying the Israelite concept of tithe. See Guthrie, "Tithe," 4:654; Kaufmann, *Religion of Israel*, 190–95; Weinfeld, "Tithe," 15:1159–60; and Wilson, "Tithe," 6:578–79.

6. Explaining the inconsistencies between the concept of tithing in Deuteronomy and the Holiness Code, Driver noted, "The Deuteronomic law of tithe is . . . in serious, and indeed irreconcilable, conflict with the law of P on the same subject." See Driver, *Deuteronomy*, 169.

7. According to Wellhausen, Jacob viewed Bethel as "a place where heaven and earth meet, where the angels ascend and descend, to carry on the communication between earth and heaven ordained by God at this gate." See Wellhausen, *Prolegomena*, 32.

8. Wellhausen, *Prolegomena*, 156. In addition, Wellhausen contended that the eighth-century prophet Amos told the Israelites to pay tithes every three days rather than the prescript of every three years (Amos 4), which paralleled the same "stage of the cultus as the Jehovist." The tithe given by individuals was a "sacrifice of joy" and was a "splendid" example of public cult since there were no priests.

The Israelite Concept of Tithing

and given to the clergy (Lev 27:30-33; Num 28: 21-32; Neh 10:37-39 [Eng. 10:38-40]; 12:44-47; 13:4-14; 2 Chr 31:5).[9]

Yehezkel Kaufmann slightly adapted Wellhausen's chronological proposal. The most glaring difference was Kaufmann's placement of the Priestly source earlier than Deuteronomy.[10] The tithes in Gen 14:20, 28:22, and Amos 4:4 were considered votive and freewill tithes that belonged to the temple and the priest. In the Priestly Code, particularly Lev 27, the shift in context characterized the types of vows and devotions, as well as their "redemption and exchange." According to Kaufmann, the priestly tithe was unknown in postexilic Israel, while the Levitical tithe of the Second Temple period was an annual obligation substantiated in part to the claims in Num 18:21ff (cf. Neh 10:37-39 [Eng. 10:38-40]; 12:44, 47). Furthermore, in postexilic Israel the votive, freewill, priestly, and temple tithe no longer existed, and the Levitical tithe was a "product of midrashic exegesis." In Deuteronomy, the annual tithe was brought and consumed in the chosen city. The peculiar law concerning the annual tithe in Deuteronomy was just one example of the author's invention that related the law of centralization to the people and Jerusalem. Rabbinical Judaism realized the differentiation in Lev 27:30 and interpreted the law in light of Deut 14:24-26.[11]

Henk Jagersma provided another chronological method for interpreting the intricacies of the Israelites' concept of tithing. He believed Deuteronomy and the exile represented the turning points in the history of tithing. As a result, he divided his assessment into three groups: prior to the cult centralization of Josiah (Gen 14:20; 28:22; 1 Sam 8:15, 17; Amos 4:4), during the centralization of the cult (Deut 12:6, 12, 17; 14:22ff, 26, 28; 26:12), and the postexilic period. Prior to the concept of centralization, tithes functioned as voluntary gifts that were taken to the sanctuaries in Salem, Bethel, and possibly Gilgal (Lev 27:30ff; Num 18:21-30; Mal 3:8-10; Neh 10:37-39 [Eng. 10:38-40]; 12:44; 13:5, 12; 2 Chr 31:5-12). A shift came during the period of centralization—individuals were mandated to take their tithes to Jerusalem. In the postexilic period the tithe lost the character of being an offering, and it no longer functioned as sacrificial meals.[12]

---

9. Ibid., 156-57. By his own admission, Wellhausen noted that the prophet Ezekiel was silent concerning the tithe being a "due" in the exilic Priestly writings.

10. In his article on tithe, Weinfeld adopted Kaufmann's chronological ordering of the Pentateuchal sources. See Weinfeld, "Tithe," 15:1156-62.

11. Kaufmann, *Religion of Israel*, 190-91.

12. Jagersma, "Tithe in the Old Testament," 119-28.

The Legislative Themes of Centralization

DIACHRONIC AND EXEGETICAL ANALYSIS

In many ways, the influence of Wellhausen on the concept of Israelite tithe continues to this day, which will be evident in some of the discussions below. For the remainder of the chapter, I will examine the relevant texts within the Enneateuch where מעשר is found: Gen 14:17–24; 28:18–22; Lev 27:30–33; Num 18:21–28; Deut 12:10–11, 15–18; 14:22–29; 18:1–8; 26:12–27; and 1 Sam 8:11–17. I delimit the scope of the discussion due to the association of מעשר with the centralization mandate, save 1 Sam 8:11–17. The first texts under consideration are found in the narratives of the patriarchs Abram and Jacob.

Genesis 14:17–24

The story of Abram and Melchizedek contains the first reference to מעשר in the HB (Gen 14:20). The entire pericope (vv. 17–24) is not void of syntactical difficulties. A brief overview of the pericope will be helpful before discussing the textual specifics of vv. 17–24. Following the war with the kings of the east, Abram returns to the general proximity of Jerusalem where the king of Sodom goes out to meet him in the Valley of Shaveh (v. 17). Melchizedek, a priest of El Elyon (אל עליון) from Salem (=Jerusalem),[13] is introduced in the narrative when he brings bread and wine, as well as a blessing to Abram (vv. 14:19–20a).[14] In return, Abram gives Melchizedek a "tenth" (מעשר) of everything, which symbolizes Abram's "recognition of a proprietary claim, a sovereign right."[15] The chronology of the story suggests that the מעשר that Abram gives to Melchizedek is a "one-time tithe

---

13. Many scholars associate the ancient city of Salem with Jerusalem. Gordon Wenham provided a comparison of Melchizedek and the king of Sodom and concluded that Salem cannot be equated with Jerusalem. See Wenham, *Genesis 1–15*, 317–18. John G. Gammie offered a more complex proposal concerning the traditions associated with Melchizedek. He believed that enough plausible evidence exists to suggest Shechem was the place of origin for the traditions of Melchizedek (i.e., his blessing, encounter with Abram, and receiving of the tithe). As Shechem faded, the Melchizedek traditions were transferred to the priesthood at Shiloh then to the priesthood at Nob and finally to the priesthood in Jerusalem (via Abiathar). See Gammie, "Melchizedek Tradition," 385–96.

14. James E. Coleran argued that the bread and wine brought forth by Melchizedek was for refreshment, but it also contained a sacrificial element. The sacrificial element coupled with Melchizedek's title of priest underscored "why *he* presided at this solemn gathering." See Coleran, "The Sacrifice of Melckisedek," 27–36, emphasis his.

15. See Rad, *Genesis*, 180.

The Israelite Concept of Tithing

of the booty" and not indicative of an annual tithe to the priest (e.g., Lev 27:30–33; Num 18:21).[16] With vv. 21–24 a shift in the dialogue occurs when the king of Sodom reenters the story and demands that Abram give him the people who were captured in the war (vv. 1–16). In return for the allotment of people, the king of Sodom will allow Abram to keep the remaining booty for himself. In response, Abram declares that his oath to Yahweh inhibits him from keeping any of the booty. Thus, Abram forfeits his portion of the booty for winning the war to the impatient and demanding king of Sodom (vv. 21–24).[17]

Due to the syntactical complexity of vv. 17–24, the Melchizedek and Abram story is not without controversy. Scholars have challenged the textual cohesiveness of ch. 14 through traditio-historical criticism.[18] Most

---

16. Both Bruce K. Waltke and Victor P. Hamilton argued that the tithe was a "one-time tithe of the booty." See Waltke, *Genesis*, 235; cf. Hamilton, *Book of Genesis: Chapters 1–17*, 413. Claus Westermann, on the other hand, argued that the tithe given by Abram to Melchizedek was not a one-time tribute and should be interpreted in the "context of sedentary cult." Furthermore, the purpose of including the tithe into the narrative was "to legitimate the regular payment of the tithe by means of a single event which took place long ago." See Westermann, *Genesis 12–36*, 206.

17. There is some debate related to the timing of Abram's oath. Was the oath made prior to going to war or after his victory? Abram's oath might represent "a vow for making war," which was common in the ANE. See Croteau, "Post-Tithing View," 58–59. On the other hand, the oath occurs after the victory of the kings and Abram is already blessed. Thus, the vow could represent a secondary attachment. See Coats, *Genesis*, 120. Somewhat related to the discussion is Num 31:25–31, a text that contradicts the 1/10 offering from the booty of war described in Gen 14:17–24. In this text, the individual was to give 1/500 not 1/10 from the spoils of war (see vv. 27–29). In sum, the chronological issue related to "when" Abram made the oath does not have an immediate impact on the task at hand.

18. John A. Emerton suggested the Melchizedek portion of Gen 14 was inserted later, probably during the united monarchy. He argued that the introduction of the king of Sodom in v. 17 was interrupted immediately by the emergence of Melchizedek (v. 18). By removing the Melchizedek story from the narrative (vv. 18–20), a connection could be made between v. 17 and vv. 21–24. These verses were inserted into ch. 14 in an effort to encourage the Israelites to create a worshipful fusion of Yahweh with the cult of El Elyon. In doing so, Jerusalem would be recognized as the religious and political capital of Israel. Moreover, David would be viewed as being from the "ancient royal and priestly status of Melchizedek." See Emerton, "Riddle of Genesis XIV," 403–39. Several other scholars have dated Gen 14:18–20 to the united monarchy. See Anderson, *Sacrifices and Offerings*, 82–86. Harold H. Rowley suggested the text was an "aetiological legend" that depicted Abram's submission to the ancient priesthood of Salem (=Jerusalem) and should be dated to the united monarchy. See Rowley, "Zadok and Nehustan," 113–41. Westermann also viewed vv. 18–20 as a later insertion. For Westermann, the rationale for separating vv. 18–20 from the remaining verses was based purely on the etiological

scholars identify the abrupt introduction of Melchizedek into the narrative flow. In fact, by omitting vv. 18–20 from the story, v. 17 and vv. 21–24 seem to continue the narrative dialogue between the king of Sodom and Abram; however, to advocate the traditio-historical arguments concerning vv. 18–20 simply ignores the textual intentionality of the larger pericope and the literary artistry depicted by the narrator, particularly the literary comparison between Melchizedek and the king of Sodom.[19]

McConville provided valuable insight into the complexity of the Melchizedek narrative. He maintained that vv. 17–24 must be interpreted in light of the larger patriarchal narratives. Along these lines, four significant elements are present in the narrative. First, the relationship between Abram and the political environment is a key component in the story since the patriarch is presented as a major figure in international affairs (e.g., his relationship with the kings of Salem and Sodom). Second, vv. 17–24 are related to the larger narrative about the relationship between Abram and Lot (ch. 14), the motif of Lot and Sodom (chs. 13; 18–19), and Abram's occupation of the land (ch. 13). Third, the patriarchal narrative in ch. 14 is concerned with religion. Thus, the narrator focuses on the God of Abram rather than the man. The intrusion of Melchizedek is offset by the priest-king's proclamation that the military victory by Abram is a gift from God

---

goal. He suggested that by starting from the presupposition that the episode was etiological, "then it is to be seen in the context of the thinking of circles in the early monarchy which wanted to anchor the new form of worship in the old traditions of ancient Israel. These circles did not shrink from indirectly juxtaposing Yahweh, the God of Israel from Egyptian times, alongside El who was worshiped at a Canaanite sanctuary." See Westermann, *Genesis 12–36*, 207. Yet another unique traditio-historical assessment questioned whether the date of the Melchizedek narrative was the same as the "tradition layer" of the king of Sodom in vv. 17, 21–24. In sum, Michal Peter concluded that vv. 17–24 contained two additions, v. 18 concerning Melchizedek and the "tithe tribute" in v. 20. He concluded the Melchizedek story was inserted later but certainly was passed along orally before being inserted in the text. See Peter, "Genesis XIV 19," 114–20. John Van Seters argued the priestly-kingship role held by Melchizedek exemplified the later Hasmonaean aspirations of becoming both kings and "high priests." Thus, he suggested the Melchizedek narrative was representative of the priesthood of the Second Temple. See Van Seters, *Abraham in History and Tradition*, 307–8. Desmond Alexander provided a concise discussion regarding the limitations of traditio-historical criticism as it pertains to Gen 14. See Alexander, *From Paradise*, 39–41. McConville has written a more in-depth critique of the traditio-historical interpretation of Gen 14, particularly the works of Emerton, Westermann, and Van Seters. See McConville, "Abraham and Melchizedek," 94–109.

19. Similarly, McConville suggested that the "double encounter" in vv. 17–24 presented coherence questions, but the inclusion of the Melchizedek incident must be understood as intentional. See McConville, "Abram and Melchizedek," 111.

The Israelite Concept of Tithing

(v. 20); therefore, the possession of the land is an illustration of God's gracious gift. Thus, the gifts of Abram to the two kings (i.e., Salem and Sodom) must be viewed in conjunction. Abram recognizes the gifts of God and as a result he returns a portion (מעשר), whereas the narrator presents the king of Sodom as having enough false bravado to give gifts that Abram refuses.[20]

From a textual and syntactical perspective, the subject of the verb נתן in v. 20b is ambiguous with regard to "who" is the individual offering the tithe: "And *he* gave to him a tithe from everything" (ויתן-לו מעשר מכל). The narrator leaves the subject of the verb נתן unclear.[21] The ambiguity has led to several interpretations. For example, if the subject of נתן is Abram, then his tithe to Melchizedek (v. 20b), on the surface, appears to contradict vv. 22–23, which states that the patriarch will forfeit the military booty to the king of Sodom. With such an interpretation one question still remains: How can Abram give Melchizedek a tenth of the military booty when vv. 22–23 clearly indicates the patriarch forfeits his share of the loot? Second, one could surmise that since Melchizedek is blessing Abram and Yahweh (vv. 19–20a), the Canaanite priest-king offers a tenth of everything to Abram. By Melchizedek giving Abram a tenth of all his belongings, the tension between vv. 20b and 22–24 appears to be alleviated.[22] Unfortunately, such an interpretation does not align itself with the larger purpose of the text.

That the narrator includes the story of Melchizedek in ch. 14 is dubious, yet a close reading of the text introduces some viable questions and some insights regarding the overall purpose of the pericope. First, a close reading reveals that the narrator presents Abram and Melchizedek as protagonists and the king of Sodom as the antagonist.[23] Second, the narrator

---

20. McConville, "Abram and Melchizedek," 111–16. By way of conclusion, McConville noted, "Abram's presence on the world-stage will be characterized by his understanding that all wealth and power is a gift of God; he will hold fast to the specific promises of the God whom he knows, rather than try to force them; . . . he enters a claim that the God who is known in Canaan as Elyon is none other than the God whom he has met as Yahweh" (p. 116).

21. The LXX inserts Abram in verse 20b.

22. Robert H. Smith argued that Melchizedek was the subject v. 20b and not Abram. See Smith, "Abram and Melchizedek," 134.

23. Robert Chisholm Jr. suggested that biblical narrators, at times, utilized literary techniques that diminished the perspective (i.e., limited) of a character compared to an "omniscient, divine perspective." Naturally, the narrator's limited portrayal of a character was for rhetorical purposes. The difficult task, however, is recognizing the narrator's use of rhetorical purposes since texts are not always formally marked, thus making the

87

The Legislative Themes of Centralization

uses geography as a literary tool in the story. For practicality purposes, the geographical implications of the story will be discussed first. In the story, the narrator omits the route taken by Abram following the defeat of the kings from the east. Geographical markers play an important role in ch. 14, particularly in vv. 1–15. From a narrative perspective, v. 16 signals a closing of the story that chronicles Abram's military efforts against the kings of the east, and a literary shift occurs in v. 17 with the use of "after his return" (אחרי שובו).

Equally important in the narrative shift is the inclusion of the Valley of Shaveh, the only geographical marker in vv. 17–24. The previous verses are replete with geographical locations, whereas the final pericope is nearly void. Due to the void of geographical locations in vv. 17–24, save the Valley of Shaveh, the narrator could be using the valley as literary tool. According to 2 Sam 18:18, the Valley of Shaveh is near Jerusalem. Verse 17 explains that the king of Sodom comes out to meet Abram in the Valley of Shaveh, which geographically speaking is a significant distance from Sodom.[24] Thus, the Valley of Shaveh might represent the narrator's use of irony since the king of Sodom "gives" Abram his portion in v. 21. The king of Sodom does not have royal or military jurisdiction in the Valley of Shaveh. Thus, his demands are unwarranted since he is not the king of the Valley of Shaveh. In short, it appears that the narrator might be using the Valley of Shaveh as a tool of irony since the demands of the king of Sodom are ruled out of place.

As for Melchizedek, he is introduced as the priest-king of Salem, possibly the archaic name of Jerusalem. If this is correct, then the presence of Melchizedek should not be viewed as being out of place (i.e., an example of later insertion). The gifts of bread and wine from Melchizedek to Abram would be appropriate since the patriarch defeated the hostile kings from the east, who possibly terrorized the Canaanite priest-king. Thus, the narrator is using the geographical marker of the Valley of Shaveh to heighten the scene that will unfold in vv. 17–24, particularly with regard to the contrast between Melchizedek and the king of Sodom.[25]

---

interpreter rely on contextual clues. See Chisholm Jr., "Rhetorical Use," 404–14. Literarily, the narrator appears to be limiting the perspective of the king of Sodom for rhetorical purposes, primarily to emphasize Melchizedek and the deity El Elyon.

24. Scholars admit that the exact location of Sodom is uncertain, but the general consensus is that the ancient city is located near the Dead Sea.

25. That the king of Sodom and Melchizedek go out to meet Abram outside Salem is the only common element shared between the two men in the story. It is possible that the narrator is contrasting the relationship of the two kings. Melchizedek is portrayed as

The Israelite Concept of Tithing

Character development is the next important element of the narrative. Verse 17 introduces the king of Sodom coming out to meet Abram. Melchizedek is introduced in the following verse when he too comes out to meet Abram. The introduction of Melchizedek is coupled with the accompaniment of his gifts and his relationship with El Elyon (v. 18). As the king of Sodom disappears briefly from the narrative, the narrator begins to construct the specifics about Melchizedek. First, the Canaanite priest-king blesses Abram and El Elyon (vv. 19–20). Thus, the narrator is describing the priest-king as gracious yet also as religious through the proclamation to Abram and El Elyon.

Immersed in the narrator's portrayal of Melchizedek is the sovereignty of El Elyon, the God that orchestrated Abram's military victory (v. 20a). If this assessment is correct, the narrator is presenting Melchizedek as a gracious priest-king who has found protection due to the military efforts of Abram. A case can be made that Abram controlled all the land he conquered, including the Valley of Shaveh. If so, then Melchizedek's gifts and blessing are appropriate, and the declaration that the military victory as a gift from El Elyon sheds new light on Abram's tithe. The tithe given to Melchizedek could possibly be the land the priest-king inhabits. By Abram recognizing the sovereignty of El Elyon in his military ventures, he returns (=tithes) the land to Melchizedek. In other words, Abram's tithe to Melchizedek is actually the gift of land, not booty from his military exploits. From this perspective, then, Abram is introduced as freely associating himself with El Elyon through worship, as well as associating the Canaanite deity with Yahweh. The entire relationship between Abram and Melchizedek, therefore, establishes a hierarchy: deity–humanity–land.

The return of the king of Sodom is short and also contains a touch of irony (v. 21). The king of Sodom's demand for the people captured in the military battle is ironic since the king is clearly out of place, particularly geographically. In short, the king is violating the geographical space of the Valley of Shaveh and Salem, which in turn indicates he has no justification for his demands. Literarily, however, the demands of the king serve to move the narrative focus to Abram's declaration of obedience and worship of El Elyon (vv. 22–24).

The above literary-critical remarks are an attempt to uncover whether the narrator imbedded narrative clues for interpreting Gen 14:17–24. The

---

the one offering a blessing to both Abram and El Elyon, whereas the king of Sodom is portrayed as abrasive and entitled with no mention of affiliation to a deity.

The Legislative Themes of Centralization

relationship between the protagonists and the antagonists, as well as the role of geography, does seem to provide valuable insight into the narrator's purpose. Both the literary and traditio-historical critic must answer one question when examining the text: Will the importance of tithing lose its patriarchal origins if the cultic stipulations are stripped away from the narrative?[26] From a literary-critical perspective, the answer is no. That being said, the omission of the tithe from the story would diminish the description of El Elyon's sovereignty and Abram's coalescing of Melchizedek's deity with the patriarchal Yahweh.

Genesis 28:18–22

Genesis 28 describes Jacob's departure from Beer-Sheba to Paddan-aram in search of a wife. While traveling, Yahweh reveals himself to Jacob in a dream and promises to give the land in which he sleeps to his descendants. Furthermore, Yahweh promises that his sovereign hand will remain upon Jacob throughout his travels until he returns to the land (vv. 12–15). Jacob wakes from his sleep and declares the presence of Yahweh in this place and names the place Bethel (v. 17).[27]

---

26. For some traditio-historical scholars the answer is yes. Several scholars have argued that the inclusion of the tithe in Gen 14:20b played an important role in establishing the theme later in Israel's history. Naturally, advocates of this view date the Melchizedek portion of Gen 14 late but recognize the theological significance of the story. For instance, Gary Anderson suggested that the inclusion of the tithe in Gen 14 established an archaic precedent for the Israelite to recognize Jerusalem and the temple as the "legitimate place of worship" and the "new cult center." See Anderson, *Sacrifices and Offerings*, 82, 84. Similarly, John Skinner suggested the payment of tithe by Abram to Melchizedek formed a "religious bond of a common monotheism" and established a precedent for giving tithes to the Jerusalem sanctuary. See Skinner, *Genesis*, 269.

27. The proclamation of the land is given first to Abram (12:6) under the oak of Moreh near Shechem. After building an altar to Yahweh, Abram then relocates to Bethel (vv. 8–9) and later returns after his sojourning in Egypt (13:2–4). The identification of Bethel in 28:17 is slightly different. Jacob appears to have no knowledge of the Abrahamic episode at Shechem and Bethel. Though the narrator does not specifically indicate Jacob's awareness to the holy location, one cannot simply dismiss the two stories (Gen 12–13; 28:10–22) as being from different narrative strands or sources. Along these lines, Van Seters argued that the tithe described in ch. 28 had the temple of the exilic community in mind. Furthermore, the inclusion of the voluntary tithe in ch. 28 was actually a "specific Deuteronomic institution" that was birthed from the centralization of worship. See Van Seters, *Prologue to History*, 301.

Recognizing the spiritual significance of his dream and the land in which he resides, Jacob erects the stone that he slept upon and anoints it as a *massebah*. After erecting the stone pillar, Jacob vows that he will remain obedient "if" (אם) Yahweh will be with him, keep him going in the right direction (שמרני בדרך הזה), and give him provisions of food and clothing (v. 20). The rationale for Yahweh's provision upon Jacob is so that when he returns Yahweh will be his God (והיה יהוה לי לאלהים) and the *massebah* will represent the house of God (v. 22a). The final portion of v. 22 introduces the second important reference to tithing in the Enneateuch. Upon returning to the land, Jacob vows to give Yahweh a tenth of everything he possesses if he is protected on his journey from his father's house.[28]

Although the *Sitz im Leben* of Gen 14:18–20 and 28:22 are drastically different, both contain important etiological characteristics in that they encourage the descendants of the patriarchs to follow in the footsteps of Abram and Jacob by giving tithes.[29] In Gen 14:17–24, the narrator emphasizes that Abram gives a tenth of everything (=land?) to the priest-king Melchizedek, whereas the latter text reveals that Jacob's tithe is dedicated to Yahweh himself.[30] Together, the narrator highlights that Israel's greatest patriarchs support the priests, king, and creator through tithes.

Leviticus 27:30–33

Leviticus 27 functions as the appendix to the Holiness Code (Lev 17–26). The chapter is comprised of various laws, with much of the chapter dedicated to vows. Of particular importance to the study is the priestly material regarding tithes (vv. 30–33). These verses begin with the proclamation that the entire tithe (כל-מעשר) of the land from seed and fruit is dedicated and holy to Yahweh (v. 30). The proclamation is interrupted by v. 31, which introduces the concept of redeeming a tithe at the cost of adding a fifth to

---

28. It should be noted that the text never specifically states that Jacob gave his tithe. I am assuming that he did give a tithe. As to whether Jacob actually tithed is speculation.

29. Cf. Jagersma, "Tithe in the Old Testament," 124. According to Weinfeld, Gen 14:17–24 and 28:10–22 contained different purposes. In the former text, the institution of tithe was related directly to the royal sanctuary in Jerusalem, which traced back to Abraham and the traditions of the south, whereas 28:10–22 linked Jacob, the ancient hero of the northern tribes, with Bethel. See Weinfeld, "Tithe," 15:1157–58; cf. Milgrom, *Leviticus 23–27*, 2422.

30. There is some debate whether Abram gave a tenth of everything he owned or all the military booty.

The Legislative Themes of Centralization

the original gift. Similar to the first tithe proclamation, v. 32 continues the impetus that every tenth animal from the herds and flocks that pass under the herdsman's staff is holy to Yahweh. The section on tithing closes in a somewhat contradictory manner. With regard to the tithing of herds and flocks, an individual shall not question the condition (i.e., good or bad) of the gift nor exchange it; yet, in the next phrase, an individual who does exchange the tithe, both the original and the replacement are counted as holy. This declaration that both tithes are holy suggests that once something is dedicated to Yahweh, the gift is shrouded in holiness. Lastly, the tithe in Lev 27:30–33 appears to be voluntary in nature.[31]

Numbers 18:21–28

The concept of tithing continues to develop in Num 18. This chapter outlines the duties of Aaron, the priests, and the Levites.[32] After describing the duties, Yahweh differentiates between the portion and inheritance enjoyed by the sons of Israel and the Levites. Yahweh is the portion and inheritance of the Levites and not the land. The sovereign dictum is followed by the prescription for acquiring Yahweh's gift (vv. 21–28). To the Levites, Yahweh gives every tithe (כל-מעשר) in Israel as an inheritance because of the serious nature of serving within the tent of meeting (vv. 21–24). In v. 25, Moses is directed by Yahweh to tell the Levites to give an offering to the Lord from the tithe of the people to Aaron and the priests (v. 28)—a "tithe from the tithe" (מעשר מן-המעשר).[33] This "novel provision" is an addition

---

31. See Lundbom, *Deuteronomy*, 486.

32. Many commentators date Num 18 later than Deuteronomy, thus, making the laws regarding the tithe for the priests dependent on Deut 14:24-27. See Budd, *Numbers*, 204; and Levine, *Numbers 1–20*, 450. Driver suggested Num 18 characterized the tithe as the "maintenance of the priestly tribe," whereas the tithe in Deuteronomy was the "property of the lay Israelite." See Driver, *Deuteronomy*, 169–70. Additionally, Jeffrey Stackert argued that nine lexical correspondences existed between Num 18:20–32 and Deut 14:22–29, proving the dependence of the former on the latter. Central to the correspondence was the בכל-מקום in Num 18:31, which Stackert interpreted as a correspondence to the centralization motif in Deut 14:23. See Stackert, *Rewriting the Torah*, 165–91.

33. Jacob Milgrom argued the tithe in Num 18 was mandatory rather than voluntary. He based his arguments on four evidences. First, the verb לקח in v. 26 should be translated as "take by force," implying the Levites were not dependent on the "whims" of the landowners. Second, if the tithes were representative of charity, an ongoing risk would be involved by working at the sanctuary. Third, a voluntary tithe would never produce enough provisions to feed 8,580 males from the tribe. Fourth, Babylonian history

to the law of the tithe: the priests are not excluded from supporting the cult and priesthood.[34] Furthermore, the "tithe from the tithe" is to be the best portion (lit. "from all the fat," v. 29) and given to the Levites (contra Deut 14:28ff).

Deuteronomy 12:10–11, 15–18

A complete portrait of מעשר cannot be acquired without examining the Deuteronomic innovation of the concept. In short, Deuteronomy represents a turning point in the "history of tithing" in the HB[35] in that the laws concerning the tithe and firstlings become social institutions.[36] The Deuteronomic concept of tithing includes two points: the tithe as a meal and the provisions of the tithe every third year (14:28; 26:12). To understand better the concept of tithing in Deuteronomy, several texts must be examined (12:10–11, 15–18; 14:22–29; 18:1–8; 26:12–27).

The first reference of מעשר is related to the "inauguration of centralization" (12:5).[37] The mandate to destroy the idolatrous locations, altars, and deities is concluded with the a posteriori monotheistic worship of Yahweh, which is outlined by conditions. The setting of this law requires the Israelites, once in the land of Canaan, to continue their obedience to Yahweh through burnt offerings, sacrifices, tithes, and first fruits. Collectively, these offerings and tithes represent the people's praise for Yahweh's grace and benevolence (12:10–11, 15–18). The inclusion of tithes within the list of offerings differs somewhat from the previous references to מעשר. For example, in Num 18, Yahweh differentiates the regulations surrounding the

---

demonstrated that a centralized government instituted an annual sacral tithe to support the sanctuary personnel. See Milgrom, *Leviticus 23–27*, 2422–23.

34. See Levine, *Numbers 1–20*, 452. He also added that the "tithe of the tithe" was an act of desacralization. For similar argument see Weinfeld, "Tithe," 15:1160–61.

35. Jagersma, "Tithe in the Old Testament," 119. He argued that Deuteronomy and the exile represented the two turning points in the history of tithing in the HB. Further emphasizing the turning point in Deuteronomy, he noted, "It is clear that the Deuteronomic tithes differ from those mentioned in all other books of the Old Testament in which tithes are nowhere explicitly looked upon as a gift or offering in connection with a meal."

36. Weinfeld, *Deuteronomistic School*, 290.

37. Levinson used the phrase "inauguration of centralization." See Levinson, *Deuteronomy and the Hermeneutics*, 24.

The Legislative Themes of Centralization

Levites and offerings, whereas in Deuteronomy, Moses explains the importance of tithe for the Levites and priests.

In 12:13–19, the law dictates the requirement for centralization and allowance for secular slaughter by individuals. Moses commands the people not to offer burnt offerings haphazardly at any place, but rather the offering should be given "in the place which Yahweh will choose" (במקום אשר־יבחר יהוה, v. 14). The final law (12:20–28) explains the condition for "inauguration of secular slaughter."[38] In this law, a special provision is given to individuals who live too far from the central sanctuary. In such cases the individual can consume the secular sacrifice in the local provinces; however, the prohibition against consuming blood and the prohibition against unclean animals, still applies to the secular sacrifice (12:18, 20–23). On the other hand, the consumption of a מעשׂר from grain, wine, firstling, or flock must be taken to the chosen place of Yahweh.

Deuteronomy 14:22–29

In Deut 14:22–29, the focus is shifted from the clean and unclean food laws to tithes. The transition may seem out of place, but the basic premise of the foods laws is to emphasize holiness. Following the same accord, the command to tithe the first fruits every year is another form of worship and obedience. The dietary and tithe laws are related through the holiness theology dictated in the motif for eating. The concept of the tithe functioning as a feast is a Deuteronomic invention.[39] The provision of מעשׂר in vv. 22–29 is related directly to the concept of centralization. In fact, the מעשׂר of seed, grain, wine, oil, and firstlings of the flock must be eaten in Yahweh's presence at the central sanctuary. The מעשׂר in ch. 14 is not a gift to the temple or an individual. Instead the tithe is a joyful meal thanking Yahweh for a "good harvest."[40] In short, vv. 22–23 represents the "basic tithe

---

38. Ibid., 24.

39. McConville, *Deuteronomy*, 246. See also Driver, *Deuteronomy*, 168–69 and Nelson, *Deuteronomy*, 184–86.

40. North, "עשׂר," 11:406. Tigay argued that Deuteronomy presented tithes as being obligatory for the Israelites. See Tigay, *Deuteronomy*, 141; cf. Jagersma, "Tithe in the Old Testament," 118.

commandment for the lay Israelites"[41] and reiterates the need to teach the fear of Yahweh continually.[42]

The Deuteronomic motif directs the people to the future location of Yahweh's chosen place (v. 24) with one caveat. If an individual lives too far from the chosen place of Yahweh, he is to sell the first fruits and bring the money to the central sanctuary, then purchase whatever his appetite desires. The use of the preposition מן in v. 24 functions as an absolute comparative and emphasizes a "quality of too high a degree."[43] In other words, if the burden of bringing the tithe offering is too overwhelming, the sale of the offering will suffice as long as the individual visits the central sanctuary and purchases a tithe offering with the money (vv. 24–26).

In vv. 27–29, a new motif or provision is introduced concerning the tithe offering. Moses commands the people to remember the Levites since they have no lot in life. Every third year the people of every town shall bring the portion reserved for the Levites, sojourner, orphan, and widow.[44] This new motif is significant in relation to the Levitical tithe in Num 18. In Deut 14:22–27, the command is to give during the festivals. Thus, these verses serve as a reminder of their responsibilities to protect and provide for the Levites. With vv. 27–29, the command is to protect the *personae miserables* in an act of obedience and it serves as a reminder of Yahweh's benevolence throughout the short history of Israel. Furthermore, the triennial tithe is given to individuals who do not own land. The uniqueness of the triennial tithe must be interpreted in light of the cultic reforms introduced in Deut 12:19. With the abolishment of provincial sanctuaries and their cultic officials, the need for tithes to maintain the institutions is no longer needed. Thus, the addition of the Levites among the list of *personae miserables* makes the tithe a sacred gift rather than a mandatory one (vv. 27–29).[45]

Since ch. 14 describes a tithe given at the central sanctuary every year and the triennial tithe to the *personae miserables* and the Levites, one major

---

41. Stackert, *Rewriting the Torah*, 166.
42. Lundbom, *Deuteronomy*, 484.
43. Williams and Beckman, *Hebrew Syntax*, 121.
44. Concerning the triennial tithe, David L. Baker described Deut 14:28–29 and 26:12–13 as a "major innovation compared with the conventional understanding of tithes in the ancient Near East and the Bible." See Baker, *Tight Fists or Open Hands?* 247. Crüsemann described the triennial tithe as the "first known tax for a social program" since it abolished the "traditional state tax" by dividing the direct contributions between the social program and the central shrine. See Crüsemann, *The Torah*, 215–19.
45. See Milgrom, *Leviticus 23–27*, 2424. See also Guthrie, "Tithe," 4:654.

The Legislative Themes of Centralization

question arises: Does the triennial tithe represent a second tithe? There are some scholars who suggest these verses represent a second tithe.[46] Along these lines, Milgrom explained that the idea for the "first tithe" and the "second tithe" derived from the contradiction between Num 18:21–24 and Deut 14:22–27. The rabbis recognized the tension between Priestly writings and the Deuteronomic law code; thus, they interpreted them as two different tributes. The first tithe was given to the Levites, and the second was brought to Jerusalem and consumed at the sanctuary. Though this form of argumentation appeared to alleviate the tension, the excise of 20 percent of yield was extremely high and would pose financial problems.[47] Furthermore, the use or purpose of the triennial tithe probably differed from the tithes of the previous two years. Thus, the tithes as described in Deuteronomy might have different purposes.[48]

Deuteronomy 18:1–8

In Deut 18:1–8, Moses emphasizes the rights of the Levitical priests due to their lack of inheritance within Israel.[49] Yahweh is the priests' only inheritance, linking them to the land forfeiture (v. 2; cf. 10:9).[50] As a result, Moses commands the people of Israel to look after the Levites' well-being. Any Levite could relocate to the place which Yahweh will choose and continue to minister in his name (vv. 1–8). The decision of the Levite to relocate to Jerusalem is a personal choice (אות נפשו, v. 6). Moreover, the priests are to have equal portions to eat (לבד ממכריו על-האבות) since their inheritance is Yahweh. The phrase לבד ממכריו על-האבות in v. 8 is "notoriously difficult,"

---

46. For example see, Verhoef, "Tithing—A Hermeneutical Consideration," 115–27 and Craigie, *Book of Deuteronomy*, 233–34; Additionally, others advocate a three-tithe theory. See for example, Croteau, "Post-Tithing View," 64–65.

47. Milgrom, *Leviticus 23–27*, 2426. Several other scholars advocate the one-tithe theory. See Driver, *Deuteronomy*, 167–71; McConville, *Deuteronomy*, 252, 254; Nelson, *Deuteronomy*, 187; Block, *Deuteronomy*, 358–59; and Cole, *Numbers*, 293.

48. Guthrie, "Tithe," 4:654; cf. Jagersma, "Tithe in the Old Testament," 119. Baker suggested the triennial tithe was used obviously for social purposes and underscored another avenue for the Israelites to serve Yahweh. See Baker, *Tight Fists or Open Hands?* 248.

49. Deuteronomy 18:1–8 is a natural extension of Num 18. See Averbeck, "מעשׂר," 2:1046.

50. See McConville, *Deuteronomy*, 297. Yahweh being the inheritance of the Levites is a Deuteronomic concept. Several Deuteronomic and Deuteronomistic texts represent this theological concept: Deut 10:9; 18:2; and Josh 13:14, 33.

but it describes the Levites as being disposed of property.[51] The rights of the Levites in vv. 1–8 seem at odds with the demands of the triennial tithe for the Levites in 14:27–29 and 26:12. A distinction can be made between the formulaic descriptions of the Levites.

Deuteronomy 26:12–27

Deuteronomy 26:12 is similar to the triennial tithe for the Levites, the sojourner, the fatherless, and the widow in 14:27–29. The demand for the triennial tithe in ch. 26 is actually part of a larger liturgy that prepares the people for entering the land of Canaan. The historical credo in vv. 5–9 concludes with the phrase "a land flowing with milk and honey." In vv. 10–11, Moses brings the first fruits of the land promised by Yahweh and demands a tithe every three years. Thus, the Deuteronomic concept of tithing is related loosely to the land motif in the so-called DH. The introduction of the triennial tithe possibly preserves the old notion that connects the Levite with the tithe and, more importantly, it establishes a relationship between tithing to individuals void of land and Deuteronomic land theology.[52] In other words, the tithe in Deuteronomy acknowledges Yahweh's ownership of the land and produce while it provides support to both the Levites and the *personae miserables*.[53]

1 Samuel 8:11–17

Samuel is introduced as a young boy who grows in his faith (1 Sam 3–4) as compared to the depraved situation within the house of Eli. The narrator introduces the ark of the covenant besiegement at the hands of the Philistines, which concludes with its return and the reemergence of the prophet Samuel (1 Sam 7:5ff). Next, the narrator captures the elders' displeasure with Samuel and his rogue children. The outcome results in the demand by the elders for a king. Again, the narrator uses irony, this time to describe the situation surrounding Israel's transition from a theocracy to a monarchy. The Philistine gods, city-kings, and armaments could not overcome the power of the Israel's Lord. Following a brief celebration for the exiled

---

51. See McConville, *Law and Theology in Deuteronomy*, 73.
52. Milgrom, *Leviticus 23–27*, 2424.
53. Cf. Herron, "The Land, the Law, and the Poor," 79.

ark of the covenant, the people of Israel yearn for a king rather than continuing to live in accordance to Yahweh. The grief experienced with the capture of the ark manifests itself into joy upon its return. Unfortunately, the jubilation for the return of Yahweh into the presence of the Israelites is subsided by the narrow-minded desires of the people.

From this historical background, the prophet Samuel vehemently opposes the people's demand for a king (1 Sam 8:11–17). In an attempt to dissuade the people of Israel, Samuel explains what a king will impose upon the people: military armaments (vv. 11–12), manual labor of women (v. 13), a tenth from the fields and vineyards (vv. 14–15), forced labor of male and female servants and livestock (v. 16), and a tenth of the flocks and slaves (v. 17).[54] Though the noun מעשר is not used in 1 Sam 8, similar prescriptions generally associated with the concept of tithing (צאן) are found in the chapter. However, the inclusion of עשר ("tenth") in vv. 15 and 17 replaces the Deuteronomic concept of מעשר. Samuel warns the people that the king will take a tenth of everything, which is reserved usually for the Levites (see Lev 27:30–33).

Thus, the concept of tithing in 1 Sam 8:11–17 represents a distinct shift from the Pentateuch. Though in the Pentateuch the tithe has various recipients, the purpose remains constant—honor and worship of Yahweh. In 1 Sam 8, the tithe becomes a state regulation mandating the offering of material to the king, the royal estates, and the temple. Both in scope and purpose, the tithes mentioned in 1 Sam 8 reflect a different character. The tithes serve as the only text in the Enneateuch that stipulates the tithe being given to the king.[55]

A SYNCHRONIC READING OF THE ISRAELITE CONCEPT OF TITHING

Since the source-critical interpretation controls the interpretative landscape of the Israelite concept of tithing, the question remains whether a synchronic reading will provide any new insights to the discussion. Though

---

54. Anderson explained that 1 Sam 8 contained similarities between the economic and judicial texts from Ugarit. See Anderson, *Sacrifices and Offerings*, 88–90; cf. Vaux, *Ancient Israel*, 140–41.

55. Richard Averbeck recognized the stark difference in the purpose of the tithe, particularly in 1 Sam 8. Thus, he postulated, "One could argue that at least part of the underlying rationale of the Levitical tithe was the recognition of the Lord's theocratic kingship in Israel." See Averbeck, "מעשר," 2:1038.

The Israelite Concept of Tithing

source-critical scholars have alleviated some of the textual tension, approaching the biblical texts from a synchronic perspective can provide a viable alternative to the traditional source-critical arguments. Several questions are at the heart of this quest. Can the laws and narratives concerning the tithe be harmonized? To what extent can a synchronic reading be an effective method for studying the concept of tithing?

The answer to the first question, at least from the perspective of source-critical scholars, appears to be "no" since the recipients of the tithes vary. Similarly, traditio-historical scholars contend that the various recipients, coupled with the inconsistency of placement and products, suggest divergent traditions encapsulated in the Pentateuchal law codes. Along these lines, Milgrom explained, "There is no recourse but to confront the discrepancies and contradictions in the Pentateuchal tithe laws head-on. To ignore them or smooth them over only blocks the disclosure of a vital chapter in the development of the religious history of ancient Israel."[56] From the outset it must be stated that the biblical texts regarding tithes in the Enneateuch contain discrepancies, particularly in regard to the recipients of the tithes.[57]

The answer to the second question represents an alternative to the source-critical and traditio-historical scholars. Adopting a synchronic reading of the biblical text assumes a canonical and holistic approach that in hindsight might shed new light on the issue. Along these lines,

---

56. Milgrom, *Leviticus 23–27*, 2434.

57. Other attempts have tried to find a relationship between the apparent contradictory traditions of tithes. First, Milgrom provided a diachronic analysis that relied heavily on source criticism. He argued that the redeemable tithe in Leviticus was aligned closely with the status of the third year tithe in Deuteronomy. Numbers, following the legislative material in the Priestly writings, assigned the tithe to the Levites and described it as being "set aside for Yahweh." The third year tithe in Deuteronomy underscored that the tithe was once entitled to the Levite (=Numbers) but now to the owner. In short, Milgrom suggested that the tithe beneficiary went through two changes: "From the sanctuary to the Levite to the owner." See Milgrom, *Leviticus 23–27*, 2425. McConville, on the other hand, offered a harmonistic treatment of the concept of tithes. He maintained that the tithes in the various sources actually encompassed a single tithe law. Deuteronomy, according to McConville, recognized the Levites' right to the tithe, which conferred with Numbers: offerings given to the entire tribe of Levi (Deut 18:1); the phrase "the Lord is their inheritance" was an indicator of the Levites' rights to "certain dues" (Deut 18:2); and the Levites were "disposed of property" (Deut 18:8). Thus, he concluded that the tithe laws in Deuteronomy legislated a "festal meal." One that took into account that not all the tithe would be consumed, but a "due proportion" would go to the sanctuary. See McConville, *Law and Theology*, 68–87.

The Legislative Themes of Centralization

Baker argued, "It would seem that the final editor of the Pentateuch did not consider the three laws to be contradictory, even though he must have been aware of the differences," and biblical scholars must recognize that the "laws are not comprehensive. . . . Some things would have been taken for granted because of earlier laws that were assumed to be known, others because of common law or common sense."[58] Baker correctly points out that the contradictions in the three law codes do not substantiate a source-critical division of the tithe. In fact, a unity in the Israelite concept of tithing can be found amidst these contradictory laws, but the references must be interpreted in light of "one basic tithe institution."[59] Thus, the synchronic reading below will examine the biblical texts from the assumption that one basic tithe institution exists in the history of Israel and the contradictions must be interpreted with the canonical purpose(s) of each book fueling the endeavor.

The origin of the Israelite tithe is ingrained in the patriarchal narratives of Genesis (14:17–24; 28:18–22). In the first patriarchal cycle, the interaction between Abram and Melchizedek and the appearance of מעשׂר is highly symbolic. The appearance of מעשׂר introduces a new customary precedent for worshiping Yahweh. Similarly, in the Jacob cycle, the concept of tithing is symbolic from a nationalistic point of view. Returning to his homeland, Jacob promises to tithe a tenth of everything for Yahweh's protection from his brother Esau. Both of these texts contain etiological characteristics that intertwine the concept of tithing with two of Israel's patriarchs. Additionally, these two patriarchal stories represent an early precedent, as well as the rationale for worshiping Yahweh.

Following the patriarchal stories, the concept of tithing in Israel's history, at least to source-critical scholars, appears contradictory. The *Sitz im Leben* of Leviticus is Mount Sinai. After receiving the Book of the Covenant, the Israelites are given directives that will guide them in their pursuit of holiness. In many ways, Leviticus is the theological paradigm for worshiping Yahweh, setting apart the Israelites as a nation of priests. The above *Sitz im Leben* of Leviticus must be kept in mind when discussing the tithe (Lev 27). According to ch. 27, all of the tithe—seed, fruit of the land, and the firstborn of the flock—is dedicated and holy to Yahweh (27:30, 32). Additionally, the

---

58. Baker, *Tight Fists or Open Hands?* 244.

59. Ibid., 245. According to Milgrom, the tithe was originally a "religious tribute" that was "channeled" to the court and supervised by royal authorities. See Milgrom, *Leviticus 23–27*, 2422.

The Israelite Concept of Tithing

tithe can be redeemed by adding a fifth to the original gift (v. 31). The ability to redeem the tithe is unique to Leviticus and must be interpreted in light of the wilderness experience and future worship of Yahweh. Situations might arise that hinder an individual from offering a tithe, which will require the redeeming of the original gift. In such cases, the individual must tithe an additional fifth to the original offering at a later time. The original tithe, though redeemed by an individual, is still the property of Yahweh.

Numbers is a record of the wilderness testing and rebellion of the Israelites. This tumultuous period in Israel's history is instrumental in molding the people's relationship with Yahweh. In short, the book is a diary of Israel's early struggles within the covenant. Intertwined in this wilderness experience is the priesthood (i.e., the Aaronite priesthood and the Levites, chs. 3–4). The descendants of Levi are responsible for protecting, erecting, transporting, and regulating worship in the tent of the meeting. Though the priesthood does not take center stage in Numbers, they are in the background. The concept of tithing builds on this perspective. The tithes of the people are to support the priesthood since they are actually the ones responsible for protecting, erecting, transporting, and regulating worship in the tent of meeting. The dictum that the priesthood tithe from the tithes underscores the unity of the Israelites. Even the descendants of Levi are required to give a tenth to Yahweh. The tithe in Numbers is differentiated between the priesthood and the sons of Israel. Yahweh is the portion and inheritance of the priestly order and, as a result, all of the tithes are given to the priesthood. Yet, the priesthood is commanded also to tithe from the tithe (18:21–28).

On the other hand, Deuteronomy presents a different point of view concerning the issue of tithing. The tithe in Leviticus is related to the idea of being set apart, and in Numbers it is tied inherently to the tent of meeting, especially the role of the priesthood. In Deuteronomy, however, the concept of the tithe is understood best as a "sacral levy" that helps preserve and upkeep the central sanctuary.[60] Thus, the dissimilarities between Numbers and Deuteronomy are not that different. The tithe in Numbers supports the priesthood—those responsible for the tent of meeting—whereas in Deuteronomy, the tithe supports the future centralized sanctuary. The triennial tithe (Deut 14:22–29) establishes a literary link with Num 18:20–32 and Deut 12:19. First, the triennial tithe reiterates Yahweh's benevolence toward those displaced with no lot in life, which is similar to the physical

---

60. Cf. McConville, *Time and Place*, 76–77.

The Legislative Themes of Centralization

displacement of the Israelites in the wilderness (Num 18:20–32). Second, the triennial tithe is related also to the centralization of the cult. The Levites are associated with the *personae miserables*, thus making the triennial tithe non-mandatory but rather a sacred gift (cf. Deut 18:1–8).

The difference between Deut 14:27–29 and 18:1–8 is not a significant shift in theology. As stated above, the purpose of ch. 14 is to continue the theological maxim of holiness, yet the purpose of ch. 18 is to provide theological and social parameters for worshiping Yahweh (i.e., the provisions of the Levitical priests, abominable practices of magic, and the office of the prophet). Due to the theological variances in scope and purpose, the tension between chs. 14 and 18 are simply superficial. The narrator is constructing his theology of cultic centralization by interweaving laws and application. As a result, any tensions at a micro level must be viewed through the macro purpose of the narrator's impetus on cultic centralization. In short, Deuteronomy shifts the focus of the tithe. The yearly tithe is to help the central sanctuary and the triennial tithe functions as a gift to the Levites, similar to the days in the wilderness, echoing in the Levitical priesthood pericopes in 18:1–8 and 26:12–27.[61]

In the so-called DH, the concept of tithing relatively disappears from the narrative focus. The lone reference to tithing is 1 Sam 8, following the return of the ark of the covenant from exile in Philistia. More importantly, however, is the inclusion of the tithe in Samuel's speech opposing the people's demand for a king. Samuel explains that a king will burden the people through military requirements, implement manual labor for both men and women, and take a tenth of the produce from the fields as well as from the flocks and slaves. In many ways, Samuel's prophetic description continues the development of the tithe in Israel's history. The patriarchs symbolically give to Yahweh a tenth of everything they own, including land. In Leviticus, the tithe represents the people's loyalty to Yahweh and establishes them as being set apart. In Numbers, the tithe is given to the priestly order due to their role with and in the tent of meeting. In Deuteronomy, the tithe shifts from the transportable tent of meeting to the future centralized sanctuary. The tithe supports the temple and the growing number of Levitical priests, particularly through the triennial tithe. Thus, the next logical progression is the forced tithe (=tax) by the king that controls the social, political, and religious life of Israel.

---

61 Ibid.

5

The Israelite Festivals

THE FESTIVAL CALENDAR OF Israel depicted in the Pentateuch can be described as convoluted.[1] The five festival calendars in the Pentateuch—Exod 23:14–17; 34:18–26; Deut 16:1–17; Lev 23; and Num 28–29—all differ to some degree. Each calendar describes the "dates and durations" with two providing liturgical direction (i.e., Lev 23; Num 28–29). Traditionally, the calendars in Exod 23:14–17 and 34:18–26 are viewed as being the oldest. The similarities between these two calendars are evident, particularly with regard to the order and specificity of the pilgrimage feasts: Unleavened Bread, Weeks, and Booths. The calendar in Deut 16:1–17 also includes these three pilgrimage feasts; however, the "ritual regulations," dates, and durations are emphasized more so than the accounts in Exodus. The most obvious difference in Deut 16:1–17 is the pride of place given to the Passover. The Passover in Deut 16:1–17 is no longer a family rite, but rather a pilgrimage feast. The Deuteronomic account also combines Passover with the Feast of Unleavened Bread, which is actually never mentioned in the text. The prohibition of leaven in the ritual alludes to the feast (vv. 3–4, 8; cf. Exod 23:15; 34:18). The calendars in Lev 23 and Num 28–29, on the other hand, are more concerned with the precise time and duration of each feast.

---

1. Levine explained, "A reconstruction of the development of the biblical festivals has by and large eluded modern scholarship primarily because the priestly laws of the Torah, which provided most of the detailed information on festival observance, cannot be dated precisely." See Levine, *Numbers*, 263.

The Legislative Themes of Centralization

The emphasis on liturgical regulations (i.e., time and duration) replaces the harvest times associated with the feasts in the other calendars.[2]

Initially, the festivals were religious observances that occurred in local homes and regional shrines (cf. Exod 23:14–17; 34:18–23). With the centralization mandate (Deut 16:1–17), the importance of these pilgrimage feasts increased dramatically. In Deut 16:1–17, the three annual pilgrimage feasts—Passover/unleavened bread (מצות), harvest (קציר), and ingathering (אסף)—are relocated to "the place which Yahweh will choose." Moreover, in the Deuteronomic account, as mentioned earlier, the Passover (פסח) and the Feast of Unleavened Bread (מצות) were assimilated into one festival.[3] It should be noted that Passover is omitted in earlier calendars and, yet, combined with unleavened bread in the later ones.[4]

For the most part, these major festivals, save the Passover, did not represent "a religious event" but instead "religious character."[5] The origin and observance of these festivals is somewhat unclear due to the insignificant details related to them. The Hebrew term חג was reserved for the three annual pilgrimage feasts (see Exod 23:14–17; 34:18–23).[6] As noted by their titles, these pilgrimage feasts were related directly to agriculture and, therefore, not restricted to a specific date within the calendar system. In other words, the feasts of unleavened bread, harvest, and ingathering could vary (minimally speaking) year-to-year due to weather and harvest.[7] Any attempt at discovering the meaning of the festivals must begin with questions

---

2. See Hartley, *Leviticus*, 376–77. It should be noted that in ancient Israel, scholars are not sure of the set dates for the festivals. In fact, the dates associated with the festivals early in Israel's history were not tied to specific dates but rather to harvests. Variations in the names of two festivals—Weeks/Harvest and First fruits/Pentecost—might reiterate this way of life.

3. Daniel Block opposed the argument that Deuteronomy combined Passover with the Feast of Unleavened Bread. See Block, *Deuteronomy*, 385–86. See also McConville, *Law and Theology*, 99–123; idem, "Deuteronomy's Unification," 47–58; idem, *Deuteronomy*, 270. The assimilation of Passover with the Feast of Unleavened Bread in Deuteronomy will be discussed below.

4. Hartley, *Leviticus*, 378.

5. Vaux, *Ancient Israel*, 468. Naturally, Passover is related directly to the exodus event and the Feast of Unleavened Bread in Exod 12–13. The celebration of the exodus from Egypt loses its luster later in Israel's history.

6. The root of חג literally means "procession, round dance, or festival." See *HALOT* 1:289. Additionally, חג is related to the Arabic ḥajja, which means "to pilgrimage." See Haran, "Festivals," 6:1237.

7. Vaux, *Ancient Israel*, 471. For a similar argument, see Armerding, "Festivals and Feasts," 301.

The Israelite Festivals

surrounding their etiologies and chronology.[8] Given the pride of place for the combined Passover and the Feast of Unleavened in Deuteronomy, the majority of the emphasis will be given to these two feasts.[9]

The watershed of Israel's salvation is rooted in the deliverance and subsequent exodus from oppressive Egypt. The Passover is related closely with the salvific deliverance of the people. The purpose of the Passover is to offer sacrifice to Yahweh and introduce Moses as Israel's intermediary who will lead the people out of bondage.[10] The Passover is introduced as a celebration and commemoration in which the people become a covenant community of Yahweh.[11] Subsequently, the Passover also represents an "expression of holiness" by the people whom Yahweh liberates from Egypt,[12] and it functions as the ritual model for the future generations of the Israelites.[13]

The biblical festival of Passover is derived from the semantic domain of פסח, which assumes two homonymous roots: "to pass by/spare" (e.g., Exod 12:13, 23, 27; Isa 31:5) and "to walk with a limp/be lame" (2 Sam 4:4; 1 Kgs 18:21, 26).[14] The semantic domain of פסח, however, is expanded with the etymological description of it being a cultic nocturnal observance.[15] In

---

8. Traditionally speaking, the complexity of Israel's calendar has been explained along traditional lines. Three calendrical traditions are preserved in the Pentateuch: the Book of the Covenant (Exod 23:14–19), Deuteronomy (16:1–16), and the ritual legislation (Lev 23). See Levine, *Numbers*, 153.

9. I decided to focus on the Passover/Feast of Unleavened Bread due to its role in Deuteronomy. Additionally, I recognize the nomenclatures of the three pilgrimage feasts within the Pentateuch, but due to the scope of the chapter these issues will not be discussed. Another reason I focus on the Passover/Feast of Unleavened Bread is due to the limited occurrences of the other pilgrimage feasts. For a discussion on these issues, see Armerding, "Festivals and Feasts," 301–4.

10. Rowley, *Worship in Ancient Israel*, 47. Similarly, Driver suggested the Passover, at least as described in Exod 12–13, was clearly a sacrifice, but more specifically, it represented "a sacrifice *sui generis*." The procedures accompanying the Passover sacrifice resembled other sacrificial offerings. For example, the Passover meal was related loosely to the peace offering, and the intimate portrait of blood in the ceremony is similar to a sin offering. See Driver, *Book of Exodus*, 407.

11. Craigie, *Book of Deuteronomy*, 24.

12. McConville, "Deuteronomy's Unification," 55–56. McConville went on to describe the events surrounding the exodus and the Passover as a time for rejoicing in light of the people's deliverance.

13. Haran, *Temples and Temple Service*, 318.

14. Otto, "פסח," 12:4–5; cf. Rylaarsdam, "Passover," 3:663.

15. Ibid., 12:8.

fact, the words of Wellhausen seem to allude to Israel's expansion of פסח into a cultic ritual: "It is not because Jehovah smote the firstborn of Egypt that the Passover is afterwards instituted; on the contrary, it is instituted beforehand, at the moment of the exodus, in order that the firstborn of Israel may be spared."[16]

Beyond the literary structure of Exod 12–13 a consistent portrait of Passover is challenging.[17] Miniscule textual evidence, coupled with the inconsistencies in data, has challenged scholars for decades. Describing the dubious characteristics surrounding the biblical Passover, Childs proclaimed, "Few problems in the Old Testament have called forth such sustained scholarly research as has that of the Passover."[18] A simple perusal of the scholarly contributions concerning the Passover reveals attempts that overemphasize the textual insufficiencies or place too much attention on the ancient traditions underlying the various biblical perspectives on the festival.[19] For most scholars, the pathway for discovering the etiology of the Passover resides in both source and traditio-historical methods.[20] Thus,

---

16. Wellhausen, *Prolegomena*, 102.

17. See Exod 12; 23:14ff; 34:18–26; Num 9:2–14; 33:3; Deut 16:1–8; Josh 5:10–11; and 2 Kgs 23:23. Other non-Enneateuchal references to the Passover can be found in Ezek 45:21ff; Hos 2:11; 9:5; 12:9; Amos 5:21; 8:10; Isa 30:29; 2 Chr 8:13; 30; 35:1–19; and Ezra 6:19ff. Extra-biblical references to the Passover shed limited perspective on the biblical festival. The Aramaic letters from Elephantine, however, provide valuable depictions of the Israelite understanding of Passover. Hananiah, the Persian king, commanded the Jews of Elephantine to observe the Passover, which would suggest that the festival was not observed (*AP* 21:6). Several of the elements in Hananiah's letter contained parallels to ancient Israelite traditions: the command not to [eat] anything (Exod 12:15, 19; Deut 16:3–4); the partaking of unleavened bread for a week (Exod 12:15, 18–19; 13:6–7; Lev 23:6; Deut 16:3–4); the restriction of work during Passover (Exod 12:16; Lev 23:7–8; Deut 16:8); and the relationship between the sunset and the feast of Unleavened Bread (Exod 12:18; Deut 16:7–8). Rowley believed the omission from celebrating the Passover was a reaction to the Josianic reforms. Following the discovery of the book of the law in 2 Kgs 22:8, Josiah regulated the observance of the Passover to Jerusalem (Deut 16:1–8). This theory suggested that the Jews of Elephantine did not observe the Passover due to the injunction imposed by Josiah—hence the letter by Hananiah ordering its observance. See Rowley, "Papyri from Elephantine," 258.

18. Childs, *Book of Exodus*, 186.

19. Recently, Benjamin Kilchör provided a thorough summation, beginning in the nineteenth century to the present, of scholarly arguments concerning the Passover and the Feast of Unleavened. See Kilchör, "Passah und Mazzot," 340–67. Due to the vastness of the topic, evidenced by Kilchör's article, I will not be able to examine every argument or contribution. Attention will be given to the broader and more mainline arguments.

20. Today, many scholars regularly adhere to the source-critical division of Exod

The Israelite Festivals

before examining the relevant texts, I will summarize several significant contributions to the study of the Passover.

For Wellhausen, the chronological genesis of פסח was Deuteronomy.[21] He argued the פסח in Deuteronomy was not only the first textual reference to Passover but also the literary foundation for interpreting the sacrifice of the firstlings (Exod 13; 34; Deut 15).[22] Furthermore, he believed Deuteronomy established the occasions for the sacrificial feasts at Jerusalem: Easter, Pentecost, and at the Feast of Tabernacles. By centralizing the three feasts, Deuteronomy required the Israelites to offer sacrifices, pay dues, and celebrate feasts within the auspices of the Jerusalem temple. The arrangement of the three festivals within the calendar was also intentional. Passover was designated to the month of Abib, which directly coincided with corn being in the ear (Exod 9:31–32). Pentecost occurred during the harvest of wheat and the autumn festival after the vintage was complete.[23]

Advocating the theory postulated by de Wette, Wellhausen argued that Josiah published Deuteronomy and ratified the book as the covenant for the people. The command to keep the Passover (2 Kgs 23:21–22) rested upon the tradition of Deut 16 rather than Exod 12. Wellhausen described this tradition as "the new unity of the cultus" and "an exemplification of it." Additionally, Wellhausen viewed the Josianic reforms as the background

---

12–13. Most notable, according to these theorists, is the Priestly material (12:1–20, 28, 40–51; 13:1–2). In addition to P, other scholars have posited the remaining verses to J and some remaining variants of Deuteronomistic redaction: the Elohist source (12:21–23, 27b, 29–39) and the Deuteronomistic redactor (12:24–27a; 13:3–16). Though the scholarly consensus supports a source-critical interpretation of Passover, Judah B. Segal criticized the proponents of interpreting the Passover with a source-critical hypothesis. The weakness of a source-critical hypothesis, according to Segal, was in the application of the method. By scrutinizing each source account in an effort to discover every specific aspect of the Passover ritual, source-critical scholars overlook the manner in which the biblical documents supplement each other. As an alternative to the source-critical approach, he argued for a visualized setting or situation that confronted the biblical "compiler." This compiler of the HB was responsible for selecting and incorporating the various passages that supported the narrative or highlighted a specific aspect of the ritual. See Segal, *Hebrew Passover*, 72–77.

21. He explained, "The elaboration of the historical motive of the Passover is not earlier than Deuteronomy, although perhaps a certain inclination to that way of explaining it appears before then." See Wellhausen, *Prolegomena*, 88.

22. Ibid., 87. The connection between the Passover and the sacrifice of the firstlings corresponded with the sacrifice of Abel the shepherd; cf. Van Seters, "Place of the Yahwist," 179; idem, *The Life of Moses*, 123.

23. Ibid., 87–90.

The Legislative Themes of Centralization

for the coalescing of Passover and the Feast of Unleavened Bread.[24] Though Exod 12 presents the biblical origin of the Passover, many scholars have followed the Wellhausenian theory that the Israelite festival has semi-nomadic origins.[25] The scholarly interest in the etiology of the Passover has concluded by in large that the origins of the festival antedate the biblical exodus.

Johannes Pedersen argued that the Passover was a legend (Exod 1–15) preserved within the various narratives of Exodus. The Passover legend depicted an event originating with the people of antiquity and established a connection with its origins. A legend simply cannot form an existence instantly, but rather it must be amplified and must evolve over years. For this reason, attempting to divide the Passover legend into literary sources was futile due to the inconclusive clues to the history of the legend. The Passover legend continued to be "perpetually transmitted" to the future generations of Israelites in the land of Canaan. The primary purpose of the Passover feast was to commemorate the departure of the Israelites from the

---

24. Ibid., 105–7.

25. See for example Warren Moulton's treatment of the Passover in the *Dictionary of the Bible*. For Moulton, Passover was like the other great feasts in Israelite history. The biblical event described in Exod 12 represented the biblical origin but not the actual derivation of Passover. He postulated that the biblical Passover was an example of Israel's religion that "takes up, transforms, and appropriates an existing institution. We might expect to find some starting-point for conjecture in the name Passover, but it proves to little aid." See Moulton, "Passover," 3:688. Though Driver adopted Wellhausen's semi-nomadic origin for the Passover in his commentary on Exodus, he emphasized, "The significance of an institution does not depend necessarily upon what it was in its origin; it may depend equally upon what it came to be, and upon the ideas of which, as years went on, it came gradually to be regarded as the expression." See Driver, *Book of Exodus*, 410–12. Rowley suggested the origin of Passover could be traced to the "observance of the religion of Yahweh among the Kenites" prior to Moses. See Rowley, *Worship in Ancient Israel*, 47. Although his commentary provides a nice summary on the scholarly arguments regarding the Passover, Childs provided only a glimpse into his etiological interpretation of the Passover. For Childs, the Priestly material in Exod 12–13, particularly the description of the Passover, has been influenced heavily by the later cultic ceremony, evidenced by material retrojected into the original narrative. From this perspective, the Priestly account of the Passover reflected a lengthy oral tradition that emerged from the years of cultic practice. See Childs, *Book of Exodus*, 192–93. De Vaux believed the Passover was a pre-Israelite sacrifice evidenced by the rituals involved, as well as the absence of a sanctuary, priest, and altar. In addition, the dress of the men partaking in the ritual was indicative of herdsmen apparel. See Vaux, *Ancient Israel*, 435–38, 487; idem, *The Early History of Israel*, 366–67. Van Seters argued that Exod 12:1–28 was an example of priestly historiography that introduces the historical etiology of the Passover. See Van Seters, "Place of the Yahwist," 172.

The Israelite Festivals

oppressive land of Egypt. The deliverance of the Israelites from Egypt was not the summation of the Passover legend because the narrative included a sequel emphasizing the humiliation of the Pharaoh (Exod 15). In sum, the Passover legend consisted of three specific elements: the foundation of the Israelite nation, particularly with the aid of its early leaders; the inauguration of Yahweh's work within the newfound nation; and the transportation of a people of bondage in a foreign land to a historic land with a centralized temple that housed its deity.[26]

The relationship between the Passover and comparative religions is another popular avenue among biblical scholars. From this point of view, the *Sitz im Leben* of the Passover, particularly the literary strand in Exod 12:1–28, is placed in the cultural realm of semi-nomadic wanderers who relied heavily on the seasonal vegetation. Within this nomadic lifestyle, the Passover festival served to protect the semi-nomadic people when migrating from desert conditions to abundant land. The sequestering of migratory safety was recognized as a viable parallel to the exodus event. Thus, the dramatic deliverance of the Israelites from the land of Egypt and their emergence into the land of Canaan became synonymous with the historical migratory cycle of the semi-nomadic peoples.[27]

Another theory concerns the coalescence of the Passover with מצות. Though postulated by Wellhausen, the intricacies of the argument are preserved in alternative theories regarding the literary history of Passover. Hans-Joachim Kraus described the coalescence of the two festivals as an attempt by the Dtr to abolish the Canaanite influence upon the cultic *familiae*, which included the programs of reform initiated by Hezekiah and Josiah. The Dtr's emphasis extended as far back as Josh 5:10–11 in an attempt to represent the Passover as an ancient festival at Gilgal. Thus, the Passover was combined with מצות into one ceremony that celebrated the great watershed from Egypt and the crossing of the Jordan River.[28] Another

26. Pedersen, "Passahfest und Passahlegende," 161–75; idem, *Israel*, 393–407.

27. See Rost, "Weidewechsel und altisraelitischen Festkalendar," 205–16. Noth found Rost's hypothesis of "historicization" illuminating and as a result adapted the basic tenet of the Passover being pre-Israelite. See Noth, *History of Pentateuchal Traditions*, 66–69. Benjamin N. Wambacq adopted much of Rost's hypothesis; however, he suggested that the actual blood ritual was instituted when a semi-nomadic group arrived at a desirable settlement rather than before setting out on a pasturing expedition. See Wambacq, "Les origines," 206–24. Similarly, von Rad was influenced by Rost's apotropaic argument that semi-nomadic people instituted the festival in an attempt to influence demons. See Rad, *OTT* 1:253.

28. See Kraus, "Passah-Massot-Festes," 47–67.

The Legislative Themes of Centralization

theory suggested that the Passover and מצות were not conjoined until the final Deuteronomistic redaction in exile.[29]

Judah Segal maintained the Passover was a New Year festival that was in primitive stages, performed at a local shrine. With the settlement of the land of Canaan, the Passover became a "solemn communal meal" at the local shrines (e.g., Judg 21:19). The context of families celebrating the Passover implied male adults only, particularly circumcised males. Circumcision not only represented an outward sign of membership within the community but also served as a *"rite de passage"* into communal life.[30]

Although the focus up to this point has been on the Passover, a few remarks are needed regarding the relationship between the Passover and the Feast of Unleavened Bread (מצות). Scholars continued to question the relationship between the Passover and the Feast of Unleavened Bread, particularly in Exodus and Deuteronomy.[31] Within the biblical narrative, the implementation of the Passover is introduced first in Exod 12:1–20 with the Feast of Unleavened Bread only briefly being mentioned in vv. 17–20. In addition, the biblical account provides the guidelines of the feast in Exod 13:3–10. Although both festivals are mentioned in Exod 12–13, it is generally accepted that the Passover and the Feast of Unleavened Bread represent two separate ancient festivals.[32] The apparent connection between the two festivals has birthed several theories. The Israelites possibly adopted the Feast of Unleavened Bread after settling in the land of Canaan.[33] Such a theory takes into account the pastoral characteristics of the Passover and the distinguishable agricultural characteristics of the Feast of Unleavened Bread. The fact that unleavened bread was eaten at the Passover sacrifice might be the primary rationale for conjoining the two festivals later

---

29. See Kutsch, "Erwägungen zur Geschichte," 1–35.

30. Segal, *Hebrew Passover*, 114–35.

31. Halbe, "Passa-Massot," 147–68; Wambacq, "Les Massôt," 31–54; idem, "Pesach-Massôt," 499–518; Van Seters, "Place of the Yahwist," 167–82; Cooper and Goldstein, "Exodus and Massôt in History and Tradition," 15–37; Weimar, "Pascha und Massot," 61–72; Levinson, "Hermeneutics of Tradition," 269–86; and McConville, "Deuteronomy's Unification," 47–58.

32. Segal challenged the view that the Passover and the Feast of Unleavened Bread were separate. See Segal, *Hebrew Passover*, 92ff. Van Seters, on the other hand, dated the separation of the Passover and the Feast of Unleavened Bread to the exile. See Van Seters, *Life of Moses*, 124.

33. See Van Seters, *Life of Moses*, 113; cf. Segal, *Hebrew Passover*, 110.

The Israelite Festivals

in Israel's history.³⁴ The various traditions associated with the festivals of Israel and Judah possibly highlight parallel strands of development that are differentiated by sociopolitical factors in the northern and southern kingdoms. Such a hypothesis is tenable due to the two calendrical traditions, northern and southern.

The northern calendar, according to Bernard R. Goldstein and Alan Cooper, seemed compatible with the lunar Canaanite calendar, meaning the day began at dusk. Furthermore, the Feast of Unleavened Bread originated in the north as a festival of national identity. In the southern region, Judah followed the solar year calendar and the day began at dawn. In sum, Goldstein and Cooper believed the R^{JE} conjoined the northern Feast of Unleavened Bread and Passover to create a "prima facie case for unity."³⁵

DIACHRONIC AND EXEGETICAL ANALYSIS

Attempting to understand the Israelite calendar or calendars is difficult. The above adumbrations highlight the scholarly discussion and interpretation of the Passover. Like the previous two chapters, in the following pages I will examine the relevant texts within the Enneateuch related to the Passover/Feast of Unleavened Bread: Exod 12; 23:14–19; 34:18–26; Lev 23; Num 9:1–14; Num 28–29; Deut 16:1–17; Josh 5:1–12; and 2 Kings 23:21–23.

Exodus 12

Passover and the Feast of Unleavened Bread are described in Exod 12:1–20. The narrator depicts the implementation of the Passover in vv. 21–28, which is assumed by many scholars to be an older tradition (vv. 21–23, 27b=E; vv. 24–27a=Dtr). The chapter begins with a declaration from Yahweh to Moses and Aaron that the current month (lit. "this month") will become the first in the new festival calendar. The narrator does not provide the name of the month, Abib, until 13:4. The name Abib is the preexilic month that is replaced later by the exilic name Nisan.³⁶

---

34. Bokser, "Feasts of Unleavened Bread and Passover," 6:756.

35. See Goldstein and Cooper, "Festivals of Israel and Judah," 19–31. See also Goldstein and Cooper, "Exodus and Massôt," 15–37.

36. Since Exod 12:1–20 is considered to be from the Priestly source, most scholars argue that the month described by the narrator was Nisan. In addition, Joel Weinberg argued that the inclusion of לבית-אבת in Exod 12:3 was a key indicator of the Priestly

The Legislative Themes of Centralization

According to Exod 12, on the tenth day of the month, the Israelites are to take an unblemished, one-year-old male lamb and remove it from the sheep and goats. Four days later, the obedient Israelites will assemble themselves into families and kill their lambs in the evening. The blood from the lambs shall be put on the two doorposts and the lintel of each house. The flesh must be roasted, not boiled in water, and eaten that night with unleavened bread and bitter herbs.[37] Any remaining food must be burned (vv. 1–10). The manner in which the people shall eat the food is outlined in vv. 11–13. The participating parties must gird their loins and have sandals on their feet and staff in hand. The meal must be consumed in haste for "it is Yahweh's Passover" (פסח הוא ליהוה).[38] Collectively, the specificity regarding preparation and regulations of the sacrifice, the emphasis and role of blood in the ritual, and the expedient nature of consuming the meal describe an "atmosphere of drama."[39] The atmosphere of drama comes full circle with the divine proclamation in vv. 12–13. The vengeance of Yahweh upon the inhabitants of Egypt cannot be suppressed. The sign of blood on a home will cover the atonement for that family. Upon seeing the blood, Yahweh will pass over (פסחתי עלכם) that house. The actions of Yahweh shall become a "festival to Yahweh" (חג) for future generations (לדרתיכם) to keep as an ordinance forever.[40]

---

version of the Passover ritual. See Weinberg, "Das BĒ IT 'ĀḆŌT im 6.-4," 400–14. Blenkinsopp built upon Weinberg's premise by adding that the "father's house" reference in v. 3 was "a form of social organization characteristic of the post-exilic rather than the pre-exilic period, and one which it would therefore be reasonable to surmise took shape in the Babylonian diaspora." See Blenkinsopp, *The Pentateuch*, 156. בית-אבת contains a priestly emphasis does find support from biblical texts. The idiomatic phrase is found primarily in the texts with a priestly focus: Gen 31:30; Exod 12:3; Num 1:2, 4, 18, 20, 22, 24, 26, 28, 30, 32, 34, 36, 38, 40, 42, 44, 45; 2:2, 32; 3:15, 20; 4:2, 22, 29, 34, 38, 40, 42, 46; 17:17, 21; 26:2; 34:14; Ezra 10:16; Neh 10:35; 1 Chr 5:13, 15, 24; 7:2, 4; 9:9, 13, 19; 12:31; 23:11, 24; 24:4, 30; 26:6, 13; 2 Chr 17:14; 25:5; 31:17; and 35:4, 12.

37. Eating at night does not follow the traditional norms found in the ANE. This fact is supported by the absence of nocturnal consumption of other sacrifices described in the HB. See Haran, *Temples and Temple Service in Ancient Israel*, 320.

38. The phrase פסח הוא ליהוה (Exod 12:11, 27; Lev 23:5; Num 28:16) was distinctive since the narrator did not use a verb of action like other texts that describe the Passover in terms of action: "keep" (Num 9:2), "offered" (Deut 16:2), "killed" (2 Chr 35:6), and "eaten" (2 Chr 30:18). See Rylaarsdam, "Passover," 3:666.

39. Haran, *Temples and Temple Service*, 320.

40. The command to observe the Passover forever implies the ritual was to be viewed as a "festival to Yahweh." See Pedersen, *Israel*, 385; cf. Haran, *Temples and Temple Service*, 347. Levinson argued the centralization mandate in Deuteronomy transformed the

The Israelite Festivals

Verses 14–20 interrupt the narrative somewhat. For source-critical scholars, these verses represent the oldest narrative in the HB.[41] The festival follows the Passover and lasts seven days. The festival begins in the evening on the fourteenth day of Abib and lasts until the evening of the twenty-first day (=Feast of Unleavened Bread). The people are commanded to eat only unleavened bread. The first and last days of the assembly are holy; therefore, no work is to be done by the people. Individuals can consume food prepared only by their hands, and if leaven is discovered, the penalty is expulsion from the congregation.

Exodus 23:14–19 and 34:18–26

The first two accounts of the Israelite calendar are found in Exodus. The *Sitz im Leben* of Moses' receiving the Book of the Covenant is the theophany at Mount Sinai. The law code is the oldest legal corpus in the HB and traditionally identified as being the work of the Elohist.[42] Exodus 23:14–19, like 34:18–26, describes the three pilgrimage feasts in the same order: the Feast of Unleavened Bread, the Feast of Harvest, and the Feast of Ingathering. The emphasis is "distinctly agricultural." The Passover event is obviously missing in the account; however, one internal aspect hints at the Passover. Verse 15 describes that the Feast of Unleavened Bread should be kept for seven days, coinciding with Exod 12:17–20.[43]

Exodus 34:18–26 has been described as the work of a redactor using JE.[44] The relationship between Exod 23:14–19 and 34:18–26 is apparent from a cursory reading of the two texts. It has been suggested that this relationship exists because both texts are "variants of the same law."[45] Both pericopes outline a cultic festival calendar giving particular attention to the

---

Passover sacrifice into a pilgrim festival. See Levinson, "Hermeneutics of Tradition," 283.

41. For example, Eissfeldt labeled vv. 14–20 as *Laienquelle* (i.e., L source), the oldest narrative in the HB. The *Laienquelle* was characterized by crude and primitive elements. See Eissfeldt, *The Old Testament*, 195.

42. Critical scholars have questioned the authenticity of the Book of the Covenant. For example, Patrick described the law code as an "independent document" consisting of two older sources (i.e., a northern document and E) combined and later inserted by redactors into the larger Sinaitic narrative. The law code, however, was older than the other biblical legal codes. See Patrick, *Old Testament Law*, 64–66.

43. See Armerding, "Festivals and Feasts," 305.

44. See Childs, *Book of Exodus*, 604–8.

45. See Propp, *Exodus 19–40*, 617. For a similar argument see Durham, *Exodus*, 461.

The Legislative Themes of Centralization

Feast of Unleavened Bread, the Feast of Weeks, and the Feast of Booths. But, when discussing the issue of Passover, 23:14–19 and 34:18–26 present an interesting disparity.[46] In Exod 23:14–19, פסח is not used, whereas in the latter text, פסח occurs in v. 25. Although פסח is absent in 23:14–19, the text appears to present an unexpected literary and theological depiction of Israel's festivals (v. 15).

Additionally, in both texts the narrator introduces a law concerning the offering of blood that cannot be combined with leavened bread, coincidentally this resembles the Passover sacrifice (e.g., Exod 23:18; 34:25). This sacrifice is differentiated from the other three cultic feasts. More importantly, the offering in 23:18 is described as a "feast" (חגי, lit. "my feast"). Though the verse does not include פס, there is no reason to assume the Passover sacrifice is not the focus. In fact, the literary relationship between 23:18 and 34:25 further proves the Passover in the former text. The sentence structure and syntax are nearly exact in these verses. In 23:18 the law states that an individual "shall not slaughter for sacrifice" (לא-תזבח), whereas 34:25 changes the verb to "shall not slaughter" (לא-תשחט). The structure of the final clause is different in each verse. Though the literary message is similar, the structure is different, evidenced by the insertion of חג הפסח in 34:25.[47] Moreover, the literary similarities between 23:14–19 and 34:18–26, particularly in the verses discussed above, substantiate the theory that the narrator is describing the Passover sacrifice in both texts.[48]

---

46. The absence of פסח in Exod 23:14–19 is not the only significant difference between the texts. Verses 14 and 17 form an inclusio around the concise cultic festival calendar. The replicated vocabulary of שלש and שנה in these verses form brackets around the cultic feast laws. An inclusio around the cultic festival calendar is not found in Exod 34:18–26. Additionally, the phrase שלש פעמים בשנה in v. 24 parallels 23:17 (cf. Exod 34:23, 24; Deut 16:16).

47. The designation of Passover as a festival (חג) was unique to Exod 34:25. See Moulton, "Passover," 684; cf. Driver, *Deuteronomy*, 188; Armerding, "Festivals and Feasts," 303, 305.

48. Haran argued that Exod 23:14–19 and 34:18–26 were parallel in content, yet represented two independent literary formulations. See Haran, *Temples and Temple Service*, 327.

Leviticus 23

Leviticus 23 has been described as the "first comprehensive calendar."[49] Similar to Exod 23:14–19 and 34:18–26, Lev 23 describes the Passover and three pilgrimage feasts (vv. 4–22; 33–36) as well as several additional events: the Sabbath (v. 3), the Feast of Trumpets (vv. 23–25), and the Day of Atonement (vv. 26–32). The designation חג is only used in reference to the Feast of Unleavened Bread (v. 6) and the Feast of Tabernacles (v. 34). Additionally, there is no reference to the men appearing three times a year (contra Exod 23:14, 17; 34:24).[50]

Levine noted the relationship between Lev 23 and Deut 16, particularly with regard to מצות. Both texts mandate the paschal sacrifice be made at the sanctuary. Given this connection, Levine argued that Lev 23 was dependent on Deut 16. A major difference, however, is found in the time that the sacrifice is offered. Leviticus 23 records the paschal sacrifice as taking place in the afternoon (Lev 23:5; cf. Exod 12:3) not after sunset (Deut 16:6).[51] Of note, Lev 23 provides a "new element" into the Passover and Feast of Unleavened Bread celebrations: the "sheaf" (עמר) as an offering along with a lamb for a burnt offering (vv. 10–12).[52]

Numbers 9:1–14

Exodus 12 and Numbers 9:1–14 are the only textual references to the Israelites "observing" the Passover in the Pentateuch.[53] In fact, Exod 12:1–13, 21–27 and Num 9:2–5 are parallel in detail and scope. The similarities between the two Passover stories are characterized generally as being part of Priestly writer's preservation of the festival.[54] The most important aspect of the Passover narrative in Num 9 is the introduction of the unique provision for individuals deemed unclean during the Passover feast. For this reason,

---

49. Armerding, "Festivals and Feasts," 306.
50. See Levine, *Numbers 1–20*, 267.
51. Ibid., 267.
52. Wenham, *Book of Leviticus*, 303–4.
53. A cursory mention of the Passover being the fifteenth day of the first month when the Israelites came out of Egypt is found in Num 33:3. It is significant since the narrator omits any mention of the Feast of Unleavened Bread (cf. Num 9:1–15).
54. The Priestly origin of Num 9:1–14 has been suggested by many scholars. See Budd, *Numbers*, 96; cf. Gray, *Numbers*, 82–83.

The Legislative Themes of Centralization

Num 9:1–14 has been called the "Supplementary Passover."[55] For these unclean individuals, the feast will be postponed one month and should provide an appropriate length of time for regaining the status of being clean (vv. 12–13). The inclusion of a second Passover has no direct impact on the calendar since, in reality, it describes a "'make-up' date for the individual pilgrim."[56] The narrative also includes the glaring omission of the Feast of Unleavened Bread.[57]

Numbers 28–29

In many ways, Num 28–29 are related to Lev 23.[58] These chapters are not calendars but rather a "compilation" of all the sacrifices offered by the Israelite community during the year. The compilation is based on the calendar.[59] Furthermore, the chapters seem to acknowledge the previous Pentateuchal texts related to sacrifices, feasts, and the Israelite calendar.[60] For this reason, these chapters have been dated late in Israel's history.[61] Along these lines, Levine explained, "What Leviticus 23 had formulated as a general rule, establishing the essential requirement of offerings by fire in the public cult, Numbers 28–29 spell out in detail, specifying which burnt offering is to be

---

55. Gray, *Numbers*, 82. Other scholars have adopted this view in recent years.

56. Chavel, "Second Passover," 9. The broader theory of the "second" Passover proposed by Simeon Chavel incorporated two other key Deuteronomic elements—the centralization of the cult and the Passover. He theorized, "The law of the Second Passover represents a Jerusalem priesthood living in the unintended fallout from the centralization of the cult, unwilling to give up on the Passover as an annual temple rite" (p. 23).

57. Broadly speaking, Wellhausen suggested that the three feasts, along with the burnt and sin offerings in the Priestly source, depreciate in value to the extreme point that each loses its "natural spontaneity" and ultimately becomes an exercise in religion. See Wellhausen, *Prolegomena*, 100.

58. See Ashley, *Book of Numbers*, 561; cf. Snaith, *Leviticus and Numbers*, 312. Gray argued that Lev 23 and Num 28 were based on a "lost festal calendar." See Gray, *Numbers*, 404.

59. Noth, *Numbers*, 219. See also Levine, *Numbers*, 153.

60. Ashley, *Book of Numbers*, 561.

61. Several scholars have argued that Num 28 was postexilic. See Vaux, *Ancient Israel*, 473; Noth, *Numbers*, 219–20; Budd, *Numbers*, 314–15; Gray, *Numbers*, 404; and Levine, *Numbers 21–36*, 393.

brought on each occasion."⁶² Given its summation of the festival calendar and relation to Lev 23, it is only important that I highlight the text.⁶³

Deuteronomy 16:1–17

Deuteronomy 16 discusses the ancient festivals of Passover/Feast of Unleavened Bread, Feast of Weeks, and the Feast of Booths (vv. 1–8). In Deuteronomy, the proscription of local sanctuaries changes the way in which the Israelites observe the pilgrim festivals. The ancient festivals are celebrated at local sanctuaries, but vv. 1–17 abolish the ancient tradition. The relationship between the Passover and the concept of centralization in Deuteronomy has birthed several interpretations. The celebration possibly functioned as a "memorial of the Exodus" with the older pre-Mosaic meaning being superseded.⁶⁴ The festival calendar was not simply replaced in Deuteronomy but became a revolution.⁶⁵ The Passover was reduced to a meal at the central sanctuary and signaled the start of the Feast of Unleavened Bread.⁶⁶ The Deuteronomic account represents a later program that elevated Passover to the status of pilgrimage festival and as result replaced the Feast of Unleavened Bread described in Exod 23:14–17 and 34:18–26.⁶⁷ Though various theories have been proposed concerning the Passover, the

---

62. Levine, *Numbers 21–36*, 394.

63. Through the years scholars have offered differing views and dates for Num 28–29. Since these chapters are summaries, I am not concerned with the source-critical issues. Several scholars have provided excellent source-critical assessments. See Gray, *Numbers*, 401–7 and Levine, *Numbers 21–36*, 394.

64. Rowley, *Worship in Ancient Israel*, 118; cf. Pedersen, *Israel*, 387. According to Levinson, the centralization of the Passover assimilated into the "normative system of Temple sacrifice." As a result, the original distinctiveness associated with the ritual was lost. See Levinson, "Hermeneutics of Tradition in Deuteronomy," 279.

65. Levinson, *Deuteronomy as the Hermeneutics*, 53–56. In short, Levinson argued the authors of Deuteronomy combined Exod 13:3–10 and 23:15–18 into a new innovative revolution or "new Passover." In doing so, the Passover in Deuteronomy is transformed from a "local domestic observance" into a "pilgrimage festival." For Levinson's complete analysis, see pp. 53–97; cf. Nelson, *Deuteronomy*, 205–6.

66. Bokser, "Feasts of Unleavened Bread and Passover," 6:758.

67. This theory is closely related to Levinson's argument. The major difference is Levinson's emphasis on Deuteronomic innovation and revolution. See Halbe, "Erwägungen zu Ursprung," 341. Volker Wagner made similar argument when he argued the Passover was interpolated with the Feast of Unleavened Bread in Deut 16:1–8. Moreover, he interpreted the Deuteronomic Passover as an innovation during the reforms of Josiah rather than as an ancient festival. See Wagner, "Das Pesach," 481–98.

The Legislative Themes of Centralization

rudimentary purpose of the festival laws in general is to underscore the gracious giving of the land by Yahweh, but in return the people must give back a portion of its produce.[68]

Moses commands the people that upon entering the land of Canaan, the Passover must be celebrated in the month of Abib. Each family is to offer a sacrifice in the place which Yahweh will choose for his name to dwell (v. 2).[69] Furthermore, the Israelites can now choose a sacrificial animal from the flock or the herd. The relationship between the Passover and the Feast of Unleavened Bread is strengthened in vv. 3–4. The remaining portion of the chapter describes the procedure of observing the Passover at the place chosen by Yahweh: the sacrifice must be offered in the evening at sunset; the sacrifice shall be cooked and eaten in the place chosen by Yahweh; and the next day the people are to return to their tents (vv. 3–8).[70] The Deuteronomic account of the Passover allows the Israelites to boil the meat rather than simply roasting. Boiling the meat is a traditional custom of cooking by settled peoples (cf. Judg 6:19; 1 Sam 2:13; Ezek 46:24).[71] The preposition אל introducing the centralization motif functions spatially and indicates the localization of the Passover at the future sanctuary ("but at the place").[72]

Next, Moses outlines the Feast of Weeks and the Feast of Booths (vv. 9–17). During both feasts, the Israelites are to include the Levite, sojourner, orphan, and widow. The celebration will be at the chosen place

---

68. McConville, *Law and Theology*, 13.

69. Noting the recurrence of the centralization motif, Haran explained, "The brief statement concerning the chosen place, contained in v. 2, was apparently not enough for the writer. Inasmuch, when he had discharged the task of citing the main law and dealing with it (vv. 3–4), he found it necessary to come back to the centralization of worship and to urge it at length (vv. 5–8)." See Haran, *Temples and Temple Service*, 336.

70. Eckart Otto argued that vv. 4b, 5–7 interrupted the context of 16:1–8 with the demand for centralization as well as the incorporation of the Passover in association with the Feast of Unleavened Bread. Thus, vv. 1–8 conjoined the mandate for centralization and the unified festivals, providing the "framework in a diachronic perspective." See Otto, "פסח," 12:15–16.

71. See Haran, *Temples and Temple Service*, 321.

72. Arnold and Choi, *Biblical Hebrew Syntax*, 100. Wambacq argued the older Passover tradition was not the same as the Josianic celebration. With regard to the Passover, Josiah commanded the people to observe the celebration "as it is written in this book of the covenant" (ככתוב על ספר הברית הזה, 2 Kgs 23:21), which for Wambacq differentiated the Deuteronomic form of the Passover from the older tradition (Exod 12). The celebration, therefore, was one of the main reasons Josiah suppressed the local sanctuaries. See Wambacq, "Les origines," 223–24.

The Israelite Festivals

and will serve as a reminder of the people's Egyptian bondage.⁷³ In v. 17, Moses commands that individuals give gifts from their hands (איש כמתנת ידו) according to their ability. The word "gifts" (מתנת), a derivative of נתן, is only used seventeen times in the HB and once in Deuteronomy. According to McConville, the use of מתנת in v. 17 is deliberate and harnesses the concept of Israel's "reciprocal giving." Together, the giving of Yahweh and the Israelites' response serves as two parts of a "single reality."⁷⁴

Joshua 5:1–12

Joshua 5 is a pivotal chapter in the history of Israel. The Israelites' spiritual vitality decays during the forty years of onerous wandering in the wilderness. This time in the wilderness also heightens their attention to Yahweh's demands prior to entering the land of Canaan. The symbolism in Josh 5 directly relates the second generation of Israelites with their ancestors who transgressed through the barren wilderness. After crossing the Jordan River, the Israelites find themselves on the brink of a new adventure. The land of Canaan awaits the downtrodden and weakened people. The surrounding nations ominously look upon the actions of both Israel and Yahweh. Before reveling in the fulfillment of Yahweh's promise to Abraham, the second generation must overcome the years of living outside the covenant of Yahweh, particularly circumcision. Yahweh commands Joshua to circumcise every adult male with knives of flint, which symbolically will remove the sins of the previous generation (vv. 3–4). The ceremonial act of circumcision takes place at Gibeath-haaraloth (lit. "place of the foreskin") but is changed later to Gilgal (vv. 3, 9).

The actions in Josh 5 punctuate for the future generations of Israelites how Yahweh's actions are just and appropriate with regard to his chosen people. With the reproach of Egypt and the wilderness rebellion repudiated, Yahweh allows the Israelites to keep the Passover in the land of Canaan. The people are allowed to eat from the produce of the land, unleavened cakes,

---

73. The spatial relationship between Passover and the Feast of Unleavened Bread has been debated within scholarship. Following the observance of Passover at the central sanctuary, the people would return to their homes and celebrate the Feast of Unleavened Bread. See Driver, *Book of Exodus*, 405–6; Haran, *Temples and Temple Service*, 338; and Sailhamer, *Pentateuch as Narrative*, 262. Other scholars have suggested that the Israelites simply inhabited tents surrounding the central sanctuary during the Feast of Unleavened Bread. See Pedersen, *Israel*, 388.

74. McConville, *Law and Theology*, 13.

The Legislative Themes of Centralization

and parched grain (v. 11). Obviously missing from the Joshua account is the presence of a paschal lamb, the conjoining sacrifice, and the Feast of Unleavened Bread.

2 Kings 23:21–23

Much has been made of the relationship between Deuteronomy and the "book of the law" that ignited the reforms of Josiah in 2 Kgs 22–23. If the discovery of "the book of the law" in 2 Kings 22 is some form of Deuteronomy, then the Josianic reforms directly affects Israel's traditional liturgical celebrations. Prior to the discovery of "the book of the law," the Israelites celebrated the Passover at various local shrines. Due to the "dangerous subversions" of Israel's relationship with Yahweh, these shrines are abolished under Josiah's reign. As a result, the observance of the Passover is relegated to the temple in Jerusalem. Such an act introduces humanization and "deritualization" to some extent.[75]

In 23:21–23, the narrator explains that a considerable length of time transpired between proper observances of the Passover. In v. 21, Josiah commands that all the people of Israel keep the Passover sacrifice as described in "this book of the covenant" (ספר הברית הזה). The failure to prepare and keep the Passover according to the law of Yahweh antedates the "days of the judges that judged Israel" and the days of the kings of Israel and Judah. The narrator appears to be forming a literary link between Deut 16, Josh 5, and 2 Kgs 23 by summarizing the Israelites' futile attempts to observe the Passover over the centuries. During these rebellious years, the observance of the Passover, along with the other festivals, fell dormant in most parts of the nation, save the districts where pastoral and wilderness life continued to thrive. The transition from transient life (e.g., Pentateuch) to a sedentary life (e.g., Judges) coincides with the deterioration of the Israelites' observance of the Passover.[76]

The spiritual climate during the time of Josiah establishes the relationship between the Passover depiction in Deut 16 and 2 Kgs 23:23. With the centralization of the Passover sacrifice by Josiah, the king of Judah attempts to ratify the Passover from the traditional liturgical celebrations. Furthermore, the narrator explains that Josiah, in the eighteenth year of his reign,

---

75. Nelson, *Deuteronomy*, 203–8.
76. See Wellhausen, *Prolegomena*, 93.

The Israelite Festivals

offers "this" Passover sacrifice to Yahweh in Jerusalem.[77] The restriction to observe the Passover in Jerusalem is in accordance to the Deuteronomic law code (16:2, 6, 7).[78]

A SYNCHRONIC READING OF THE FESTIVAL CALENDAR

A synchronic reading of the festival calendar, and particularly Passover and the Feast of Unleavened Bread, must take into account the inconsistent portrait within the Enneateuch. Additionally, the Enneateuch contains limited textual evidence that alludes to or discusses the Passover. The combination of textual inconsistencies and minuscule textual references has led many scholars to advocate a diachronic reconstruction of the Passover. For example, Wellhausen argued the Passover account in Deuteronomy represented the earliest historical motive of the festival.[79] Thus, the other Pentateuchal references to the Passover must be interpreted in light of Deuteronomy rather than vice versa. Also related to the dilemma is the relationship between the Passover and the Feast of Unleavened Bread in Exodus and Deuteronomy. The primary objective of this inquiry is to answer one pertinent question: Can a synchronic reading of the Passover/Feast of Unleavened Bread theme in the Enneateuch provide a viable alternative to the traditional diachronic renderings?

The earliest literary reference to the Passover is Exod 12:1–20, a pericope generally identified as Priestly. In this textual account, the Passover signifies the new festival calendar. The month of Abib is mentioned in Exod 13:4. On the fourteenth day of the month a one-year-old male lamb is to be sacrificed and the blood smeared on the doorposts and lintel of the house. The blood functions as the atonement for the family. Each subsequent year,

77. Wambacq differentiated the Deuteronomic form of the Passover from the older tradition (Exod 12). The celebration described in 2 Kgs 23:21–23 was one of the main reasons Josiah suppressed the local sanctuaries. See Wambacq, "Les origines," 223–24.

78. Going somewhat further, Driver argued that the observance of the Passover described in 2 Kgs 23:23 continued until the destruction of the temple in C.E. 70. See Driver, *Book of Exodus*, 407.

79. Wellhausen, *Prolegomena*, 105–7. Since Wellhausen's treatment of the Passover, little has changed concerning the relationship between Exod 12 and Deut 16. For example, Haran argued the Passover, as described in the Elohist and Priestly writings, presented the paschal sacrifice being given without a temple—an "optical illusion" that linked the biblical tradition of the Passover with the Israelites' departure from Egypt. In fact, the original setting of the Passover was with the temple. See Haran, *Temples and Temple Service*, 348.

The Legislative Themes of Centralization

the family shall keep the Passover in remembrance of Yahweh passing over and sparing the house. The Passover is alluded to elsewhere in Exodus. Both 23:14–19 and 34:18–26 summarize the cultic festival calendar. The former text is void of an explicit reference to the Passover, though an argument can be made that the narrator alludes to the festival since syntactically 23:18 and 34:25 are virtually identical.

Closely related to Exod 12 is the Passover narrative in Num 9:1–14. The narrative in Num 9:1–14 slightly modifies the Passover feast in an effort to accommodate unclean individuals. In the case of an individual being unclean, the Passover can be postponed by one month. The shift in the festival calendar due to issues of uncleanness does not impact the cultic festival calendar—historically or theologically. In short, the Passover accommodation in Num 9:1–14 represents the benevolence of Yahweh to the Israelites during their wilderness experience.

Much attention has been focused on the textual inconsistencies concerning the presentations of the Passover in Exod 12 and Deut 16. Naturally, the most glaring difference between the two textual traditions is the centralization mandate in Deut 16. In Deuteronomy, a thematic shift occurs in regard to the pilgrim festivals. On the surface, the ancient festival traditions appear to be abolished by the Deuteronomic concept of centralization. The Passover tradition in Deuteronomy also permits the Israelites to choose an animal for the sacrifice from the flock or the herd (16:2), whereas the account in Exod 12:5 specifically requires a lamb from the sheep or goats. Additionally, the Deuteronomic account ignores the specific characteristics regarding the sacrificial animal. In the Exodus account, the lamb is to be a year old without blemish (v. 5).

The discrepancies between Exod 12 and Deut 16 have led to a variety of theories, many of which rely heavily on a diachronic interpretation. Though the interpretive efforts of others have furthered the discussion on the apparent inconsistencies between Exod 12 and Deut 16, a synchronic reading of the material might actually provide a convincing argument. An overarching safeguard must be put in place when approaching the biblical text—whether from a strictly diachronic or synchronic perspective—that is, all biblical text(s) under examination must be interpreted (i.e., textually, historically, and theologically) in accordance to the surrounding pericopes. Naturally, some scholars will dismiss such an argument on the grounds of the HB being a collection of disjunctive sources. That the HB is comprised of multiple sources is certainly true; however, the final literary structure of

The Israelite Festivals

the HB must take a higher precedent over etiological concerns of individual sources, which actually constitute a larger composite literary work.[80]

An informed synchronic approach must be the starting point when discussing the inconsistencies between Exod 12 and Deut 16. Miller made a strong argument that the canonical presentation of the Passover in Exod 12 clearly emphasizes how the event began as a "family feast" that was consumed in the בית-אבת (v. 3) and later expanded into an inclusive Israelite celebration (Deut 16:1–8).[81] A synchronic reading of the Passover in the Pentateuch progresses logically. The option to choose an animal from the flock or herd is representative of an agrarian lifestyle, which is exactly what Deuteronomy envisions. The shift to celebrating the Passover, as well as the other festivals, at the central sanctuary continues the theological development of Israel's faith in Yahweh. The inhabitance of the land of Canaan will bring forth many challenges, particularly the Israelites' religious preservation. The celebration of the Passover and the other festivals only continues the theme that Deuteronomy contains a liturgical component that requires every faithful Israelite to continue and foster a monotheistic relationship with Yahweh. Thus, the centralization mandate concerning the Passover serves two purposes. First, the celebration of the Passover at the central sanctuary is compatible with the land and liturgical themes of Deuteronomy. Second, the cultic observance of the Passover at the central sanctuary functions as a conservation of Yahwistic monotheism.[82]

In short, Exod 12 is intended to be read as the derivation of the Passover. As the Israelites flee Egypt following the Passover, a caveat is made for unclean individuals during the wilderness experience (Num 9). Deuteronomy, on the other hand, looks forward to the inhabitance of the land of Canaan and modifies the earlier Passover observance to a new *Sitz im Leben*. The inconsistencies between Exod 12 and Deut 16 are not mere

---

80. At a rudimentary level, this argument is essentially the basis of Childs's original canonical context argument.

81. Miller, *Religion of Ancient Israel*, 69. Miller dated the transition of the Passover from a "family feast" to an inclusive Israelite celebration prior to the monarchy, but the festival diminished during the deplorable conditions of the monarchic period.

82. Von Rad provided an interesting point of reference when interpreting Exod 12 and Deut 16, even in light of the festival's alleged apotropaic function. Over the years, generations of Israelites kept the Passover, but the question remained concerning their motivation for keeping the ritual. In essence, the performing of the ritual connected each generation to the saving history of Yahweh and the observance of Passover was an "actualization of Yahweh's redemptive action in history." See Rad, *OTT* 1:253; cf. Vaux, *Early History of Israel*, 369.

The Legislative Themes of Centralization

representations of differing sources but rather an example of the evolution of the Israelite religion through the various historical periods.

Unfortunately, only two references to the Passover occur in the so-called DH. Joshua 5 represents a new period in Israel's history. The crossing of the Jordan River into the land of Canaan is symbolized first by the circumcision of the second-generation males and then the observance of the Passover. The celebration of the Passover in the land of Canaan is the first observance of the festival since the originating sacrifice in Egypt. The final reference to the Passover is found in 2 Kgs 23:21–23. The discovery of "the book of the law" ignites the reforms of Josiah, including the reinstitution of the Passover. The narrator obviously discredits the earlier attempts of observing the Passover. In the end, the literary history of the Israelites chronicles how the Passover becomes simply dormant once the people inhabit the land of Canaan.

In many ways, a literary connection can be made between Exod 12 and Josh 5 as well as Deut 16 and 2 Kgs 23. First, the observance of the Passover precipitates a new period in Israel's history—the crossing of the Sea of Reeds and freedom from Egyptian slavery. Likewise, the observance of the Passover in Josh 5 represents yet another historical period in Israel's history—the inhabitance of the land of Canaan. The crossing of the Jordan River, though it precedes the observance of the Passover, is theologically similar to the crossing of the Sea of Reeds. In Deut 16, the observance of the Passover is described as taking place at a central sanctuary. A synchronic reading of Deuteronomy reveals a prophetic undertone to the law code, especially the mandate for the centralization of the cult.

At this point, the synchronic reading of Deuteronomy connects with the diachronic arguments posited by scholars over the centuries. Through a synchronic reading, the exilic audience of the Enneateuch, particularly of the Kings corpus, would have recognized the prophetic tone of the centralization mandate in Deuteronomy and equated it with the reforms of Josiah (2 Kgs 22–23). Thus, the observance of the Passover in 2 Kgs 23:21–23 is related to Deut 16, not only literarily and theologically but also historically. With Josiah apparently being the only Israelite king to institute a centralized observance of the Passover, the biblical narrator creates a literary link between Deuteronomy and the reforms of Josiah.

6

The Judiciary Officials

OUTSIDE THE BOOK OF Judges, various individuals function in that capacity of a judge: Yahweh as judge (Gen 18:25; 31:53; Exod 5:21; 12:12; Judg 11:27), humanity as judge (Gen 19:9; Judg 2:17), Moses as judge (Exod 2:14), Samuel and his sons as judges (1 Sam 8:1–5), Absalom as judge (2 Sam 15:4), and Solomon as judge (1 Kgs 3:16–27). The office of judge in the history of Israel is related closely with the verb "to judge" (שפט).[1] In most cases, the noun "judgment" (משפט) is used in reference to the office of judge. Ironically, only a few verses contain both the noun "judgment" (משפט) and the verbal form "to judge" (שפט).[2] Another group of individuals closely associated with the office of judge is the "officials" (שטר) from the tribes.[3] Together, the judges and officials function as the secular and civil gatekeepers among the Israelites and should be distinguished from city elders.[4]

---

1. Josh 8:33; 23:2; 24:1; Judg 2:16–19; 3:10; 4:4; 10:2–3; 11:27; 12:8, 9, 11, 13, 14; 15:20; 16:31; 1 Sam 3:13; 4:18; 7:6, 15, 16, 17; 8:1, 2, 5, 6, 20; 2 Sam 7:11; 15:4; 1 Kgs 3:9, 28; 7:7; 23:22.

2. Gen 18:25; Deut 16:18; 25:1; 1 Kgs 3:28; 7:7; Isa 1:17; 16:5; Jer 5:28; Ezek 7:27; 16:38; 23:24, 45; 44:24; Zech 7:9; 8:16; Lam 3:59.

3. The noun שטר occurs in the Enneateuch several times: Exod 5:6, 10, 14, 15, 19; Num 11:16; Deut 1:15; 16:18; 20:5, 8, 9; 29:9; 31:28; Josh 1:10; 3:2; 8:33; 23:2; 24:1. In Exod 5, the biblical narrator uses שטר to describe the Israelite "foreman" over the forced laborers under Pharaoh's dominion, which is slightly different from the Deuteronomistic use. See *HALOT* 2:1441.

4. Weinfeld, "Judge and Officer," 81; cf. Lundbom, *Deuteronomy*, 520.

The Legislative Themes of Centralization

DIACHRONIC AND EXEGETICAL ANALYSIS

Thus, the purpose of this chapter is to summarize the significant texts that will help construct the rationale and purpose of these two offices. Attention will be given to the following texts: Exod 18:13–27; Num 11:1–17; 25:1–5; Deut 1:9–18; 16:18–20; 17:2–7; 25:1–3; Judg 2:11–23; 1 Sam 7:3–6, 15–17; 8:1–3; 2 Sam 15:1–6; and 1 Kgs 3.

Exodus 18:13–27

The reunion of Moses and his family is the literary backdrop of Exod 18. The placement of the current chapter is somewhat perplexing since the preceding and following chapters are somewhat different in literary scope.[5] Exodus 17 concludes with a battle between the Israelites and the Amalekites at Rephidim (vv. 8–15). Chapter 19 begins with the people of Israel leaving Rephidim and entering the wilderness of Sinai (vv. 1–2). Sandwiched between these chapters is Exod 18, providing valuable insights into the court and judicial system of the Israelites. The reunion between Moses and his family emphasizes the miraculous works of Yahweh in delivering the people from Egyptian bondage (18:1–12). A literary shift occurs in 18:13, signified by "and the next day" (ויהי ממחרת). The focus of the chapter is shifted to the establishment of the court and judicial system (vv. 13–27).

The language of 18:13–27 is pre-Deuteronomic in origin and function. After the shift in v. 13a, the narrative continues with Moses sitting and judging the people for many hours (וישב משה לשפט את-העם). Jethro reappears in the narrative by questioning Moses concerning his practices of judging the people alone (לבדך) "from morning to evening" (מן-בקר עד-ערב). The opening clause of the riposte given by Moses is somewhat confusing since he is functioning similarly to a diviner. Moses maintains the people came to him so that he would inquire of God (לדרש אלהים). The next clause introduces the second function of Moses as judge—he rules on disputes between individuals (vv. 15–16). The final clause of Moses' riposte emphasizes his basic rationale for being a judge: "I make them know the statutes of God and his law" (הודעתי את-חקי האלהים ואת-תורתיו).[6]

---

5. Van Seters provided a thorough assessment of the literary discontinuity of Exod 17–19. See Van Seters, *Life of Moses*, 208–19.

6. The placement of Exod 18:13–27 between the narratives at Rephidim (ch. 17) and Mount Sinai (ch. 19) introduces several difficulties. Van Seters argued that the establishment of the courts and judges in ch. 18 was not void of chronological and functional

The Judiciary Officials

Jethro counters Moses with a negative assessment due in large part to his concern for his son-in-law's physical and emotional stability (v. 18). Verses 19 and 20 echo the first and third clauses in vv. 15–16. Jethro challenges Moses concerning his ability to judge the entire nation. He suggests that Moses appoint officials (שׂרי) to judge (שׁפט) the people at all times (v. 21). Additionally, these officials must be trustworthy and unwilling to take a bribe. The implementation of these officials would allow Moses freedom from the overbearing weight of being the primary judge. In fact, the officials would judge the people at all times (בכל-עת) and bring only the most pressing issues to Moses. In doing so, the burden on Moses would be lessened, and the people would find solace within their allotted groups (vv. 22–23).

In summation, the instillation of the court and judicial system outlined in Exod 18 precedes the laws regarding judicial procedures in Deuteronomy, both conceptually and chronologically. The most obvious difference in Exod 18 from the other Enneateuchal texts addressing the judicial system is the absence of the Deuteronomistic "officials" (שטרים) and "the judge" (השפט). In short, Exod 18 is pre-Deuteronomic in theory, practice, and vocabulary.

Numbers 11:1–17

Although the burden placed on Moses is introduced in Exod 18, the narrator continues to develop the system of the court and judges. Interestingly, לבדך is used several other times outside of Exod 18, particularly when emphasizing the burden of the people upon Moses. Following the departure from Mount Sinai in Num 11, the people instantly begin to complain, requesting meat, fish, and produce (vv. 1–6). The manna provided by Yahweh is no longer sufficient for the people. With animosity mounting, Moses questions Yahweh for the harsh circumstances bestowed upon him as

---

difficulties. First, Moses was described as a judge who ruled on the disputes of the people (v. 16). Second, Moses was viewed as a "source of divination" who people utilized as an avenue to "inquire of God." From a chronological standpoint, the act of being a source of divination presupposed the primary objective of the tent of meeting introduced in 33:7–11. A third tension in the text was Moses' ability to "make known the statutes of God and his law" (v. 16). Again, the actions of Moses seemed to presuppose the theophany at Mount Sinai, the Book of the Covenant, and the communal relationship between Moses and Yahweh in the tent of meeting (Exod 34:29–35). See Van Seters, *Life of Moses*, 213–15.

The Legislative Themes of Centralization

leader. To plead his case, Moses briefly summarizes his accomplishments, as well as the areas of his inability to meet the growing requests of the people (vv. 10–15). That Moses is no longer able to sustain the demands and duties bestowed upon him is reiterated by Yahweh's command to gather seventy elders (זקני העם) and officers (שטרי). These men help Moses temporarily share the burden of the people (vv. 16–17).[7]

Numbers 25:1–5

Following the recommendation of Jethro, Moses apparently appoints judges over the tribes of Israel. In many cases, the implementation of these individuals into the office of judge can be substantiated in simple, terse verses scattered through the Enneateuch. One such example is found in Num 25:5. Immediately after the Balaam cycle (Num 22–24), the people of Israel dwell in Shittim and commit apostasy by worshiping Baal of Peor. The inclusion of the phrase "the people began to play the harlot to the daughters of Moab" (ויחל העם לזנות אל-בנות מואב) forms the relational circumstances that will lead to the moral deviation by the people of Israel. As a result of the harlotries, the Moabites are able to coerce the Israelites to offer sacrifices and worship their pagan gods (vv. 1–2). Additionally, the Israelites become partial to Baal of Peor.[8] As a result of the idolatrous acts, Moses commissions the judges of Israel to kill the individuals who have yoked themselves with Baal of Peor (v. 5). This unique story portrays one of the roles of the judges of Israel—an executioner.

Deuteronomy 1:9–18

Much of the first four chapters of Deuteronomy are a summation of the wilderness experience in Numbers. Thus, the material in 1:9–18 reiterates

---

7. Similarly, Deut 1:9 and 12 emphasize Moses' inability to "endure/bear" (לא-אוכל) the people because of their toil (טרחכם) and burden (משאכם). As a result of Moses' inability to bear the burden of the people, he is directed to select wise men from each tribe to be over the people (Deut 1:13; cf. Exod 18:13–27; Num 11:14, 17). Martin Rose provided a lengthy comparison of the various accounts of the courts and the judicial system (Exod 18:13–27; Num 11:16–22, 24–25; Deut 1:9–18). See Rose, *Deuteronomist und Jahwist*, 224–63.

8. The unique use of the Niphal verb "to join" (יצמד) is a rare example of the Niphal ingressive-stative. The narrator uses the verb to emphasize the people of Israel's emotional attachment to Baal of Peor. See *IBHS* 385, 391.

the narratives in Num 11:14, 17 and 25:4–5. In short, these verses reiterate the inability of Moses to function as "the" judge for all the people due to the overwhelming burden of the people (cf. Num 11:14, 17). Additionally, the appointment of wise men, chiefs, and judges parallels Exod 18:13–27.

Deuteronomy 16:18–20

The preceding texts portray a minute glimpse into the system of the courts and judges in the history of Israel. Within the Deuteronomic law code, 16:18—18:22 forms a unified section that deals with the religious and civil officials: local courts (16:18; 17:2–7), a central court (17:8–13), the king (17:14–20), the Levitical priesthood (18:1–8), and the prophet (18:15–22).[9] These chapters function similarly to a "constitutional proposal" regarding the concepts about the judge, king, priest, and prophet. The contextual emphasis is on the selection process, the functions, the obedience owed to the individuals, and the mechanisms of succession. In each subsection, the concept of centralization substantiates the constitutional proposal by regulating various offices within the land.

Following the account in Deut 1:9–18, Moses discusses the establishment of civil positions, particularly judges and local officers (Deut 16:18–20).[10] The participle "to judge" (שֹׁפְטִים) at the beginning of v. 18, "you shall appoint judges and officers," functions as a substantive noun along with the absolute noun שֹׁטְרִים.[11] The purpose of these civil positions is to protect justice within the towns inhabited in the land. Each town is to appoint judges and officers according to the division of the tribes. These civic officers judge the people with "righteous judgment" (מִשְׁפַּט־צֶדֶק). Moses demands the civil officers not pervert justice by showing partiality or by accepting bribes (cf. 27:19, 25). The installation of the civil offices will help the people live justly, since obedience is the only way the people will inherit the land of Yahweh. The beginning of v. 20 contains the emphatic repetition

---

9. See Lohfink, "Functions of Power," 336–52; cf. Knoppers, "The Deuteronomist," 334; idem, "Deuteronomy and the Deuteronomistic History," 397; Sonnet, *Book within the Book*, 71; Dutcher-Walls, "Circumscription of the King," 603; Hagedorn, "Deut 17,8–13," 540; and Block, "Burden of Leadership," 263.

10. Lundbom, *Deuteronomy*, 520.

11. *IBHS* 614.

The Legislative Themes of Centralization

צדק צדק, meaning "perfect justice" or "justice alone."[12] The phrase, in many ways, summarizes a Deuteronomic ideal.[13]

Deuteronomy 17:1–13

Deuteronomy 17 is related closely to 16:18–20. The local courts in 16:18 are developed in 17:2–7 and further clarified with the centralized court system in 17:8–13.[14] In 16:18–20 and 17:2–7, Moses continues the theme of forbidden forms of worship. Any blemished or lame offering is considered an abomination to Yahweh. Furthermore, an individual who breaks the covenant of Yahweh by worshiping or serving other gods shall be stoned to death at the city gate. To break the covenant carries the idea of transgressing or trespassing the covenant (vv. 2–3). The use of אשר לא-צויתי (lit. "which I [Yahweh] did not command") at the end of v. 3 is possibly a litotes, a figure of speech that expresses a positive idea through negation. Moreover, the phrase can be a denial of something others proclaim as true. The phrase (אשר לא-צויתי) probably rejects any suggestion that other gods can be worshiped in conjunction with Yahweh.[15] Within the broader context of the so-called DH, the Israelites are commanded not to become disloyal to Yahweh by transgressing the covenant through worshiping other gods (cf. Josh 7:11, 15; 23:16; Judg 2:16–20; 2 Kgs 18:12).[16] An individual guilty of committing an abomination to Yahweh is sentenced to death. Before issuing the death sentence, two witnesses must bring evidence against the individual accused of transgressing the covenant (vv. 2–7).

The following pericope (vv. 8–13; cf. 19:17–18) continues to develop the institution of priests and judges. The concept of centralization affects the outcome of ritual justice when witnesses are unavailable. If a case is too baffling for the civil or religious leaders to determine an outcome (כי יפלא

---

12. Driver, *Deuteronomy*, 201; cf. Weinfeld, *Deuteronomic School*, 273; Tigay, *Deuteronomy*, 161; and Nelson, *Deuteronomy*, 212.

13. Similarities possibly exist between Deut 16:18 and the reforms of King Jehoshaphat in 2 Chr 19:5–11. See Rad, *Deuteronomy*, 114; cf. Weinfeld, "Judge and Officer," 65–67; Miller, *Deuteronomy*, 141–43; and Lundbom, *Deuteronomy*, 521.

14. Many commentators identify 17:18–23 as the centralized court system: Craigie, *Book of Deuteronomy*, 251; Mays, *Deuteronomy*, 266; Tigay, *Deuteronomy*, 163–66; and McConville, *Deuteronomy*, 281. On the other hand, Block dismissed the notion that vv. 18–23 functioned as the centralized court system. See Block, *Deuteronomy*, 408.

15. See Tigay, *Deuteronomy*, 462.

16. Weinfeld, "ברית," 2:261.

ממך דבר למשפט), then the case is to be transferred to the central sanctuary. At the central sanctuary, the Levitical priests and "the" judge will hear the injunction and decide the proper sentencing. The singular "judge" (השפט) possibly means the court contained one lay judge.[17] On the other hand, the singular השפט might represent all the lay judges or simply the head of the lay judges.[18] In any case, once the verdict is given, the people must obey the decision of the priests and the judge. Any individual who ignores the verdict must be purged from the community to suppress any future actions of defiance.

Deuteronomy 25:1–3

Deuteronomy 25:1–3 contains the "procedure for the administration of corporal punishment."[19] The regulation addresses a dispute between two men. The reason for the dispute is not mentioned in the text. To settle the dispute, both men are brought to the law court to receive a legal judgment and punishment. All punishments come from a ruling judge or court. In addition, two punishments are bestowed upon the guilty party. First, the judges decide whether or not the offence warrants corporal punishment. Second, if corporal punishment is the verdict, then the judges regulate the number of lashes the guilty individual is to receive. Corporal punishment is carried out in the presence of the judge. By doing so, the judge is able to determine whether the punishment is too lenient or extreme. Even in judgment, the dignity of the guilty party is considered.[20]

Judges 2:11–23

As mentioned earlier, the book of Judges, in many ways, is the theological antithesis of Deuteronomy. Whereas Deuteronomy prepares the people to live in the land of Canaan, Judges reveals the anarchic reality of the Israelites living in the land. The theological prudence demanded by Yahweh

---

17. The word שפט is another example of Deuteronomic and Deuteronomistic language (Deut 17:9, 12; 19:17, 18; 25:2; Judg 2:18, 19; 11:27; 2 Kgs 23:22).

18. Tigay, *Deuteronomy*, 165. Andrew D. H. Mayes interpreted "the" judge as a Deuteronomic innovation that supplemented the old traditional practice of priests serving as civil magistrates. See Mayes, *Deuteronomy*, 268–69.

19. Driver, *Deuteronomy*, 279–88; cf. Craigie, *Book of Deuteronomy*, 312.

20. Ibid., 288.

The Legislative Themes of Centralization

reverberates through Deuteronomy and Joshua, yet it becomes a distant memory in Judges. Sadly, the theological apex of Joshua is surpassed by the incumbent failures of the tribes of Israel in Judges. With the raising up of charismatic leaders (i.e., the judges), Yahweh introduces the stark contrast between faithful obedience under the leadership of men of faith (e.g., Moses and Joshua) and the Yahwistic ideals that lead to punishment, subjugation, and anarchy.

The role of the judges during the tribal amphictyony differs from other periods in Israel's history. Emphasis is given to the social, political, and spiritual turbulence of the tribal amphictyony period in Judg 2:11–23. The underlying circumstance of Yahweh's judgment and implementation of judges (vv. 16–17) is the people's harlotry (זנו). Yahweh shrouds each judge in divine protection and, at times, imparts the spirit upon him.[21] Delivering the oppressed Israelites is the primary objective for the judges; however, when the judge dies, the people of Israel regress into the temptations of the land and once again find themselves being subjugated by another opposing nation (vv. 18–19).[22]

1 Samuel 7:3–6, 15–17; 8:1–3

A literary comparison between Samson and Samuel uncovers dramatic parallels between the two men. Both are born to mothers who are stricken with barrenness for a period of time (Judg 13:3; 1 Sam 1:5). The parents dedicate their child as a Nazirite (Judg 13:4–5; 1 Sam 1:26–27). A message from Yahweh is revealed to both women (Judg 13:6ff; 1 Sam 1:11; 3:1). In addition to the similarities, the narrator also highlights the differences between the men. The narrator introduces Samson as an egotistical and selfish man who shuns the traditions and faith. These qualifications of Samson eventually lead to his demise (14:1ff). Samuel, on the other hand, is introduced as a faithful young boy who is astute to the voice and calling of Yahweh (1 Sam 1:11; 3:1).

The comparison becomes more important when Samuel's actions are recognized as being similar to those of the judges during the tribal

---

21. "The spirit of Yahweh upon him" (עלי רוח יהוה) is a unique phrase that is applied specifically to Othniel (3:10) and Samson (14:6, 19; 15:14).

22. Due to the scope of the chapter and material found in the idolatry subsection above, I will not discuss the intricacies of each major and minor judge. More important to the current discussion is the office of judge rather than the individuals.

amphictyony period (1 Sam 7:3ff).[23] Though his last act of valor includes Yahweh's mediation, Samson should be considered a failure in regard to his task as a judge. In fact, the mere declaration of Samuel as a judge in Mizpah (1 Sam 7:6) underscores the narrator's plot development—Samuel becomes the replacement for Samson. In fact, Samuel restores the land and cities captured by the Philistines (vv. 13–14). This description of Samuel's actions is consistent with the scope and task of the judges during the tribal amphictyony period. Samuel's judicial domain consists of a yearly cycle to Bethel, Gilgal, Mizpah, and Ramah (vv. 15–17). Yet, the spiritual proclivity of Samuel apparently leads to his judicial tenure.

In 1 Sam 8, a narrative shift is employed with the description of Samuel being old (v. 1). Recognizing his limited ability as a judge, Samuel commissions his sons, Joel and Abijah, to be judges over Israel. His sons, however, do not follow the same spiritual commitment as their father. In fact, they are described as perverting justice (v. 3).[24] The encumbering health of Samuel and the insurmountable acts of Joel and Abijah create a methodological shift in the Israelite cult. The theocratic view of leadership in the Hexateuch is replaced with a monarchic government in the Samuel and King corpuses (vv. 4–5; cf. 12:1–2).[25]

2 Samuel 15:1–6

The designation of Samuel as a prophet and judge is accurate based on the narrator's depiction. The capacity to which Samuel functions as judge extends somewhat beyond the Deuteronomic description (cf. Deut 16:18ff). Due to the old age of Samuel and the deplorable actions of his sons, the Israelites yearn to be like the other surrounding nations. With the establishment of the monarchy, the role of the judge returns to the Deuteronomic

---

23. Note the Deuteronomistic language of 1 Sam 7:3, particularly שבים אל-יהוה (cf. Deut 30:10; 2 Kgs 23:25; Hos 6:1; 7:10; 14:3) and הסירו את-אלהי (cf. Deut 11:16; Josh 24:14, 23; Judg 10:16).

24. The Deuteronomistic idiomatic phrase לא-הלכו בניו בדרכו describes the behavior of Joel and Abijah (cf. 1 Sam 8:5; 1 Kgs 11:33; 2 Kgs 21:22; Jer 2:23).

25. Samuel vehemently opposed the people's desire for a king (1 Sam 8:6–18). The prophet criticizes the people's desire at Mizpah, one of his four judicial centers. In his creedal message, Samuel proclaims the sovereignty of Yahweh during the exodus, which is overshadowed by the people's desire for a monarchy rather than a theocracy (1 Sam 10:17–19; 12:6–8). Moreover, in his farewell address, Samuel equates the current generation with the unfaithful generation of the tribal amphictyony period (1 Sam 12:9–12).

ideal. The brief narrative on Absalom's clever plot to thwart David's reign substantiates this fact. After being away from Jerusalem and his father, Absalom returns with revenge, hatred, and deception in his heart. In 2 Sam 15:1–6, Absalom recognizes his father's oversight in not implementing a judicial system. As a result, Absalom, along with fifty men, arise early each day and stand in the gates of the city. The men hear the judicial cases of the people and make rulings (v. 3).

Ironically, the people of Israel desire a king rather than live under the judicial constraints of Samuel and his sons (1 Sam 8:1–3); yet, decades later, King David fails to implement the Mosaic judicial system that will meet the needs of the people (cf. Exod 18:13–26). Absalom uses his father's oversight of establishing a judicial system to enact his coup d'etat and is able to steal the hearts of the people (v. 4–6). In short, the narrator, in this brief pericope, explains how David ignores both the Mosaic precedent and the Deuteronomic innovation while Absalom is aware of and sensitive to the judicial system.[26]

1 Kings 3

The transition from David to Solomon is not without turmoil. Although the narrator's portrait of Solomon is ironic in some regard, some focus is given to the king's purer motives. One example of Solomon's good intentions is found in 1 Kgs 3:9: "Give to your servant an understanding heart to judge (לב שמע לשפט) your people, in order that I may be able to discern between good and evil." Solomon earnestly prays to have the knowledge imparted upon him to judge the people accordingly. The second part of v. 9 reveals that at the current time no one is able to judge the people of Yahweh. It appears that Solomon assimilates the duties of the judicial system, at least the office of judge, under his role as head of the monarchy (cf. 1 Kgs 7:7). To emphasize this point, the narrator introduces a story involving two harlots and their dispute over the maternity of a child (1 Kgs 3:16–27). Naturally, the narrator uses the story to heighten the fact that Solomon is the wisest man in Israel (v. 28), but it is cast within the framework of the kingship functioning as an instrumental office of the judicial system. Thus, the depiction of Solomon serving as a judge counters the Deuteronomic constitution (16:18—18:22).

---

26. Polzin suggested a similar interpretation of Absalom's betrayal of David. See Polzin, *David and the Deuteronomist*, 149–50.

The Judiciary Officials

A SYNCHRONIC READING OF THE JUDICIARY OFFICIALS

The literary depiction of the judiciary officials is not as convoluted as the previous themes. The origin of the judiciary officials resides in the narratives attributed to Moses. In many ways, Moses functions as the archetype of the Israelite judiciary system. In Exod 18:13–27, Moses is described as judging the people of Israel alone. Additionally, the primary task of Moses' being judge is to settle disputes between individuals (vv. 15–16) and to declare the statutes of Yahweh. Jethro realizes the difficulty in the task embraced by Moses. Thus, Moses is encouraged to appoint officials to judge the people, which in turn will lighten his burden. Even with implementation of officials, Moses will retain his status as the chief official/judge. The burden of being the leader of the people manifests itself in the wilderness. In one such case, Moses complains to Yahweh concerning his inability to satisfy the requests of the people (Num 11: 1–15). For a temporary period of time, Yahweh allows seventy elders and officers to share Moses' burden of the people (vv. 16–17). Following the Balaam cycle, the people of Israel commit apostasy with Baal of Peor. Yahweh commands Moses to enlist the officials and judges from the tribes to purge the evil from the presence of the people (25:4–5). The sharing of the burden by Moses and the officials and judges in Num 25 coincides with Jethro's suggestion in Exod 18:13–27.

The introduction to Deuteronomy reiterates much of the above material. The abominable acts of the people result in the judgment of Yahweh by means of the judges. Again, Moses is considered "the" chief judge of all the people (1:8–12). One minor difference is found between Exod 18 and Deut 1. In Exod 18, Moses succumbs to the suggestion by Jethro to appoint wise, God-fearing, and unflappable men as officials (שׂרי) to rule over thousands, hundreds, fifties, and tens. The Deuteronomic narrator slightly changes the description of the officials (שׂרי) in Deut 1:15. Underscoring this fact, the narrator uses the titles ראשי שבטיכם and ראשים twice to describe the office of שׂרי ruling over thousands, hundreds, fifties, and tens. In Deut 1:15–16, the Deuteronomic narrator deviates from the role of שׂרי to "judge the people at all time" (ושפטו את-העם בכל-עת). In fact, the narrator charges the judges (lit. "ones judging," שפטיכם) to be nonpartisan toward individuals and unwavering when issuing judgments. Moreover, a case that is too difficult for judgment will be brought to Moses.

Up to this point, the textual depiction of the judiciary offices is miniscule. With the Deuteronomic law code, however, the judiciary offices are

135

The Legislative Themes of Centralization

described in more detail. The more elaborate depiction coincides with the purpose of Deuteronomy in Israel's PH. Since Deuteronomy anticipates the inhabitance of the land of Canaan, the constitutional characteristics introduce a new paradigm shift, specifically in the civil and religious arenas (16:18—18:22). The first establishment of the constitutional proposal is the civil positions of judges and local officers. These civil officials represent the grassroots level in the land of Canaan. The requirements of these officials are to protect justice by showing no partiality or perverting justice (16:18–20). Deuteronomy 17:1–13 provides the parameters in which these civil officials function within the social structure of Israel. The judges and officials are to uphold justice and punish individuals guilty of abominable acts against Yahweh (vv. 1–7); yet, if a specific case proves too difficult or void of witnesses, the case will be transferred to the Levitical priest and the judge at the central sanctuary (vv. 8–13; cf. 19:17–18; 25:1–3). The precise status of the judge at the central sanctuary is unknown, but his function appears to be superior to the local judges—possibly a Mosaic archetypal judge who supersedes local tribal judges.

The judicial procedures carried out at the central sanctuary (vv. 8–9) portray a heightened and prospective augmentation of the court and judicial system described in Exod 18:13–27 and Deut 1:13–17. In the former case, Moses is the primary judge of difficult cases, recapitulating in the Tetrateuch summation in Deut 1:13–17. Deuteronomy 1:9–12 reiterates the inability of Moses to function as "the" judge for all the people due to the overwhelming burden of the people (cf. Exod 18:18; Num 11:14, 17). The prospective focus undergirds vv. 8–9 and continues in Deut 17 and 18, particularly in relation to the restrictive laws concerning the king (17:14–20) and the laws regarding the defamation of the people through pagan divination (18:15–18).

The substratum of officers and judges is established in the various Pentateuchal strands discussed above. In the narrative structure of the so-called DH, these judicial offices become part of the theological metanarrative. Beginning with the covenantal ceremonies in Deuteronomy and Joshua, the appearance of officers and judges emphasizes the significance of these officials in the lives of the Israelites. In Deut 31:28, Moses assembles all the elders from the tribes (כל-זקני שבטיכם) and the officers (שטריכם) before uttering his song (Deut 32). Prior to the assembly, Moses demands that the people obey "this book of the law." A similar list is found in the building

The Judiciary Officials

of the altar at Mount Ebal (Josh 8:33; cf. Deut 27:4–5) and the covenantal ceremonies in Josh 23:2 and 24:1.

The theme of monotheism in the Pentateuch reaches a climax in Deuteronomy and is continued in Joshua. The covenantal ceremonies in these two books, in many ways, epitomize Israel's theological dictum of monotheism. The tribal amphictyony, on the other hand, signifies yet another historical period as well as theological paradigm in Israel. The theological dictum of monotheism in Deuteronomy is replaced with the spiritually apathetic, and yet melodramatic, narratives in Judges. The responsibility of the spiritual apathy and, at times, depravity of the Israelites during the tribal amphictyony falls on the shoulders of human judges. The judges of the tribal amphictyony must be differentiated from the Pentateuchal judges. In Judges, the Israelites no longer heed the monotheistic dictum of the previous generations (2:16–17). Thus, Yahweh sends judgment upon the people through means of subjugation to other nations. Yahweh raises up judges to deliver the people from oppression upon hearing the cries of the people (vv. 18–19). In short, the judges of the amphictyony period are categorically different from the Pentateuchal local judges serving in Israelite cities. Moreover, a Mosaic archetypal judge is never mentioned in Judges.

The proclivity for sinfulness in Judges subsides somewhat in the introductory chapters of the Samuel corpus. In many ways, the life of Samuel is antithetical to the diabolical portrait of the Israelites in Judges. Though Samuel functions similarly to the judges of the amphictyony (1 Sam 7:3ff), the so-called DH does not contain much information concerning the judiciary officials. The people's rejection of Samuel and his sons in favor of a king substantiates this fact (1 Sam 8:1–5). The only other references to the judiciary officials are to Absalom and Solomon. First, Absalom, along with fifty men, functions as a local judge issuing verdicts within city gates (2 Sam 15:1–6). Absalom uses the role of judge to dislodge David's stronghold as king. Inasmuch, the narrator uses the Absalom narrative to slight David for not implementing a judicial system. Second, the narrator illustrates the depth of Solomon's wisdom by presenting him as the ruling judge over the issue of a disputed maternity (1 Kgs 3:16–27).

The above synchronic reading provides an important glimpse at the judiciary officials in the Enneateuch. In the Pentateuch, the judiciary officials lighten the burden on Moses and provide a civil judicial system at multiple levels of Israelite life, evidenced by the Deuteronomic implementation of a Mosaic archetypal judge at the central sanctuary. The role of the judge shifts during the amphictyony period. The individuals are selected by Yahweh to deliver his oppressed people. The rise of Samuel continues along the pathway of the judges in the amphictyony period since he delivers them from the Philistines. He is responsible also for returning of the Pentateuchal ideal of a judge, that is, serving at the local level.

The two obscure references to the judiciary functions of Absalom and Solomon should be viewed as related. The fact that David did not utilize judges at the local level becomes an area of weakness that Absalom exploits. The request of Solomon to receive a heart to judge (1 Kgs 3:9) might be an attempt to procure the same judiciary abilities as his father. In other words, David did not create a judiciary system because he functioned as the Mosaic archetypal judge. Solomon, likewise, adopts this practice, which is supported by his prayer for a heart to judge. The arrogance of David becomes a weak point in his ability to reign. Thus, Absalom capitalizes on this weakness and divides the people. The Davidic and Solomonic example of judiciary aptitude is substantiated also by the narrator's omission of judges and officials within the royal courts and local provinces.

7

Priesthood in Israel

THE ACADEMIC QUEST FOR the origin and history of the Israelite priesthood has been described as "one of the most vexing problems" in biblical studies.[1] Obviously any thorough discussion on the priesthood should include the exilic writings. Due to the constraints of my research, the discussion concerning the Aaronite and Levitical priesthood will remain within the literary confines of the Enneateuch. Similar to other chapters, a brief overview of the prominent scholarly theories will establish the foundation for the discussion.

The genius of Wellhausen's construction of the history of Israel, though challenged and modified over the decades, continues to influence the study of the HB. His re-creation of the Israelite priesthood, however, has found widespread acceptance for the most part and has been viewed as one of the pillars of his legacy. Put succinctly, Wellhausen understood and divided the history of Israelite priesthood into three stages. The earliest stage was void of hereditary tradition and tribal affiliation. The second dated to the monarchic period and marked the genesis of the Levitical priesthood. In the final stage, the Aaronite priesthood and priestly propaganda permeated the postexilic period.[2] A closer look at Wellhausen's theory will reveal the depth of his argument.

1. Duke, "Priests and Priesthood," 646.
2. An advocate of the Wellhausenian model, de Vaux provided a clear and concise history of the Israelite priesthood under the rubric of non-Levitical priests, Levite-priests, and priests and Levites. See Vaux, *Ancient Israel*, 361–66.

The Legislative Themes of Centralization

At the basic level, Wellhausen believed the priests and the Levites in the Priestly writings in Exodus, Leviticus, and Numbers were representative of the latest stage in the evolution of Israel's priesthood rather than the earliest. Thus, the difference between the Aaronite priesthood and the Levites was substantial. The Levites were not chosen by Yahweh and did not belong to the clergy. Moreover, the equality described in the biblical accounts between the two priesthoods was insignificant.[3]

According to the Priestly source, the earliest stage of the Israelite priesthood was a hierocracy with the clergy serving as the skeletal structure, the high priest as the head, and the Yahwistic temple forming the heart.[4] In hindsight, the Priestly portions of the Pentateuch were not a reality since the period of the judges provided a more accurate portrait of the social and religious life. During the time of the judges, the Israelites no longer assembled around the priests and Levites. The people of Israel could not be described as unified since only individual tribes existed in the land of Canaan. Thus, the Priestly portions of the Pentateuch depict the high priest having central authority over the people of Israel, but in reality, the portrait should be understood anachronistically since the judges functioned as the heads over the people. Within this hierocratic society the priests did not have a *locus standi* until the centralization of the cult. Prior to the centralization of the cult, each head of the household offered sacrifices on behalf of himself and his family. These ad hoc sacrifices were performed on improvised altars constructed out of materials available. During this period of the judges the evolution of the priesthood began (e.g., Eli at Shiloh).[5]

The hierocratic argument of Wellhausen rested on textual examples when people and professionals offered sacrifices without the assistance or presence of a priest. The lives of Eli and Samuel were preclusions to the great watershed of Israelite priesthood that coincided and flourished with the inauguration of the monarchic period. Coupled with the growing prominence of the kings and the kingdom, particularly during the reign of Saul, the centralization of the political and social strata of Israel began to take form. Additionally, the Ephraimitic priesthood distinguished itself at Nob under the leadership of Ahijah the priest. During this period in Israel's

---

3. Wellhausen, *Prolegomena*, 121. Concerning the insignificance of the relationship between Aaronite priesthood and the Levites, Wellhausen argued, "Their office and their blood relationship separates them more than it binds them together" (p. 122).

4. Ibid., 127.

5. Ibid., 127–28.

history, the king, following the lead of David, appointed the priesthood and controlled the sanctuary of the ark.⁶

Deuteronomy played an important role in the monarchic period. First, Moses was presented as the archetypal priest (33:8). Second, once an official name, the title Levite became a patronymic, a rallying point for all the Levites to form a blood-kinship void of any land inheritance. In addition, the name Levite commemorated the priesthood with a hereditary heritage. This hereditary heritage of the Levites allegedly began with the inception of Israel's history with the earliest generation of Levites consisting of numerous members including Moses and Aaron. To this end, Wellhausen dismissed the notion that the priestly families of Judah during the monarchic period derived from Levi son of Jacob (Gen 44). The equality among Jacob's sons, along with the "blood-thirsty character" of Levi, overshadowed the hallowed status of the Levites living in the monarchic period.⁷

Since Wellhausen's landmark theory, several scholars have augmented his original argument while others have offered new theories concerning Israel's priesthood. The essence of the issue is the historicity of the tribe of Levi. Aelred Cody maintained that a relationship existed between the Levitical claim and the tribe of Levi, particularly through their status as "sojourners" (גרים). Contra Wellhausen, Cody argued that the name "Levi was not an appellative but a personal name which has come to be the gentilitial name of a secular tribe."⁸ That the pre-monarchical priests differed from the namesake counterparts of the monarchic period was evidenced by their serving at local sanctuaries as well as functioning as "consultors of oracles" rather than overseers of the sacral system (e.g., Judg 18:5ff; 1 Sam 14:18–42; 22:10–15; 23:9–12; 30:7ff).⁹ Thus, much of the material concerning the priesthood in Exodus–Numbers was "drawn from the liturgy of the monarchic period and applied anachronistically to the desert period."¹⁰ For Cody, the Levites were גרים with priestly specialization. Thus, they could only be understood as "a natural sociological phenomenon in the Israelite tribal system."¹¹ The Levites who lived as גרים among the tribes of Israel

---

6. Ibid., 128–32.
7. Ibid., 143–45.
8. Cody, *History of Old Testament Priesthood*, 33.
9. Ibid., 13, 29.
10. Ibid., 41.
11. Ibid., 55.

The Legislative Themes of Centralization

were analogous to ancient nomadic societies. Moreover, the Levites' status as גרים became a primary characteristic for being recognized as priests.[12]

Cross somewhat adopted Wellhausen's theory, yet he modified portions of the original argument. In short, Cross believed the biblical texts contained competing traditions from two priestly houses: the Mushite priesthood and the Aaronite priesthood. The tradition of the Mushite priesthood was rooted in the sanctuaries of Shiloh and Dan. In addition, an allied relationship between the Mushite and the Kenite priesthoods was forged at the local shrines at Arad and Kadesh. The tradition of the Aaronite priesthood, on the other hand, was related to the sanctuaries of Bethel and Jerusalem. Both David and Jeroboam enlisted priests from the competing priestly houses most likely for diplomatic interests. With the jettisoning of Abiathar during the reign of Solomon, the Mushite priestly tradition became obsolete with the Aaronite priestly tradition taking a place of prominence not only in the kingdom but also in the Priestly material in the Tetrateuch.[13]

Merlin Rehm posited another popular theory concerning the title of Levite. He suggested the group of Levites shared a common function but not always a blood relationship. It was plausible that the individual clans of the Levites (i.e., Gershon, Kohath, and Merari) shared a blood relationship, but this relationship did not necessarily extend to the other clans. Thus, Moses and Aaron would not be related even though both men were priests and from the tribe of Levi. Since the blood relationship existed only in specific clans, similarity in function became the solidifying element that led these various clans to form the tribe of Levi.[14]

---

12. Ibid., 55–60.

13. Cross, *Canaanite Myth*, 206–15.

14. Rehm, "Levites and Priests," 4:300. Building on the genealogical works of several scholars including Cross, Rehm maintained that a reconstructed history of the Levites must take three distinct periods of history into consideration: desert, tribal, and monarchy. In the desert period, the Levites were divided into three groups: Gershonites, Kohathites, and Merarites. Moses and Aaron were both descendants from Kohath. In the desert narratives, Aaron was presented as an elder—who at times made the life of Moses difficult—rather than a priest. In the tribal period, the Levites gained in number and primarily became the "keepers of the central sanctuary" and the Mosaic law, which they could expand when they saw fit. The priests serving at the central sanctuary were the Deuteronomic Levitical priests and descendants of Moses and Ithamar, probably from the lineage of the Mushites and Libnites (Num 26:58a). The Aaronites and Korahites were not influential during the tribal period. In the monarchic period, specifically during the reign of David, the Mushite Levites were invited to serve alongside the Aaronites, thus conjoining the descendants of Moses (i.e., Abiathar) and Aaron (i.e., Zadok) at the

DIACHRONIC AND EXEGETICAL ANALYSIS

The brief sketch above simply highlights the prominent issues related to the priesthood in Israel. The earliest stage of priesthood, particularly with regard to the tribe of Levi, has been questioned and described as non-Levitical, anachronistic, patronymic, and an appellative. Historically, the monarchic period represented the establishment of the Israelite priesthood and the birth of the Levites. During the postexilic period, the Aaronite priesthood flourished and dictated the social, political, and theological landscape of the people.

For the remainder of the chapter, attention will be given to the two types of Israelite priests discussed in the HB, the Levites and the descendants of Aaron.[15] Due to the fragmentary nature of the material, the textual analysis will be presented in a composite fashion rather than a chronological, literary order. Following the reconstruction of the literary depiction of the Levites and the Aaronite priesthood, the Deuteronomic portrait of the Israel's priesthood will examined.

The Levites

An attempt to construct a composite literary history of the Levites might be considered handicapped by some scholars due to the intentional omitting of prophetic and exilic writings from the discussion. I am aware that any comprehensive study of the Levites should include the breadth of Israelite literature; however, the current endeavor is not premature since the books of the Enneateuch comprise the literary history of the Israelites. Even if the theorists are correct in that the exilic writings and the Priestly source share a theological perspective, ideology, and compositional dating, the original (exilic) audience most likely differentiated between the messages

---

sanctuary in Jerusalem. See Rehm, "Levites and Priests," 4:297–310.

15. The Enneateuch contains several stories where individuals offer sacrifices to Yahweh without the assistance or presence of a priest: Abel (Gen 4:4), Noah (Gen 8:20), Abraham (Gen 22:1–13), Jacob (Gen 31:54), individual families (Exod 12), Jethro (Exod 18:12), Gideon (Judg 6:26), Jephthah (Judg 11:31), Manoah (Judg 13:16–23), Saul (1 Sam 13:9–12), David (2 Sam 24:22), Solomon (1 Kgs 3:4), Jeroboam (1 Kgs 12:32), Elijah (1 Kgs 18:20–40), Jehu (2 Kgs 10:25), and Ahaz (2 Kgs 16:13–15). The independent sacrificial acts of Saul, David, Solomon, and Jeroboam are disputed in scholarship. Theoretically, these kings could have had a priest offer the sacrifice, which would be implied within the literary context of the monarchy. Moreover, the HB records the actions of freelance or for hire Levites (Judg 17:7–13; 18; 19–20).

The Legislative Themes of Centralization

of the Enneateuch and the exilic writings. This fact is evidenced by the exilic date of the Enneateuch and more relevantly by the canonical separation (=structure) of literary histories in the HB (e.g., the so-called DH and CH). Thus, the current endeavor is valuable when discussing the priesthood in the primary history of the Israelites.

The secular origin of the Levites can be traced to the birth of Jacob's third son, Levi (Gen 29:34). In the patriarchal history, Levi is recognized not for his godliness but for his revenge and lawlessness. Together, Levi and his brother Simeon avenge the rape of their sister Dinah by killing Hamor and his son Shechem (Gen 34:25–31; cf. 49:5).[16] A transition from the secular to the religious evolves with the sons of Levi: Gershon, Kohath, and Merari.[17] In the wilderness, the sons of Levi are given a specific location surrounding the tabernacle and given charges related to the cult. The sons of Gershon are encamped behind the tabernacle on the west, and their primary charges relate to the tabernacle in the tent of meeting: the covering, screen, hangings, and the doors pertaining to the court around the tabernacle and altar (Num 3:21–25; 4:22–27). Ithamar, the son of Aaron, oversees the work of the Gershonites (Num 4:28).

The sons of Kohath are encamped on the south side of the tabernacle and are charged with "the most holy things" (קדש הקדשים), the holy objects within the sanctuary: the ark, the table, the lampstand, the altars, vessels, and the screen (Num 3:27–32; 4:4–20). The Kohathites are directed to carry

---

16. Ephraim Speiser argued the obscure and difficult phrase כלי חמס מכרתיהם in Gen 49:5 was a textual allusion to the vengeful acts of Simeon and Levi. See Speiser, *Genesis*, 365. The difficulty of ascertaining the meaning of the *hapax legomena* מכרתיהם continues to challenge scholars. Commentators and philologists alike have suggested wide-ranging interpretations, none of which has gained prominence. For example, Mitchell J. Dahood suggested that מכרתיהם was a noun from the verbal root כרת. In doing so, Dahood postulated that מכרתיהם was linked to the blades used in the circumcision act described in Gen 34:22. See Dahood, "*MKRTYHM* in Genesis 49,5," 54–56; see also Moeller, "Four Old Testament Problem Terms," 219–20. Matty Cohen translated מכרתיהם as *'leurs biens'* ("their property"), which built on the root idea of accumulation or collecting of goods. See Cohen, "*MᵉKĒRŌTĒHEM*," 472–82. Othniel Margalith challenged Cohen's conclusions that the root of מכרתיהם meant to accumulate or to collect. For Margalith, Cohen's argument overlooked the immediate context and the literary relationship between Gen 34:25, 28 and 49:5. See Margalith, "*MᵉKĒRŌTĒHEM*," 101–2. Dwight W. Young postulated the use of מכרתיהם was a pun building on the word play of כלי חמס. The audience would have recognized it as an allusion to the Simeon and Levi story in Gen 34:25–26. See Young, "A Ghost Word," 335–42.

17. Concise and expansive genealogies of Levi's descendants are given in the Pentateuch and the CH: Gen 46:11; Exod 6:16–25; Num 3:17–39; 26:57–63; 1 Chr 6:1–15; 23:13.

Priesthood in Israel

the קדש הקרשים on their shoulders (Num 7:9; cf. Josh 3:6). Elizahan, son of Uzziel, is the overseer for the house of Kohath. Eleazar, son of Aaron, is the leader of the Levites and the overseer of the sanctuary. The sons of Kohath garnish more attention in the biblical narrative due to Korah, a Kohathite of Levitical decent. He is responsible for challenging Moses and Aaron during the Israelites' sojourn to Kadesh (Num 16:1–50) in aspirations of gaining full priestly status (vv. 9–10, 40). The sons of Merari are encamped on the north side of the tabernacle, and their primary charge is its frames: the bars, pillars, bases, and accessories. In addition, the house of Merari is responsible for the pillars within and around the court and the appropriate accessories (Num 3:33–37; 4:29–34).

In his birth narrative (Exod 2:1–11), Moses is introduced as a descendant from the house of Levi (בית לוי). Although Moses is never called a priest formally in the HB, his priestly status is substantiated in several places, none more cogent than the covenant ceremony in Exod 24 and the direction of the Levites in Exod 32. In the former text Moses, Aaron, and his sons, including seventy elders of Israel, are called to worship Yahweh from afar. Moses, however, approaches Yahweh. While in the presence of Yahweh, Moses is given the words of the Lord. The next day he erects an altar and keeps half the blood in a basin while the other half he sprinkles on the altar (cf. the Aaronite priestly duties in Lev 1). Upon completing this ceremonial act, Moses reads from the Book of the Covenant (24:1–8).

The sinful acts of the people and Aaron are depicted in Exod 32. In response to the people's idolatry, Moses seeks recourse from the Levites. As a result, the Levites eradicate three thousand sinful men from the Israelites and procure a role in serving Yahweh (vv. 25–29). The following day, Moses approaches Yahweh in hopes of making atonement (אכפרה) for the people's sin, but the wrath of the Lord manifests itself through a plague (vv. 30–35). In both of these texts, the role of Moses surpasses the others present. Erecting an altar, sprinkling blood on the altar, and petitioning Yahweh concerning the atonement of the Israelites demarcate Moses clearly over and against Aaron, the elders, and the Levites. Though Moses is singled out and separated from Aaron and the Levites, the division should not overshadow the priestly acts of Moses. For this reason, Moses, a descendant of Levi, functions as a priest even without the promulgation of the title. The phrase בית לוי occurs only one other time in the Enneateuch—the blossoming rod of Aaron narrative (Num 17:16–28 [Eng. 17:1–13]). This pericope validates

The Legislative Themes of Centralization

Aaron as the leader of the priestly tribe of Israel (vv. 18, 21–23 [Eng. vv. 3, 6–8]).[18]

Following the purge of sin at the behest of Moses (Exod 32), the Levites reappear in the court of the tabernacle working under the direction and supervision of Ithamar, the son of Aaron (Exod 38:21). Though the reference is miniscule, v. 21 not only introduces the subordination of the Levites to the Aaronite priests but also implies the differentiation between the two groups. Numbers provides a clearer portrait of the Levites' responsibilities and their subordination to the Aaronite priesthood. The primary charge of the Levites is the transportation, erection, and deconstruction of the tabernacle (Num 1:47–51; 1 Sam 6:15; 2 Sam 6:1–3; 15:24; 1 Kgs 8:3–4). At the request of Yahweh, Moses summons the tribe of Levi before Aaron the priest. Once there, the tribe of Levi ministers to Aaron, and then they are given to the Aaronite priesthood for servitude. In addition, they are given the directive to act in accordance to Aaron's discretion and serve the whole congregation of Israelites concerning the tabernacle (Num 3:5–9, 32; 8:13; 18:1–6).[19] Yahweh explains to Moses that this decision is an alternative measure vis-à-vis the divine election of the Levites (vv. 11–13, 41, 45; 8:14–19), supplanting the earlier dictum that every firstborn child be dedicated to the Lord (Exod 13:1–16; 22:29b–30). Related to the divine election theme is the non-provincial statute given to the Levites at the behest of Yahweh (Num 1:47; 2:33). The Levites also are not represented in the census of the tribes of Israel (Num 1:47–49; 26:62). In addition to the election and isolation of the Levites from the other tribes, the Levites are given special allotments, provisions (Num 31:30, 47), and cities for inhabitation (Lev 25:32–34; Num 35:1–6; Josh 21) since they have no inheritance (Num 26:62; Deut 10:9; 12:12, 19; 14:27, 29; 18:1; Josh 13:14, 33; 14:3; 18:7).

---

18. Two other references to the house of Levi occur outside the Enneateuch. First, in a message of lament concerning the sins and idolatry of Jerusalem, the prophet Zechariah includes the house of Levi as one of the families that will mourn for the house of David and Zion (Zech 12:13). The final occurrence of the house of Levi is found in Ps 135:20, a hymn of praise. Here the house is commanded to bless the Lord. In addition to בית לוי, the title "the tribe of Levi" (מטה לוי) is used to describe the descendants of Levi (Num 1:49; 3:6; 17:3, 8; 18:2).

19. Haran suggested that the duties of the Levites extended beyond the confines of submission to the Aaronite priesthood. Additionally, the Levites served the people of Israel "by performing acts which do not appertain directly to the altar, such as slaughtering the sacrifices, or preparing the sacrifices for consumption after the fats had been burned in the fire." See Haran, *Temples and Temple Service*, 60.

The Aaronite Priesthood

In the Tetrateuch, Aaron and his descendants are set apart from the others within the priesthood. First, Aaron, a Levite, is introduced as Moses' helpmate (Exod 4:14).[20] Although Aaron initially functions as the mouthpiece for Moses, many of his actions suggest priestly activity: the signs he performs in wilderness with Moses (Exod 4:27–31); his presence in the Pharaoh narrative (Exod 5:1—11:10); his participation in the Passover ritual (Exod 12:43); his joining Moses when Yahweh descends upon Mount Sinai (Exod 19:24); the building and preservation of the tent of meeting (Exod 27:21; Num 3:38–39; 4:4–20); his aiding Moses in taking the census of the people of Israel (Num 1:3; 4:1–3, 34–37); and his formal blessing of the Israelites (Num 6:22–27).

In Exod 28, a theological shift occurs in the history of Israelite priesthood. Aaron and his sons (i.e., Nadab, Abihu, Eleazar, and Ithamar) are to be brought forward (הקרב) to serve as priests of Yahweh (לכהנו-לי). Sacral garments are to be made for Aaron that distinguish and exalt his status (vv. 2–40; cf. Exod 39:1–31).[21] Of importance is the breastplate that contains the names of the sons of Israel, which Aaron carries into the sanctuary. In addition, he wears the sacred lots (i.e., the Urim and the Thummim) over his heart when entering the presence of Yahweh (vv. 28–30). The sacred priestly garments also are made for Aaron's sons (v. 41).

The consecration of the Aaronite priests (Exod 29) takes place at the tent of meeting, beginning with the anointing of Aaron as the high priest (vv. 7–9). Next, a bull is presented as a sin offering (vv. 10–14) followed

---

20. The genealogical association of Aaron to the tribe of Levi is found also in Exod 6:23. Gershon Galil argued the stylistic and structural tools in the larger genealogical text of Exod 6:13–30 indirectly described two important ideas. First, the authors separated the Aaronite priesthood from the other remaining Levite families. Second, the authors described the covenant between the houses of Aaron and David. Although the authors explicitly detailed the pedigree of Aaron and Moses in vv. 13–30, the primary aim of the text was to emphasize the division of the Aaronite priesthood from the remaining Levite families, which included Moses and his descendants. This primary aim of the authors was supported by the omission of Moses' descendants from the genealogical record in vv. 13–30, and the authors utilized different genealogical patterns—syntactical formulas—when comparing the accounts of Aaron's descendants and the other Levite families (cf. Rehm, "Levites and Priests," 4:299). The marriage of Aaron and Elisheba established a link between the descendants of Aaron and the descendants of Judah. Moreover, the authors used the marriage of Aaron and Elisheba as a subtle hint to the covenant between the kings of Judah and the Aaronite priesthood. See Galil, "Sons of Judah," 488–95.

21. Cf. Sarna, *Exodus*, 177.

The Legislative Themes of Centralization

by a burnt offering of the first ram (vv. 15–18). Aaron and his sons are consecrated next with the offering of the second ram. Blood is applied to the right ears, thumbs, and big toes (vv. 19–34), symbolizing the dedication of the entire body to Yahweh. Following the consecration of Aaron and his sons, the Israelites celebrate the ordination of these men for seven days (vv. 35–41). This celebration serves as a ritualistic reminder for future generations since Yahweh will meet his people at the tent of meeting. The election of Aaron and his sons to the office of high priest solidifies the covenant between Yahweh and the Israelites by providing chosen intermediaries between the divine and his people (vv. 42–46). In continual fashion, the ministerial responsibilities of Aaron and his sons are described in Exod 29 (cf. Lev 8).

The height of the Aaronite narrative occurs in Exod 32 when Aaron erects an altar and creates a golden calf for the people of Israel. Though the idolatrous acts of Aaron are examined in more detail in ch. 3, it would be remiss not to highlight the irony of golden calf narrative within the larger, literary structure of Exodus. Aaron and his sons are consecrated to Yahweh (Exod 28) and given specific ministerial responsibilities (Exod 29–31), and yet, in the first glimpse of Aaron functioning as the high priest, he orchestrates an abomination to Yahweh (32:1–35). Leviticus describes in great detail the responsibilities of the sons of Aaron. Chapters 1–7 introduce the various procedures and types of offerings the Israelites are required to offer.[22] The sons of Aaron are at the center of the Israelite sacrificial system since they are responsible for protecting and facilitating the worship of Yahweh. In chs. 8–10, the consecration of Aaron and his sons is revisited, which is followed by the first sacrificial convocation at the tent of meeting with Aaron presiding as high priest. Like the narrative in Exodus, an ironic twist follows the consecration of Aaron and the convocation of public worship. Nadab and Abihu, the sons of Aaron, die as a result of their unauthorized and unholy offering before Yahweh (ch. 10; cf. Num 3:4). In addition to

---

22. Noted scholar Anson F. Rainey described the sacrifices introduced in Leviticus as both prescriptive and descriptive in nature. For the most part, Lev 1–7 provides prescriptive information, whereas ch. 8 is descriptive. The prescriptive sacrifices in 1:1—6:7 can be divided into two groups, those having "a pleasing odor" and those for making atonement to Yahweh. This first group consists of the burnt offering (ch. 1), cereal offering (ch. 2), and the peace offering (ch. 3), each of which expresses a right relationship with Yahweh. The primary purpose of the latter group, consisting of the guilt and sin offerings, is atonement. In 6:8—7:38, the prescriptive section moves from didactic in nature to administrative. See Rainey, "Sacrifice and Offerings," 5:201–2.

the sacrificial system, Yahweh commands Aaron to explain the conditions regarding clean and unclean status (chs. 11–15; 17:1–16). The first fifteen chapters of Leviticus build in anticipation to the primary responsibility of Aaron functioning as the high priest, the Day of Atonement (ch. 16). One day a year the sins of the Israelites can be expunged through Aaron's mediation before Yahweh. More important to the discussion is the primary guideline appropriated to both the Aaronite and Levitical priesthoods, which are governed by the dictum "they shall be holy to their God" (21:6).

Numbers continues the literary construction of the Aaronite priesthood by emphasizing several important elements. First, the hereditary nature of the high priest is interwoven within the genealogy of Aaron with his sons being called "the anointed" (המשחים) who will serve as priests of Yahweh (3:1–3; 20:22–29; cf. Exod 6:23–25). Second, the Levites are given to Aaron and his sons as servants in performing the duties of the sanctuary (3:5–10; 8:5–13, 19–26). Third, Moses, along with Aaron and his sons, encamp on the east side of the tabernacle. Unlike the other descendants of Levi, these men are charged with the rites within the sanctuary as well as the preservation of the holy things within the tent of meeting (3:38–39; 4:4–20). Fourth, in the blossoming rod narrative, Yahweh elects Aaron and the house of Levi as his chosen tribe (17:16–28 [Eng 17:1–13]). Fifth, like the Levites, Aaron and his descendants are given no inheritance, yet Yahweh will be their portion (18:20). The final detail concerning the life of Aaron characterizes the priest along with his sister Miriam rebelling against Moses (12:1–11).

Unlike Exodus–Numbers, Deuteronomy devotes little to the overall portrait of Aaron. His idolatrous actions at Mount Sinai (9:20) and his death on the mountain (10:6; 32:50) are reiterated only for historical purposes. The so-called DH contains limited references to Aaron, which can be categorized by four subjects: the historical material concerning the allotment of Levitical cities in the land of Canaan (Josh 21); the ministry of Aaron in Egypt (Josh 24:5; 1 Sam 12:6, 8); the death of Aaron (Josh 24:33); and genealogical references (Judg 20:28).

The "Levitical Priests" of Deuteronomy

The isolation of the Deuteronomic presentation of the Israelite priesthood from the discussion above should underscore its importance within the larger discussion. Driver astutely observed the distinction between the

The Legislative Themes of Centralization

priests and the Levites in the Priestly laws of Leviticus and Numbers. Deuteronomy, on the other hand, implied that all members of the tribe of Levi were qualified to serve and function as priests.[23] In his monumental commentary on Deuteronomy, he expanded his initial observation concerning the differences in the Priestly material and Deuteronomy:

> The term "Levite," it must always be remembered, has in Dt. a different meaning from "Levite" in P. In P it denotes the members of the tribe, *exclusive* of the priests, the descendants of Aaron; in Dt. it denotes *all* members of the tribe, without distinction. The "Levites" of P are inferior members of the tribe, who are assigned various subordinate duties in connection with the Tabernacle (Num 3–4; 18:1–7), but are peremptorily forbidden to intrude upon the office of priest (Num 4:20; 16:7b–11, 40; 18:7). In Dt. this sharp distinction between priests and the common Levites is not recognized; it is implied (18:1a) that *all* members of the tribe are qualified to exercise priestly functions.[24]

Coupled with Wellhausen's priesthood theory, Driver initiated the discussion of the Deuteronomic concept of priesthood. Put succinctly, more than any other book of the Enneateuch, Deuteronomy uses more designations, some of which are strictly Deuteronomic, to describe the priesthood: "the Levite" (הלוי),[25] "the Levites" (הלוים),[26] the priest(s) (כהן),[27] "the priests the sons of Levi" (הכהנים בני לוי), "the tribe of Levi" (שבט הלוי), and the "Levitical priests" (הכהנים הלוים).[28] Canonically, the idiomatic phrase הכהנים הלוים appears first in Deuteronomy (17:9, 18; 24:8; 27:9), two times in Joshua (3:3; 8:33), and ten times in the exilic writings.[29]

As noted above, the discussion of the priesthood in Deuteronomy extends beyond the idiomatic הכהנים הלוים. For this reason, a laconic schema of the various characteristics associated with the Deuteronomic description

---

23. Driver, *Introduction to the Literature*, 82.
24. Idem, *Deuteronomy*, 219, emphasis his.
25. See Deut 12:12, 18, 19; 14:27, 29; 16:11, 14; 18:6; 26:11, 12, 13.
26. See 10:9; 18:7; 27:14; 31:25.
27. See Deut 17:9, 12, 18; 18:3; 19:17; 20:2; 21:5; 24:8; 26:3, 4; 27:9; 31:9.
28. According to Rehm, the various designations of the priesthood in Deuteronomy all allude to or parallel the Deuteronomic phrase "Levitical priests" (הכהנים הלוים). See Rehm, "Levites and Priests," 4:303.
29. See Ezek 43:19; 44:15; Ezra 10:5; Neh 10:29, 35; 11:20; 1 Chr 9:2; 2 Chr 5:5; 23:18; 30:27.

Priesthood in Israel

of the priesthood will portray clearly the textual intricacies within the book.[30]

1. An individual who serves as priest (10:8; 17:9, 18; 18:6–7; 21:5; 24:8; 27:9, 14; 31:9, 25; 33:8)
2. An integral part of the Israelite community (12:12, 18; 16:11, 14; 26:11)
3. An individual who has no portion or inheritance (10:9; 12:12, 19; 14:27, 29; 18:1–5; 26:12–15)
4. A member of the *personae miserables* (14:29; 16:11, 14; 26:11–13)
5. An individual who serves in some judiciary manner (17:9–13; 19:17; 21:5)
6. An individual who will keep the law, including the king's copy (17:18; 27:9)
7. An individual who ministers at the central sanctuary (18:6–7)
8. An individual who motivates the troops in preparation of holy war (20:3–4)
9. An individual who bears the ark of the covenant (31:25)

This list adequately summarizes the Deuteronomic concept of the priesthood. Many of the textual examples have been discussed or alluded to in other parts of the chapter. For this reason, attention will be given to every occurrence of הכהנים הלוים and to four of the characteristics listed above: the priest serving in some judiciary manner, the keeper of the king's copy of the law, the requirement to minister solely at the central sanctuary, and the responsibilities associated with preparing the Israelites for holy war.

Deuteronomy 17:8–13, 18

The institution of the king (17:14–20) is preceded by a pericope that discusses the institution of priests and judges. The current pericope addresses the rare occasions when legal situations arise (e.g., murder, legal issues, and assault) where making a prudent verdict is simply unattainable. Thus, if a case is too baffling for the civil or religious leaders to decide then the case

---

30. The categorical presentation was inspired by Stackert's similar treatment. Moreover, the first and third characteristics are adopted and slightly expanded from Stackert's representation. See Stackert, *Rewriting the Torah*, 201.

should be transferred to the central sanctuary (v. 8b). At the central sanctuary the Levitical priests (הכהנים הלוים) and the judge (השפט) will hear the injunction and decide the proper sentencing. Once the verdict is given, the people must obey the decision of the Levitical priests and the judge.

Two of the four idiomatic phrases of הכהנים הלוים in Deuteronomy occur in ch. 17. Included within the ways of the king (vv. 16–18) is the interesting mandate that the king will write for himself a copy of the law. The writing of a copy of the law by the king symbolizes the subjugation of the Israelite king to Yahweh. That the Levitical priests (הכהנים הלוים) are included within the kingship pericope might suggest that the priests actually wrote the copy for the king. More importantly, by linking the law of Yahweh with the priests, the Deuteronomic concept of the monarchy subjugates the king not only to Yahweh but to the priests who are responsible for the adherence and obedience to the Yahweh (vv. 19–20).

Deuteronomy 18:1–8

Deuteronomy 18:1–8 is the center of the scholarly debate concerning the Deuteronomic concept of priesthood. Several scholars have noted the relationship of this pericope with 17:8–13; however, the syntactical and theological ramifications of 18:1–8 overshadow the literary connection between the two texts.[31] Much of the scholarly discussion has focused on v. 1a when the Deuteronomic title הכהנים הלוים is followed by the phrase כל-שבט לוי ("all tribe of Levi"; cf. Josh 8:33).[32] The ambiguity of הכהנים הלוים כל-שבט לוי serves as a source of contention not only for some scholars but also Bible translators. For example, the most prominent rendering of the phrase among English translations is "the Levitical priests, the whole tribe of Levi" (RSV, NRSV, JPST, NASB, ESV, HCSB). Yet, the editors

---

31. See Levinson, *Deuteronomy and the Hermeneutics*, 98, 142–43. Nelson, on the other hand, suggested an earlier law was behind 18:1–8. The earlier law assured the Levitical priests that they would receive their portions from the sacrifices, but the present laws modified the older mandate and emphasized the privileges of all Levites. See Nelson, *Deuteronomy*, 229.

32. The author(s) of Joshua uses the idiomatic phrase הכהנים הלוים two times to describe the individuals responsible for carrying the ark of Yahweh. In 3:3 the Levitical priests carry the ark across the Jordan River. The second occurrence in Joshua follows the defeat of the Israelites at Ai (7:1–5) when Joshua builds an altar at Mount Ebal and the people of Israel along with the elders, officers, and judges stand before the ark of Yahweh and the Levitical priests (הכהנים הלוים, vv. 30–35).

of the KJV, NKJV, and the NIV approach הכהנים הלוים from a slightly different perspective. The NIV editors rendered the text "the priests, who are Levites—indeed the whole tribe of Levi." Similarly, the KJV and the NKJV translators preferred "the priests, the Levites, and all the tribe of Levi."

A cursory study of the English translations reveals a limited disparity when translating 18:1a. Within the academic sphere, scholars have capitalized on the combination of the various designations for the priesthood in Deuteronomy, specifically the title Levitical priests, and proffered differing theories. Due to the syntactical difficulties, and theological implications associated with interpreting 18:1-8, the scholarly contributions can be divided into three general categories: all Levites are priests; some Levites are priests while others do not share the same status; and the text describes three types of individuals.

The first category, all Levites are priests, was popularized by Wellhausen. At the most basic level, proponents of this theory suggest the seeming lack of syntactical features in לכהנים הלוים כל-שבט לוי (v. 1a) do not support any argument for apposition between לכהנים הלוים and כל-שבט לוי. Thus, the translation "the Levitical priests, the whole tribe of Levi" literally means every Levitical priest, and for that matter potentially every male member of the tribe of Levi, has the opportunity to serve in a priestly manner.[33] In other words, Deuteronomy obscures, if not dissolves, the divisions between the Aaronite and Levitical priesthood.

Proponents of the second category maintain Deuteronomy describes two levels of status within the tribe of Levi. Some Levites attain priestly status, while others do not. The elevated status of a Levite was the exception rather than the rule. George Ernest Wright was the first noted scholar who challenged the traditional Wellhausenian model. He argued the Deuteronomic concept of priesthood, as portrayed by the phrase Levitical priests, described two separate priestly types—the altar-clergy and the client-Levites.[34] Wright's model has not received widespread acceptance, yet it

33. See Wellhausen, *Prolegomena*, 124, 146–47; Driver, *Deuteronomy*, 219–20; and Cody, *History of Old Testament Priesthood*, 127–31. Rodney K. Duke was critical of the Wellhausian proposal. In short, he argued the structure of Deut 18:1-8 assumed a distinction between priests and Levites: the general principle was stated in vv. 1–2; an issue related to the priestly office was handled (vv. 3–5); and the concern for the Levite was treated (vv. 6–8). See Duke, "Priests and Priesthood," 193–201.

34. For Wright, the theory that Deuteronomy described two separate priestly types was based solely on a thoroughgoing interpretation of the phrase כהנים הלוים. He argued the phrase was ambiguous since there was no conjunction between the two words. From a translational perspective, Wright preferred the rendering "the priests the Levites."

The Legislative Themes of Centralization

inspired other theories. For example, Haran also argued the Deuteronomic presentation of the Levitical priests represented two types of priests—those willing to sojourn and serve at the central sanctuary and those living in the provinces removed from the central sanctuary. In the scope of Deuteronomy, then, the former represented an individual who depended on Yahweh, and the latter was viewed as an "ordinary layman."[35] Several scholars have argued the phrase כהנים הלוים did not equate all Levites as priests, but rather it emphasized the ancestral Levitical heritage of the priests in question. In other words, the title Levitical priests (כהנים הלוים) was in apposition to non-Levitical priests (i.e., כל-שבט לוי).[36] Based on syntactical and

---

His translation became the foundation to his basic argument that כהנים הלוים suggested two differing groups of priests. The first group, the priests, functioned as altar-clergy at the central sanctuary, whereas the second group, the Levites, were client-Levites "scattered throughout the country and who are classed with the sojourner 'within thy gates.'" Wright arrived at this conclusion by examining the isolated uses of Levite(s) in Deuteronomy without the accompaniment of the word priests. Thus, he surmised the priests and "the priests the Levites" were Deuteronomic references to "clergy who officiate at altar ceremonies." From this perspective, then, Wright suggested the differences between the Priestly source and Deuteronomy, espoused by some source-critical scholars, had been exaggerated. The priests and the sons of Aaron in the Priestly material described the altar-clergy at the central sanctuary while the Deuteronomists, writing after 621 B.C.E., employed the idiom "the priests the Levites" in a likewise manner. See Wright, "Levites in Deuteronomy," 325–30.

35. Haran suggested the Levite(s) who lived in the provinces outside Jerusalem did not participate in the cultic activity of the temple; thus, they could not share in the offerings of Yahweh. The proclamation that Yahweh would be their inheritance functioned similar to rule if not an abstract promise. The economic and social position of these Levites must have been difficult comparable to other downtrodden Israelites (14:29; 16:11, 14; 26:11–13). In addition, Haran argued, "There should be no doubt that the realization of the privilege of priesthood, too, is understood by J and E in exactly the same manner as by D, to wit, all the sons of Levi are potential priests and all they have to do to attain the actual priesthood is to be present at the temple. . . . The only difference between D and J or E is the matter of the centralization of the cult—whereas D acknowledges the legitimacy of only one temple, one place of worship, this being the only place where the Levites can exercise their right to the priesthood, J and E assume that there are many houses of God, where various Levitical families have already become priests and where every Levite has the option to take the holy orders." See Haran, *Temples and Temple Service*, 62 (quote pp. 68–69). For similar argument, see Vaux, *Ancient Israel*, 363 and Cody, *History of Old Testament Priesthood*, 131–32.

36. Vaux, *Ancient Israel*, 362; cf. Merrill, *Deuteronomy*, 267; Nelson, *Deuteronomy*, 231; and Lundbom, *Deuteronomy*, 544. McConville interpreted Deut 18:1–8 in somewhat of a different light than others. For him, Deuteronomy was more concerned with expressing the function and relation of the tribe of Levi to the inheritance of Israel, which would account for the distinctions made between the priests and Levites in the Priestly

exegetical analysis of vv. 1–8, the third category divides these verses into three sections with each one describing a different type of person. Thus, vv. 1–2 refer to all Levites, vv. 3–5 refers to Levitical priests, and vv. 6–8 refers to Levites who normally do not function as priests.[37] The last type is relatively new. The Levites living in their own town served the function of pastoral care: caring for the needy, presiding over the clean/unclean laws, presiding over local sacrifices, teaching, and maintaining the fidelity of the people to Yahweh. In short, the Levitical cities represented "the central sanctuary in the far-flung regions of the land."[38] The categories above are an oversimplification of scholarship. Each category contains convincing and unconvincing components.

Returning to 18:1–8, the pericope outlines the provisions for the Levitical priests. The opening portrait of the Levitical priests in vv. 1–2 parallels the description of the priests having no inheritance within Israel in Num 26:62. The priests' only inheritance is Yahweh, and the forfeiture of land is the rudimentary characteristic of their dependency upon the Lord.[39] For this reason, the Deuteronomic law addresses the purpose and rationale as to why the people of Israel must provide for and support the priests. With no inheritance of land, a Levite could relocate to the place which Yahweh will choose and continue to minister in his name (vv. 6–8). The decision of the Levite to relocate (v. 6), particularly to Jerusalem, is an individual choice (lit. "the desire of his soul," אות נפשו).

In such an event, the people of Israel are to provide the priests who minister at the chosen place equal portions to eat "besides what he receives from the sale of his patrimony" (לבד ממכריו על־האבות) since they are disposed of property. This line of interpretation follows the argument posited by Haran. There are priests willing to serve at the central sanctuary, and for these priests, the Israelites are to provide for their well-being. On the other hand, the Levites who do not minister within the confines of the cult are not privy to the priestly portions—thus, they function as ordinary

---

material but not in Deuteronomy. The phrase Levitical priests was not in apposition to "all the tribe of Levi" but rather an equivalent description. Deuteronomy did recognize the upper and lower division of the tribe of Levi, and the discrepancies between Pentateuchal sources should be overshadowed "not by historical vicissitudes" but by the theological purposes of Deuteronomy, particularly the representation of the tribe as a key member of the Israelite brotherhood. See McConville, *Law and Theology*, 142–53.

37. See Craigie, *Book of Deuteronomy*, 268; cf. Abba, "Priests and Levites," 262–67.
38. Block, *Deuteronomy*, 430.
39. McConville, *Deuteronomy*, 297.

laymen.⁴⁰ Lundbom interpreted the centralization mandate from a different perspective. He suggested that the close of local sanctuaries during the eighth and seventh centuries forced many Levites to be unemployed. Thus, the Deuteronomic mandate of centralized worship invited the out-of-work Levites to Jerusalem three times a year for the pilgrimage feasts. Once in Jerusalem, these Levites could not be denied altar service.⁴¹ From a macro perspective, the Deuteronomic author(s) appears to add a prerequisite for being a Levitical priest, that is, serve at the central sanctuary, and failure to do so alters one's status among the people.

Deuteronomy 20

Deuteronomy 20 is the only chapter that contains laws regarding holy war. The literary structure of the account is framed by an introduction (v. 1) and a conclusion (v. 9). Together, these verses bracket two independent speeches: the priest (vv. 2–4) and the officers (vv. 5–7).⁴² In v. 3 the first speech by the priest, introduced with a "*waw*-relative," is couched as a future event or situation⁴³ even though it includes four specific negated verbs: "let not your hearts be soft" (אל-ירך לבבכם), "do not fear" (אל-תיראו), "do not be alarmed" (אל-תחפזו), and "do not tremble" (אל-תערצו). The speech by the priest is framed by the basic fundamental principle of holy war: Yahweh will be with Israel in times of war; therefore, Israel shall not fear the enemy (v. 4).⁴⁴ Moreover, this priestly speech given to Israelite warriors prior to the ensuing battle reiterates patriotism and national fervor.⁴⁵ The second speech clearly shifts the focus from the spiritual to the practical with the deferrals from war pronounced by civilian officers.⁴⁶ Thus, Deuteronomy introduces yet another responsibility for the priests—a voice proclaiming Yahweh's blessing and protection during holy war.

---

40. McConville rejected the notion that Josiah's reform was the context of Deut 18:1–8. See McConville, *Deuteronomy*, 285.

41. Lundbom, *Deuteronomy*, 547.

42. Brueggemann, *Deuteronomy*, 208.

43. *IBHS* 519.

44. In his excursus, Tigay explained how war played a prominent role in early Israelite history; however, Deuteronomy seemed to emphasize a desacralized form of warfare. See Tigay, *Deuteronomy*, 430.

45. Weinfeld, *Deuteronomic School*, 45.

46. See Christensen, *Deuteronomy 1:1–21:9*, 438.

Deuteronomy 24:8

The reference to Levitical priests in v. 8 is obscure and unrelated to the others. Unlike the other references, the phrase is imbedded within a law concerning leprosy. If an attack of leprosy strikes, the people are to follow the advice of the Levitical priests since Yahweh will be the one directing them. Verse 9 recalls the Miriam story when Yahweh strikes her with leprosy for turning against Moses (Num 12:10–15). Incidentally, Aaron is present also when Miriam is leprous. A problem arises, however, with the use of Levitical priests in v. 8 when cases of leprosy are brought to the Levitical priests, but in Lev 13–14 anyone stricken with leprosy must be brought to Aaron or to one of his descendants (13:2–3). Thus, Deut 24:8 appears to no longer differentiate between the responsibilities of the Aaronite priesthood and the Levites.

Deuteronomy 27:1–10

The ceremony at Shechem, a theological watershed in Deuteronomy, chronicles the Israelites' covenantal obligations to Yahweh. Moses and the elders command the people to keep the commandments of Yahweh, particularly when they enter the land of Canaan. As a remembrance of the covenantal ceremony the words of the covenant are recorded on large stones covered in plaster (vv. 1–4, 8). Moreover, the consecration of the ceremony is established through the erection of an altar and subsequent sacrifices of burnt and peace offerings to Yahweh on Mount Ebal (vv. 5–7). In the next sequence, Levitical priests replace the elders alongside Moses (v. 9). Together, they call the Israelites to listen (שמע), for "this day" (היום הזה) they will become the chosen people of Yahweh.[47] For this reason, the people of Israel must keep the commandments and statutes of Yahweh (v. 10). The final Deuteronomic responsibility of the priests is highly significant. The priests stand with Moses during the covenantal ceremony and represent Yahweh's commitment and election of the people. In many ways, the symbolic act functions somewhat prophetically within the history of Israel. Neither Moses nor his successors will be the mediator of the covenant between Yahweh and the Israelites. The title of covenant enforcers will be

---

47. The syntactical use of שמע ישראל is highly theological since it constitutes the announcement of Israel's election and requirement of obedience to Yahweh (5:1; 6:3, 4; 9:1; 20:3; 27:9).

transferred to the priests. If so, the author(s) of Deuteronomy is conscious of the power bestowed upon the priests, which is chronicled in Lev 1–16.

A SYNCHRONIC READING OF THE PRIESTHOOD IN ISRAEL

A synchronic study of the priesthood in Israel should not be viewed as the antithesis of diachronic conclusions that continue to have a resounding effect on the current discussion. Through a synchronic reading of the priesthood in the Enneateuch, I will uncover the literary-historical message of the exilic reader. The task at hand, then, is to answer one simple question: How is the priesthood characterized in the literary history of the Enneateuch?

Above, attention is given to the textual presentations of the Aaronite priesthood and the Levites. The debate surrounding the origin of the Levites—whether historical or anachronistic—is of no consequence to a synchronic reading. A connection is formed between Levi the son of Jacob and the Levites (Gen 29:34) as well as Moses and Aaron (Exod 2:1–11; 4:14). The descendants of Levi (i.e., the Gershonites, Kohathites, and Merarites) are all given specific duties related to the maintenance, transportation, and protection of the tabernacle in the wilderness (Num 3:21–37; 4:22–34; 7:9). In the Pentateuch, both Moses and Aaron are singled out in the literary history of the priesthood. Both are Levites and important figures in Israel's early history. In fact, both play a prominent role in the Tetrateuch, evidenced by the call narrative of Moses (Exod 2:23—4:17) and the blossoming rod narrative of Aaron (Num 17:16–28 [Eng 17:1–13]). The important division between the Aaronite priesthood and subservient Levites reverberates throughout the Tetrateuch (Exod 38:21; Num 3:5–9, 32; 8:13; 18:1–6). That the Aaronite priesthood is held in higher regard goes without saying, but the division slowly dissipates in Deuteronomy and the so-called DH.

From a synchronic perspective, the syntactically difficult הכהנים הלוים in Deuteronomy signifies a theological shift in the literary history of Israel's priesthood. In short, Deuteronomy becomes the theological turning point of the Enneateuch. That Deuteronomy introduces a new description of the priesthood (i.e., Levitical priests) is highly important in a synchronic reading. Deuteronomy certainly does not differentiate between the Aaronite priesthood and the Levites. Thus, the introduction of the Levitical priests in Deuteronomy is no accident. In fact, the phrase brings up two

Priesthood in Israel

questions: Does the phrase Levitical priests suggest a coalescence of the two types of priests described in the Tetrateuch (i.e., descendants of Aaron and the Levites) under one title by the Deuteronomic author(s)? If so, does the title, Levitical priests, terminate the earlier subordination tradition of the Levites? The answers to these two questions are not found actually in Deuteronomy but rather in the literary history of the so-called DH.

Beginning in the so-called DH, the priesthood is portrayed dramatically in a different light. Gerald A. Klingbeil poignantly observed that the textual data regarding the Levites in the so-called DH contains a shift in responsibilities. In Joshua–2 Samuel, the primary responsibility of the Levites is to carry and transport the ark. With the erection and ratification of public worship at the temple, the ark no longer needs to be moved.[48] With the completion and coronation of the temple as the epicenter of the cult, the Israelite priesthood is forced to change. Since the ark is primarily stationary, the Levites begin assimilating into other areas under the patronage of the king.[49]

A cursory examination of the priesthood in the so-called DH will support Klingbeil's observation. In Joshua, the priests play a minimal role in the conquest and settlement of the land of Canaan in Joshua. The Levitical status of the priests is omitted in the narratives concerning the crossing of the Jordan River (Josh 3:6) and the fall of Jericho (6:4, 8, 9, 13, 16). In fact, the priests in Joshua are characteristically benign compared to their ancestral portraits in Exodus–Numbers. In Judges, the lack of priestly material corresponds with the Israelites' decline in spiritual vitality. The narratives that include Levitical priests (Judg 17–20) chronicle the difficult times for the priesthood during one of Israel's lowest spiritual points. These isolated narratives serve as the literary bridge to the Samuel corpus, when the spiritual complacency of the Israelites is transferred to Eli, the high priest of Shiloh.

The devotion of Hannah to Yahweh is evidenced by the dedication of her son, Samuel, at the shrine at Shiloh (1 Sam 1:1–2:10). The narrator explains that the voice and signs of Yahweh ceased for some time (3:1b), yet the young Samuel hears the voice of Yahweh and accepts the divine sign (3:2–21). Thus, the introductory chapters of the Samuel corpus parallel the spiritual depravity of the people and priests serving in the high places. With the introduction of the monarchy, the description of the priesthood

48. Klingbeil, "Priests and Levites," 812.
49. Ibid., 815.

drastically differs from the Hexateuchal portrait. The emphasis shifts to individual priests (e.g., Samuel) and the high priest (e.g., Eleazar, Abiathar, Zadok, Jehoida, and Hilkiah). De Vaux germanely noted that the Kings corpus contained the most dramatic shift with the priesthood of Jerusalem becoming the focal point.[50] Though still active in Israel's history, the priesthood receded into the background of the biblical narrative, whereas the characterization of the individual priests moved into the foreground.

Through a synchronic reading of the priesthood in the Enneateuch, a unique portrait emerges. Early in the Israel's history, the Aaronite priesthood and the Levites coexisted with the former being in the position of authority. Deuteronomy, the theological hinge between the wilderness and the land of Canaan, no longer differentiated between the Aaronite priesthood and the Levites. The diminishing focus on the priesthood at large is evidenced in Joshua. In Judges, narratives about individual priests, along with the demise of the tribe of Levi, represent a literary shift in the priesthood. In the Samuel and King corpuses, the literary focus is on individual priests and the changing roles of the high priest and not on the Aaronite and Levitical priesthoods.

---

50. See Vaux, *Ancient Israel*, 362; cf. Nurmela, *The Levites*, 17ff.

8

Centralization and the Integrated Methodology

IN CHAPTERS 3–7, I was concerned with the exegetical and syntactical analysis of the five legislative themes associated with the concept of centralization in Deut 12–18. Much of the exegetical work, though not particularly innovative, did introduce some new literary and syntactical elements overlooked by scholars. For most scholars, the assessment of the texts in Deut 12–18 should be done through the context of Josiah's centralization of the cult. Much of this chapter will substantiate this consensus. The purpose of this chapter is to revisit the five themes through the lens of Josiah's reform, but also through an exilic reading.

By way reminder, I am not concerned with determining whether Deuteronomy and, more specifically, the concept of the centralization of the cult are *originally* prophetic in nature or an example of anachronistic literature. Since the focus is on an exilic reading of the book, parts of Deuteronomy will naturally appear prophetic in nature. The book of Deuteronomy and, especially, the centralization mandate establish an important aspect within the theology of the so-called DH. Put succinctly, the Deuteronomic theologies of monotheism and land are related closely to the five legislative themes. The Israelites' disobedience and disregard for the centralization mandate and the laws governing the five themes discussed in chs. 3–7 become the foundation for the demise and devastation of the nation. Even though Josiah's reform addresses all of these themes, his reforming efforts are not enough to stave off destruction.

The Legislative Themes of Centralization

Below, I divide the chapter into three subsections. First, I will provide a brief examination of the philology of the Hebrew verb בחר. Second, a concise overview of the Deuteronomic concept of centralization will establish the literary relationship within the Enneateuch. Finally, I will discuss the implications of the concept of centralization within the Enneateuch and draw some conclusions for further study.

THE PHILOLOGY OF בחר

The historical conception of בחר is debated within scholarship. The debate is centered on the literary dating of Deuteronomy. Before discussing the issues, a philological overview will explain the diachronic development of the ancient concept of election. Within ancient Mesopotamian literature, the selection or choice of a king was paramount and emphasized by the verb (w)atû ("to seek," "to discover," or "to choose").[1] The Late Babylonian verb *beheru* ("to choose") was assimilated into Aramaic, which was imported later into Akkadian.[2] In addition, the Akkadian *bêrum* ("to choose") symbolized the most important Semitic parallel to בחר.[3]

The relationship between the Akkadian *beheru* and *bêrum* and the Hebrew בחר provides an evolutionary timeline within the ANE. The Hebrew root בחר means a "careful choice occasioned by actual needs, and thus a very conscious choice and one that can be examined in light of certain criteria, in contrast perhaps to making a selection, to deciding as an act of an especially intimate relationship, or to 'taking' (*laqach*) and 'determining' (*ho'il*)."[4]

Within the HB, the verb בחר is used 172 times, mainly in narrating events that take place in the religious sphere. The secular origin of בחר, however, does not coincide with its overt religious use. The verb is used in a variety of secular settings in the HB: the sons of God choose the daughters of men for marriage (Gen 6:2); Lot chooses the Jordan valley for inhabitance (Gen 13:11); Moses chooses men to judge the people (Exod 18:25); David chooses the stones to defeat Goliath (1 Sam 17:40); the Baal prophets choose the bull for sacrifice (1 Kgs 18:25); the carpenter carefully chooses

---

1. Seebass, "בחר," 2:73.
2. Ibid., 2:76.
3. Nicole, "בחר," 1:638–39.
4. Seebass, "בחר," 2:74; cf. Oswalt, "בחר," 100–1.

wood for constructing an image (Isa 40:20); and Job chooses death rather than life (Job 7:15).[5]

More relevant to the current discussion is the use of בחר in the religious sphere. Two scholars pioneered the explanation of בחר in the religious sphere—McBride and von Rad. In his groundbreaking work on the name theology in Deuteronomy, McBride argued for the restrictive usage of בחר in the religious sphere. According to McBride, בחר was never used explicitly in association with another sanctuary other than the temple in Jerusalem.[6] He readily admitted the precise origin of בחר was not easily decipherable; however, he argued the בחר terminology expressed the "dual election of Zion and the Davidic line," an embedded characteristic in the southern royal theology. The seeming lack of בחר terminology associated with other shrines or sanctuaries further substantiated a southern, if not Jerusalemite, cult tradition. The southern royal theology associated with בחר must not overshadow the northern origins of Deuteronomy. Thus, McBride believed the centralization program was inspired by a northern effort to reunite all of Israel at one single location, that being Jerusalem.[7]

The deliverance of the Israelites from Egyptian bondage is the greatest salvific story in the HB. Within the exodus story are two parallel events: the miracles at the Sea of Reeds and the revelation of the name Yahweh. For von Rad, the formulaic use of "Yahweh delivered his people from Egypt" was confessional, a corporate praise of Yahweh's grace. The earliest forms of the exodus confession did not include a divine utterance associated with Yahweh. In the earliest confessions, the acts of Yahweh were glorified for his deliverance and mercy. As the Israelites' history of tradition continued to develop, the confession evolved into the concept of Israel's election (בחר), which became theologically embedded in history. The concept of Israel's election came to the forefront in Deuteronomy. The deliverance from Egyptian bondage formed the foundation of Yahweh's saving acts through redemption and election.[8]

---

5. Seebass, "בחר," 2:76–78.
6. McBride, "Deuteronomic Name Theology," 198.
7. Ibid., 201–3.
8. See Rad, *OTT* 1:175–79. Similarly, Clements argued the explicit terminology of election associated with the ordinary word (בחר) was a "distinctive theological application" in Deuteronomy. Moreover, the election of Israel was united directly with Yahweh's promise of the land. This unique bond was repugnant for Israelites who believed the relationship between Yahweh and his people was based on moral responsibility. See Clements, "Jerusalem Cult Tradition," 305–8.

The Legislative Themes of Centralization

In recent years, much of the discussion regarding the Deuteronomic concept of centralization of the cult gravitates to the name theology component or the location of the chosen place (המקום). The election of the chosen place must not be separated from the five legislative themes. Inasmuch, McConville accurately noted the manner in which the Qal imperfect יבחר implied how Yahweh chose more than a place. In fact, the imperfect form of בחר is used also to choose or elect Israel (Deut 14:2), the king (17:15), and the priests (18:5; 21:5). Although the majority of the time in Deuteronomy יבחר emphasizes the place where Yahweh will establish his earthly dwelling, a common thread in Yahweh's divine choosing is his sovereign will and interaction in the lives of the Israelites.[9]

Building upon the insights of McConville, an argument can be made that the centralization of the future sanctuary is interwoven within not only the theological fabric of Deuteronomy but also the Israelite social, political, and religious sectors. In fact, the central sanctuary is the most important distinctive characteristic of Deuteronomy. Thus, a closer look at the Deuteronomic concept of centralization of the cult is in order. In Deuteronomy, the name theology idiom, and its variants, occur eight times, all of which accompany some form of the centralization motif (12:5, 11, 21; 14:24; 16:2, 6, 11; 26:2).[10] The common noun מקום occurs 401 times in the HB, with 163 of those occurrences being in the Pentateuch. In Deuteronomy מקום is used thirty-three times, twenty-two of which occur in chs. 12–18. Nineteen of the twenty-two occurrences in chs. 12–18 are in conjunction with the cen-

---

9. McConville, *Law and Theology*, 30. Like McConville, Mayes argued בחר was a pre-Deuteronomic concept that emphasized divine election; however, his interpretation of בחר differed considerably from McConville's. According to Mayes, the verb בחר was not used to denote the divine election of the people but rather of the king. Yahweh chose the Davidic line and Mount Zion. Both the Samuel corpus and the Psalter "presupposed the existence of a royal ideology connected with the Davidic dynasty which held that the king was the chosen of Yahweh." Concerning the kingship laws in Deut 17:14–20, Mayes believed the primary intention was to suppress the concept of kingship by emphasizing that only Yahweh could choose the Israelite king. Furthermore, he argued the phrase "a place which Yahweh will chose" obviously was a "stereotyped formula" and pre-Deuteronomic (see Josh 9:27). In addition, he believed the covenant and election went hand-in-hand, but the latter existed in the Israelite faith before its proclamation in Deuteronomy with the verb בחר. See Mayes, *Deuteronomy*, 60–64.

10. The importance and ramifications of the name theology are discussed in ch. 2. In this chapter, I will focus mainly on the centralization motif rather than the name theology idiom. It should be noted that the concept of "to put his name there" is found elsewhere in the HB: 1 Kgs 9:3; 11:36; 14:21; 2 Kgs 21:4, 7; 2 Chr 6:20; 12:13. Similar adaptations are also found in 1 Kgs 8:16, 29; 2 Kgs 23:27.

tralization motif. Outside chs. 12–18, only three occurrences of מקום reference the centralization of the sanctuary (23:17; 26:2; 31:11). Additionally, two of the three uses of מקום in chs. 12–18 coincide with Moses' command to destroy the "places" where Canaanites worship other gods (12:2, 3). The other use of מקום emphasizes the concept of centralization, though it is not accompanied with the traditional centralization motif. In 12:13, Moses commands the Israelites not to offer burnt offerings "at any place you see" (בכל-מקום אשר תראה); instead the offering should be made "at the place which Yahweh will choose in one of your tribes" (12:14).

The above textual remarks are important to the name and centralization theologies in Deuteronomy. The verb בחר is of more significance for the explaining the theological impetus of chs. 12–18. The common verb בחר occurs 172 times in the HB, with thirty-one of those occurrences being in Deuteronomy. More importantly, however, בחר is used twenty-two times in chs. 12–18, with twenty of those references as the pivotal verb in the centralization motif. In every centralization motif, the verb בחר is in the imperfect tense (יבחר), which anticipates the future "choosing" of a central sanctuary. The other two references of בחר in chs. 12–18 continue the theme of election, particularly Yahweh "choosing" Israel as his people (14:2) and his "choosing" the Levitical priests (18:5). The centralization motif occurs outside of chs. 12–18 only two times (26:2; 31:11). In 26:2, Moses again commands the people, once in the land, to bring the first fruits and harvest to the place that will be chosen by Yahweh (cf. 12:5–7). The latter text explains how Moses wrote "this law" and gave it to the priests and the sons of Levi. During the seventh year, at the Feast of Booths, "when all of Israel comes to appear before Yahweh your God in the place which he will choose," the law is to be read aloud to all the people (cf. 1:5; 15:1–23; 16:13–17).

In sum, the twenty centralization motifs in chs. 12–18 emphasize three theologies: election, land, and the dwelling of Yahweh.[11] The impetus of the concept of centralization is the command of obedience and loyalty to Yahweh. Below, a summary will explain the *Sitz im Leben* of each centralization motif. In doing so, it will help form the basis for interpreting chs. 12–18 within the Enneateuch as well as highlight the theological ramifications on the demise of the monarchy.

---

11. For a similar argument see Block, *Deuteronomy*, 305.

The Legislative Themes of Centralization

THE CONCEPT OF CENTRALIZATION IN DEUTERONOMY 12-18

Scholars have long discussed the compositional layers of Deut 12, making it one of the most debated chapters in the HB.[12] For decades, biblical scholars have equated the "the book of the law" (ספר התורה) in 2 Kgs 22:8 with some form of Deuteronomy. The promise by Yahweh to give the Israelites the land of Canaan is an essential theological motif throughout the book. The recurring motif also emphasizes the land as a gift to Israel. In Deuteronomy, some form of the clause "in the land that Yahweh your God gave to your fathers" becomes the common expression denoting Yahweh's benevolence (cf. Deut 12:1). The giving of the land is a promise to the fathers of Israel by Yahweh. Thus, the land motif directly connects the Israelites' obedience with Yahweh's promise.[13]

In essence, the theological sequence in Deuteronomy is Yahweh blessing the people, Israel obeying Yahweh, and Yahweh continuing to bless the Israelites. The blessings of Yahweh are presented as unconditional; however, the blessing could become conditional if the Israelites do not obey the commands of Yahweh once in the land of Canaan.[14] The literary structure of ch. 12 contains the land motif and two additional purposes. First, v. 1 introduces the law code found in chs. 12–26. The introductory phrase "statutes and ordinances" functions as the preliminary declaration that the Israelites must follow the laws to inherit the land promised by Yahweh. Second, the centralization motif "the place which Yahweh your Lord will choose" (v. 5) emphasizes Yahweh's supremacy for not only choosing the land for inhabitance but also the location for his name and corporate worship. The centralization motif occurs five times in ch. 12. The future chosen place is the antithesis of the places where the Canaanites worship (vv. 1–4, 29–32).[15]

Following the command to destroy all the places where the inhabitants of Canaan worship other gods, Moses proclaims the new religious motif:

---

12. See ch. 1, n. 15.

13. McConville, *Law and Theology*, 11. The verb נתן occurs 167 times in Deuteronomy with Yahweh being the subject in 131 of the occurrences. According to Craigie, the use of נתן in Deut 12:1 implied the certainty of Yahweh's promise. See Craigie, *Book of Deuteronomy*, 216; cf. Nelson, *Deuteronomy*, 144.

14. McConville, *Law and Theology*, 17.

15. Along these lines, Nelson aptly observed, "Deuteronomy does not present centralization as a strategy for royal political control, but as a way to eliminate apostasy." See Nelson, *Deuteronomy*, 149.

Centralization and the Integrated Methodology

"But you shall go to the place which Yahweh your God will choose from all your tribes to put his name there, to make his habitation and you shall go there."[16] Theologically, v. 5 functions as the antithesis of the Canaanite places of worship. Yahweh is giving the land to the people, but they must be obedient to his form(s) of worship. The second motif in v. 11 (והיה המקום אשר־יבחר יהוה אלהיכם) continues the land theme only through the recourse of obediently expelling the pagan people from the land. Once the inhabitants of Canaan are destroyed, Yahweh will choose a location for worship. The final two centralization motifs in ch. 12 are concerned with the offering of sacrifices. In v. 21, Moses allows individuals to kill their secular sacrifice and consume it but only if the central sanctuary is too far to travel. Verse 26 revisits the holiness motif in vv. 5–14. Again, the Israelites are commanded to bring holy things and holy sacrifices to the central sanctuary rather than offering them in their own towns. This method of offering differs from the secular sacrifices in vv. 15–25.

Deuteronomy 14 is related to the holiness laws in ch. 12. Three formulas describe the procedure for bringing a holy offering to the place chosen by Yahweh. Unlike the secular sacrifice that could be eaten in the towns, the holy tithe must be offered and consumed in the chosen, central sanctuary. If the distance is too great to transport the tithe, then Moses commands the people to turn the tithe into money and sojourn to the central sanctuary. Once there, the individual is ordered to purchase any gift to be offered to Yahweh. After exchanging the money for the gift, the individual is to enter the central sanctuary, consume the offering, and rejoice in Yahweh's bountiful blessings. All three centralization motifs emphasize the holiness of Yahweh and the priority to remain loyal in the chosen land. Similarly, Deut 15:20 continues the theme of bringing the firstborn males from the flock as a dedication to Yahweh. The family is to bring the offering "in the place which Yahweh will choose" (במקום אשר־יבחר יהוה).

Moses continues to elaborate the importance of the future centralized sanctuary by readjusting the ancient festivals: the Passover/Feast of Unleavened Bread, Feast of Weeks, and the Feast of Booths. The Israelites are commanded once a year to celebrate the Passover at the sacred sanctuary while adhering to the prescriptions of 15:20 (cf. 16:2, 6, 7). Similarly, the laws regarding the Feast of Weeks and the Feast of Booths require the

---

16. כי אם־אל־המקום אשר־יבחר יהוה אלהיכם מכל־שבטיכ לשום את־שמו שם לשכנו. תדרשו ובאת שמה. Emanuel Tov described the Qal infinitive construct לשכנו as grammatically problematic and should be translated as a noun ("habitation"). See Tov, *Textual Criticism*, 42.

The Legislative Themes of Centralization

Israelites to celebrate at the central sanctuary (16:11, 15, 16). Building upon the holiness of the central sanctuary, the issue of a dispute within a town that cannot be solved is transferred to the central sanctuary to allow the priests and the judge to give a verdict. The parties must obey the verdict of the priests and the judge (17:8, 10). The final centralization motif in chs. 12–18 declares the Levites' freedom to join the other priests at the "place which Yahweh will choose" (המקום אשר־יבחר יהוה).

THE INTEGRATING THE FIVE THEMES OF CENTRALIZATION

Up to this point, I have examined the themes in isolation. Above, I provided a theological and textual assessment of the Deuteronomic concept of centralization. What remains is the final assessment of the synchronic reading and its implications within the so-called DH and, more specifically, the literary history designated as the Enneateuch. In other words, the last interpretive step is to analyze the biblical text as a complete, unified exilic work, all the while knowing the completed work is actually a composite text with a long and varied compositional history.

The goal of what follows is an integrated synthesis of both the diachronic and synchronic approaches. I will hopefully provide another viable reading and interpretation of the Deuteronomic concept of centralization. The final assessment, though independent of any one form of scholarly influence, does find similarities in other significant works. Schmid was correct when he argued that Genesis–Joshua was structured as *Heilsgeschichte* while Judges–2 Kings was an *Unheilsgeschichte*.[17] Nevertheless, an intentional assessment of the five legislative themes centralized in Deut 12–18, along with the land motif and monotheistic overtones in the book,[18] can reveal another theological level within the so-called DH and ultimately the Enneateuch. The Deuteronomic concept of centralization either projects a prophetic message of demise and devastation in the so-called DH, or represents the work of redactors *post ex eventu* presented in a prophetic

---

17. Schmid, *Erzväter und Exodus*, 290–91.

18. McConville emphasized the theological profundity of the Deuteronomic themes of land and monotheism. With precise acumen he explained, "The religious dimension of Israel's responsibilities in the covenant is contained in the laws in Deut 12–18. . . . Israel shall worship only Yahweh, not other gods, and they shall do so at his behest (his choosing)." See McConville, *Deuteronomy*, 35.

guise. Either way, the canonical shaping of the Enneateuch positions Deuteronomy and, more importantly, chs. 12–18, as the transitional point in the PH of Israel.

In Genesis–Deuteronomy, the narrator focuses on the establishment and reestablishment of the covenantal promise. In Joshua–2 Kings, the narrator(s), using Deuteronomy as his literary source, outlines in great detail how the Israelites breached the covenant, resulting in the demise of the nation.[19] That the biblical laws tell the story of the HB is the driving force behind this theological drama.[20] The concept of centralization in chs. 12–18, specifically the five associative legislative themes, play a significant role in the demise of both the northern and southern kingdoms. The laws concerning idolatry, tithing, the festival calendar, judiciary officials, and the priesthood are interrelated politically, sociologically, and theologically. For this reason, the Israelites' breach of these various themes, some more drastic than others (e.g., idolatry), functions in many ways as a roadmap toward destruction. Thus, the complete collapse and destruction of Israel chronicled in the so-called DH make the constitutional elements of Deuteronomy appear as a utopian ideal.[21]

Several introductory remarks are needed before proceeding with the basic structural and theological argument of Deut 12–18. In Deuteronomy, the Israelites are considered holy, not because of their proximity to the sanctity of Yahweh but by their divine election.[22] As noted above, the blessing of Yahweh upon the Israelites is unconditional but becomes conditional if the people do not obey the Lord.[23] The legislative themes associated with the concept of centralization amplify this fact. The hallmark of the centralization mandate is the expulsion of the inhabitants of the land

---

19. Polzin made a similar observation when he described Deuteronomy as an "ideological and surface composition" that provided readers with a "bird's-eye view of the entire history of Israel shortly to be recounted in detail in Joshua–2 Kings." See Polzin, *Moses and the Deuteronomist*, 72.

20. See Levinson, "Right Chorale," 130–48.

21. Both Lohfink and Levinson described Deuteronomy as utopian. Levinson argued the constitutional monarchy described in Deuteronomy was a "utopian manifesto" that envisioned the delimitation of royal power. Unfortunately, the constitutional vision of Deuteronomy never became a reality. See Levinson, "Reconceptualization of Kingship," 511–12; see also Lohfink, "Functions of Power," 346.

22. Weinfeld, *Deuteronomic School*, 227.

23. See again McConville, *Law and Theology*, 17.

The Legislative Themes of Centralization

as preventive measures against assimilating the idolatrous practices into mainline Yahwism.

Within the so-called DH, the narrative describes the historical erosion of Israel's faith by comparing the sins of Jeroboam with the righteousness of Josiah. In this history, Deuteronomy incorporates the theophany at Horeb, the promulgation of the Decalogue, the oratory expansion of the Decalogue in the Deuteronomic law, and preparation for the conquest of Palestine. Collectively, these topics establish the foundation of the "real theme" of the so-called DH: the Israelites' ultimate demise in Palestine.[24] From this historical backdrop, Deut 12–18 must be understood as being rhetorically constructed. The monarchies and the Israelites systematically disregard the five legislative themes that were to be centralized in the so-called DH.

The Abrogation of Idolatry

The centralization of the cult in Deut 12 is instituted to constrict any assimilation of idolatrous worship into the relationship between Yahweh and Israel. Choosing a central sanctuary for offering sacrifices, tithes, and gifts regulates the religious practices of the people, which in turn will protect the monotheistic dictum (Deut 6:4–5). Sadly, the centrality of worship does not come to fruition until the days of Josiah. Scholars have postulated as to whether local shrines (e.g., Shiloh, Nob, Dan, and Bethel) functioned as the epicenter of Yahwism. The biblical narrative of the so-called DH, however, does not provide enough sustainable evidence for any of the theories. What is certain is the Israelites' insatiable appetite for idolatry.

In Joshua, Israel's conquest and inhabitance of Canaan are recorded in great detail. The land motif of Deuteronomy continues in 2:9, when Rahab tells the spies, "I know that Yahweh gave to you the land" (ידעתי כי–נתן יהוה לכם את–הארץ). The inhabitants of the land fear the Israelites because of Yahweh's strength (2:11; 5:1–2). Following the biblical account of the

---

24. See Noth, *Deuteronomistic History*, 91. Emphasizing this point, Noth explained, "The historical role of the Deuteronomic law, in the period of Josiah, has in fact determined the subsequent assessment of this law, especially as we see it in Dtr. Whenever Dtr. makes Moses, Joshua and others insist upon the 'law,' that is, the Deuteronomic law, and warn the people not to transgress it, and whenever he judges historical figures and events by the standard of the 'law,' he obviously means the legal ordinances concerning the worship of 'other gods' and, in the case of the monarchial period especially, the legal prescription that there should be only one place of worship; he apparently ignores the rest of the law" (p. 81).

conquest (5:13—11:23), Joshua commands the people to allot the land of Israel as their inheritance; therefore, the people divide and allocate the land to the tribes of Israel (13:6–7; cf. Deut 12:1–28). After being in the land for years, Joshua summons all the elders, judges, and officials to his presence and gives his farewell address, similar to Moses' speech (Deut 31:7–8).

The importance of Joshua's farewell address is couched in the Deuteronomic tradition. The laws in Deut 17:14–20 command the king to read the law "all his days" (כל־ימי חייו) and observe its teachings. The narrator repeats the same command but strengthens it by mandating the ruler to read the law "day and night" (יומם ולילה, Josh 1:8).[25] The use of the demonstrative pronoun "this" in the phrase "this book of the law" (ספר התורה הזה) retains the use in Deut 17:18–19, representing the narrator's deliberate editorial effort to protect the semblance between Deuteronomy and the so-called DH.[26] Joshua goes on to proclaim that Yahweh will continue to push back all the inhabitants of Canaan for the Israelites to possess the land (23:5; cf. Deut 12:1–4). Second, like Moses, Joshua commands the people to read the law and never turn astray from its teaching or assimilate the idolatrous practice of the Canaanites into the Yahwistic cult (23:6–9; cf. Deut 12:1–4, 29–32; 16:21—17:7; 18:9–14). In his final warning, Joshua commands, "Be very careful to keep your soul and love Yahweh your God. For if you indeed return and cling to the remainder of these nations remaining among you and cause you to intermarry with them, and you join them and they with you, you shall indeed know that Yahweh your God will not add to the cause of your inheritance from these people" (24:11–13).

With the covenant renewal at Shechem, Joshua gathers all the tribes and commands them to keep their faith and obey Yahweh by abolishing all the other gods worshiped by their forefathers. The people are given the choice to follow their ancestors' pluralistic religion or Yahweh (24:1–13; cf. Deut 29:1–29). The climax of the covenant renewal is Joshua's final declaration: "But I and my house will serve Yahweh" (24:15). From the above summary, Joshua definitely establishes himself as the chosen successor of Moses and mediator for the Israelites. He becomes a "prophet like Moses" by following his lead: speaking boldly against idolatry, preaching and demanding obedience to Yahweh, and renewing the covenant. In addition, Joshua and the Israelites begin the process of fulfilling Deut 12 by entering

---

25. Weinfeld, *Deuteronomic School*, 5.
26. Nelson, "Josiah in the Book of Joshua," 531.

The Legislative Themes of Centralization

the land and expelling the people. The account in Judges reveals that the Israelites did not drive out nor slaughter all the inhabitants of the land.

Judges begins with the continuation of the conquest in Canaan and its subsequent failure (Judg 1). From this vantage point, the people of Israel begin their downward spiral, which is predicted in Deut 12–18. Judges records the failures to expel all the people from Canaan. As a result, the Israelites assimilate Baalism into their pantheon. In Judges the Israelite aberration, particularly the assimilation of Baal worship, becomes detestable to Yahweh. The Israelites "forsook" (וַיַּעַזְבוּ) Yahweh the God of their fathers in order to worship Baals and Ashtaroth (2:11–15; cf. Deut 16:21—17:7). As a result, Yahweh raises up judges to save the people, but their severance with Yahweh retards the people's willingness to return to their monotheistic ways (2:16–23). The cavalier decision to ignore the judges and priests of Yahweh is an act of defiance to the civil and religious offices described in Deut 17:8–13.

The Samuel corpus records the establishment of Israel's monarchy, which follows the religious demise in Judges. Samuel is given to Yahweh for service by his parents and eventually supplants the house of Eli (1 Sam 3). Speaking out against the ways of the people, the prophet demands the renewal of obedience to Yahweh. Continued disobedience meant the impending judgment for their idolatrous practices (1 Sam 7:3–17). With the narrative focus on the birth of the monarchy, the idolatrous practices of the people simply fade into the background. Coinciding with the division of the monarchy is the nation's spiritual deterioration. The climax of the so-called DH is the Kings corpus. The royal figures in both Israel and Judah are responsible for maintaining a healthy relationship between Yahweh and the people. The role of the king, according the narrator, is the protection and promotion of the temple in Jerusalem (cultic unity and cultic purity).[27] Sadly, the Kings corpus chronicles the shortcomings of the nation, most of which are related directly to idolatry. The sins of Jeroboam, the Baal and Asherah prophets atop Mount Carmel, the destruction of Samaria, the desolation of the temple by Manasseh, and the destruction of Jerusalem and the temple are the most grotesque examples of Israel's spiritual decay. In short, these examples are the antithesis to the Deuteronomic abrogation of idolatry (Deut 12).

---

27. See Knoppers, "The Deuteronomist," 346; cf. Clements, " Deuteronomic Law of Centralization," 19.

The Israelite Concept of Tithing

In chapter 4 the examination of applicable texts reveals the Israelite concept of tithing is of minimal importance in the literary history of the Enneateuch. The Deuteronomic innovation requiring the tithe be offered at the central sanctuary radically modifies the history of tithing, making the tithe a social institution rather than religious. The tithe becomes a social meal at the central sanctuary. Additionally, the author(s) of Deuteronomy introduces the tithe given every third year (14:28; 26:12). The tithes, save the triennial tithe (Deut 14:28), are to be given at the central sanctuary as an offering of praise to Yahweh for his benevolence (12:10–11, 15–18; 14:22–26). The socialistic orthopraxis of tithing in Deuteronomy extends to the protection of the *personae miserables*, yet another reminder of Yahweh's benevolence (14:27–29; 18:8; 26:12).

The centralization mandate of the Israelite tithes apparently becomes a nonfactor. The absence of the tithe within the so-called DH possibly indicates a lack of interest or signifies a lapse in observance. A more probable understanding is indicated in Samuel's passionate denunciation of the monarchy. Though the noun מעשר is not used in 1 Sam 8:15–17, Samuel explains the threats of having a king preside over the people, this includes tithes becoming taxes. The future king will take the tithe generally reserved for the Levites and use it at his own discretion. In short, the Israelite concept of tithing will shift completely from a religious/social institution to a state regulated and controlled institution. Ironically, after 1 Sam 8, neither מעשר or עשר appear in the so-called DH.

Second Kings 22 might provide a link between tithes to the central sanctuary (12:10–11, 15–18) and Samuel's warning (1 Sam 8). In 2 Kgs 22:3–6, Josiah sends Shaphan, the scribe, to the centralized sanctuary to meet Hilkiah the high priest to count the money brought into the temple. Interestingly, the text also adds that the doorkeepers collected the money of the people. It is not difficult to infer that the collection of money was for the temple repairs.[28] Furthermore, it should be noted that scribes played an important role in the administrative aspects of the kingdom, including the temple.[29] If this is the case, then Josiah's command to Shaphan aligns itself nicely with the laws regarding the tithe in Deuteronomy and warning of

---

28. Cf. Sweeney, *I & II Kings*, 444; cf. Fritz, *1 & 2 Kings*, 398; Stevens, *Temples, Tithes, and Taxes*, 76.

29. Grabbe, "Scribes and Synagogues," 363; idem, *Priests, Prophets*, 152–71; cf. Nelson, *Faithful Priest*, 47; Miller, *Religion of Ancient Israel*, 174.

The Legislative Themes of Centralization

Samuel. In other words, 2 Kgs 22:3–7 confirms the mandate to bring tithes to the central sanctuary and the fact that the tithe became a tax during the monarchy, evidenced by the temple repairs. Even with the seemingly lack of textual references to מעשר in the Enneateuch, a connection can be substantiated between the Deuteronomic innovation and the reforms of Josiah. This connection might be used to highlight Josiah's religious sensitivities.

The Israelite Festivals

The ancient tradition of celebrating the Israelite festivals at local sanctuaries is abolished in Deuteronomy. Like the concept of tithing, the Passover, along with the other pilgrimage festivals, is subjected to the legal innovation of centralization (Deut 16:1–17). The primary purpose of the Deuteronomic Passover is to celebrate the benevolence of Yahweh, particularly the gift of land. As a measure of thanks, the people return a portion of its produce. The celebration of Passover and the Feast of Unleavened Bread, similar to the concept of tithing, become a social institution with a religious history. The people are to present the sacrificial offering at the central sanctuary, and the meal must be consumed at sunset. Both of these prescriptions—the cooking and eating of the sacrifice—must take place at the central sanctuary (16:3–8).

Following the Deuteronomic innovation of the Passover, only two occurrences of observing the Passover occur in the so-called DH—Josh 5 and 2 Kgs 23:21–23. Once the Israelites cross the Jordan River and officially enter the land of Canaan, the people observe the Passover (Josh 5:10–11). The details relating to the observance, however, are omitted from the narrative. The second reference to the Passover is instrumental in the reforms of Josiah. After the discovery of "the book of the law" in the temple, Josiah commands that all the people of Israel observe the Passover (2 Kgs 23:21).

Prior to the mandate issued by Josiah, the Passover had not been observed correctly since the judges' period (v. 22). The narrator, by referencing the period of the judges and the monarchy (v. 22), is establishing a theological and literary relationship between Deut 16, Josh 5, and 2 Kgs 23.[30] The spiritual deterioration in the judges' period obviously carries over into

---

30. Recently, Lauren Monroe came to a similar conclusion: "In the deuteronomistic formulation, both Joshua and Josiah are compared to Moses, who was unsurpassed in his faithfulness to Yahweh and who led the Israelites to freedom." See Monroe, *Josiah's Reform*, 62.

the monarchic period. The dormancy of the Passover and the offering of tithes, following the Israelites' inhabitance of the land, correspond with the mounting assimilation of idolatrous acts and beliefs. Theologically speaking, Josiah recognizes the decline in spiritual vitality among the people and as a result attempts to reinstitute the traditional liturgical celebration. By restricting the observance of the Passover to the temple in Jerusalem, Josiah becomes the only king to successfully centralize the cult.

The Judiciary Officials

The Deuteronomic role of the judicial officials builds on the other Pentateuchal texts (Deut 1:8–12; cf. Num 11:14, 17; 25:4–5). The primary role of the judicial officials is found in Deut 16:18–20 and 17:2–7. Within the social structure of Israel, local judges preside over civil cases. When a civil case is deemed too difficult to render a verdict, the case is transferred to the central sanctuary, where Levitical priests and a judge will decide the proper sentencing (Deut 17:8–13; 19:17–18). Thus, the Deuteronomic innovation of the judicial system differentiates between two levels of officials—the civil magistrates and a cultic judge. The two levels of officials described in Deuteronomy are disregarded completely in Judges. The twelve judges in the book do not function as civil magistrates or as a cultic judge overseeing the jurisprudence of Israel. These judges are charismatic leaders raised up by Yahweh to deliver the specific tribes that become oppressed by another nation.

On the other hand, Samuel in many ways exemplifies the Deuteronomic cultic judge, though his primary judicial district is Bethel, Gilgal, Mizpah, and Ramah (1 Sam 7:16–17). His sons function as civil magistrates in Beer-Sheba. The judicial difference between Samuel and his sons is evidenced by the elders' demand for a king rather than have Samuel's sons become cultic judges (8:5–6). The demise of Samuel and the rise of Saul signify the end of the Deuteronomic innovation of judicial officials. With David on the throne, Absalom capitalizes on his father's oversight by not utilizing civil magistrates or a cultic judge (2 Sam 15:1–6). Solomon perpetuates the oversight of his father David when he assimilates the responsibilities of the cultic judge within the monarchical throne (1 Kgs 3:16–27).[31]

There exist no significant points of reference to the judicial officials in the so-called DH after 1 Kgs 3:16–27. An argument can be made, although

---

31. Cf. Levinson, "Reconceptualization of Kingship," 524.

The Legislative Themes of Centralization

textually unsustainable, that the actions of Josiah in 2 Kgs 23:1–14, especially vv. 1–4, are similar to the abuses of judicial authority and power of Absalom (2 Sam 15:1–6) and Solomon (1 Kgs 3:16–27).[32] The law of the king in Deut 17:14–20 denied "essential components of royal power and prestige: supreme judicial authority and sponsorship of the cult."[33] Though the law of the king denied the judicial authority and sponsorship of the cult, in the so-called DH, it would appear that the kingship assimilated the civil and religious institutions under the auspices of the throne (cf. 2 Kgs 23:1–4). The acts of Josiah appear to be held in the highest regard by the editors of 1–2 Kings, but his oversight of the Deuteronomic limitation of power (Deut 16:18—18:22), in reality, is a failure to comply with the Mosaic ideal.[34]

---

32. It should be noted that David also functioned as the chief judiciary official. The major difference, however, is that David is not painted in a negative light for such actions (cf. 2 Sam 8:15).

33. Levinson, "Reconceptualization of Kingship," 524.

34. Such an argument challenges portions of the double redaction of the DH proposed by Cross. The basic argument of Cross was that the first redaction of the DH (Dtr[1] = cf. Noth's Dtr) contained "two grand themes." The first was the Josianic edition of the DH. In the first theme, Dtr[1] contrasted the sins of Jeroboam and the subsequent oracles and judgments that led to destruction of the northern kingdom and Samaria (e.g., 1 Kgs 13:25; 14:7–11; 16:1–4; 20:42ff; 21:17–29; 22:8–28; 2 Kgs 17:1–23). The second theme reached a climax in the reforms of Josiah since he attempted to restore the kingdom to the grandeur of David's empire (cf. 2 Sam 7). The promise to be with the Davidic dynasty in Jerusalem, the city chosen by Yahweh to put his name (1 Kgs 11:36; 15:4; 2 Kgs 8:19), juxtaposed the faithfulness of David with the aforementioned sins of Jeroboam. If 2 Kgs 17 was the climax of the first theme, then 2 Kgs 22:1–23:25 was the climax of the second theme since it was related directly to the prophecy in 1 Kgs 13:2–5. Josiah not only eradicated the "countercultus" of Jeroboam, but he also attempted to reestablish the kingdom back to the days of David, which included the north, Dtr[1] contrasted these two themes, "the sin of Jeroboam and the faithfulness of David and Josiah," with the former deriving from the old Deuteronomic covenant theology, and the latter stemming from royal ideology in Judah (i.e., the eternal promises to David). Together, the two themes of threat and promise were juxtaposed in an effort to establish the rationale for the Josianic reforms. Cross also argued that another sub-theme emerged by an exilic redactor (Dtr[2]). Dtr[2] was responsible for retouching the Deuteronomistic work to include the fall of Jerusalem. As a result, the second redaction of the DH was for the "exiles living in an age when the bright expectations of the Josianic era were hopelessly past." For Cross, the clearest example of the sub-theme was King Manasseh and his sins of syncretism and idolatry (2 Kgs 21:2–15). Similar to the thematic juxtaposition in Dtr[1], the exilic redactor compared the sins of Manasseh with the faithfulness of Josiah (2 Kgs 23:25b–27). Although the primary focus of Dtr[2] was on Manasseh, other passages addressed the exilic captives (e.g., Deut 4:27–31; 28:36, 63–68; 29:27; 30:1–10; Josh 23:11–13, 15; 1 Sam 12:25; 1 Kgs 2:4; 6:11–13; 8:25b, 46–53; 9:4–9; 2 Kgs 17:19; 20:17). See Cross, *Canaanite Myth*, 278–84, (quote p. 285). It is my contention that the exilic

Priesthood in Israel

The Deuteronomic innovation of the priesthood introduces a new paradigm shift in the religious institution of the cult. Though the book uses more designations to describe the priesthood (הלוי, הלוים, כהן, הכהנים בני לוי, and שבט הלוי), the syntactically difficult phrase Levitical priests (הכהנים הלוים) actually introduces a new paradigm. The other designations to the priesthood are equivalent, theoretically, to the Deuteronomic Levitical priests. Several innovations concerning the priesthood are worth mentioning. First, the author(s) of Deuteronomy apparently do not differentiate between the Aaronite priesthood and the Levitical priests. Second, the Deuteronomic Levitical priests are to keep the king's copy of the law (17:18). Third, Deuteronomy describes three types of priests: Levitical priests, secular Levitical priests, and active Levitical priests serving at the central sanctuary (18:1–8). Deuteronomy also describes other characteristics of the Levitical priests (see ch. 7), but the Deuteronomic innovations mentioned earlier in this chapter are particularly relevant to the so-called DH.

The so-called DH contains limited references to Aaron, which can be categorized into four subjects: the historical material concerning the allotment of Levitical cities in the land of Canaan (Josh 21); the ministry of Aaron in Egypt (Josh 24:5; 1 Sam 12:6, 8); the death of Aaron (Josh 24:33); and genealogical references (Judg 20:28). Specifically, the Aaronite priesthood and Levitical priests supplant the priestly ministry of Aaron in the so-called DH. In Joshua, Eleazar the son of Aaron and Phinehas the son of Eleazar become the chief priests (Josh 14:1; 19:51; 22:13, 31, 32; 24:33). On the other hand, Judges does not mention a chief priest in Israel but rather introduces narratives about individual Levites for hire (Judg 19–20). The Samuel and Kings corpuses primarily focus on individual priests and the high priest. In the Samuel corpus, Eli and his sons are the priests of the shrine at Shiloh (1 Sam 1–2) when the young Ephraimite boy Samuel is dedicated into the service of Yahweh (1 Sam 1–3).[35] David's sons are called priests in 2 Sam 8:18, but this reference is most likely corrupt since 1 Chr 18:17 describes David's sons as chief officials serving the king. Both Zadok

---

audience would have viewed Josiah's abuse of power like that of Absalom and Solomon.

35. If Samuel is born a member of the tribe of Ephraim as stated in 1 Sam 1:1, then the priestly characteristics of Samuel might suggest the tribe of Levi is composed of non-related priests who formed a tribe.

The Legislative Themes of Centralization

and Abiathar provide protective counsel and support to David during the rebellion of Absalom (2 Sam 17:15; 19:12; 20:25).[36]

Within the Kings corpus, the priesthood continues to evolve. During the monarchy, the priests become instrumental in the king's political decisions. For example, instead of aligning with Solomon, Abiathar establishes an alliance with Adonijah (1 Kgs 1:7, 19, 25, 42; 2:22), whereas Zadok remains faithful to David and his son Solomon (1 Kgs 1:8, 26, 32, 34; 2:35).[37] Obscure individuals like Zabud the son of Natha are described as priests (1 Kgs 4:5). When Jeroboam appoints priests to serve at his shrines at Bethel and Dan, he continues the precedent instituted by David (2 Sam 15:24–29; cf. 1 Kgs 12:31, 32). The king can exert his authority to appoint priests into service—even if they are from the non-Levite sector. In somewhat of an ironic twist, the priest Jehoida protects the young Joash during the ruse of Athaliah (2 Kgs 11–12). Last, priests begin to teach the people (2 Kgs 17:27–28).

The current discussion of the Aaronite priesthood can be described as sporadic.[38] Certainly, the narrator is concerned more with the monarchy

---

36. Interestingly, David rescues Abiathar the son of Ahimelech at Nob when Saul orders the annihilation of all priests (2 Sam 22:20–23). On the other hand, the biblical account of Zadok's ancestry is omitted in 1–2 Samuel. Lester L. Grabbe maintained the silence concerning Zadok's ancestry could not be accidental given the importance of the genealogical descent of the Israelite priests. See Grabb, *Prophets, Prophets, Diviners*, 44. In 1 Chr 5:34 [Eng. 6:8], Zadok is described as being from the line of Eleazar, a son of Aaron. The genealogy of Zadok in 1 Chr 5:34, according to Grabb, represented a "later attempt to make Zadok 'orthodox' rather than original information."

37. See Klingbeil, "Priests and Levites," 813.

38. Nelson also recognized the limited attention given to the priests in the so-called DH; however, he would not label the priests as peripheral characters. He argued the Dtr used priests in several capacities: as "redactional tools" to emphasize and rationalize ideological truths (1 Kgs 13:2; 2 Kgs 23:20); as guarantors of legitimacy (Josh 3; 4; 6); as proprietary associates in Josiah's reforms (2 Kgs 22:3, 12; 23:1, 4, 21); as redactional characters used to evaluate kings and their policies (1 Kgs 12:31–32; 13:33); and as redactional characters used to indicate the collapse of Jerusalem and the temple (2 Kgs 25:13–18). In sum, Nelson believed the priests were used by the Dtr to make a theological point. See Nelson, "Role of the Priesthood," 132–47. Elsewhere, Nelson posed a relevant question: "How does this text [Deut 18:1–8] related to Josiah's reform, if at all?" He believed the text could not be a "retrospective reflection on Josiah's resettlement of priests to Jerusalem." Instead, he suggested that vv. 1–8 represent a spontaneous decision by priests to serve at the central sanctuary. In short, he denied any connection between Deut 18:1–8 and 2 Kgs 23:8–9. See Nelson, *Deuteronomy*, 232. McConville, in an article responding to Nelson, argued that priests and the priesthood played an important role in the narrative of Joshua–2 Kings. He dismissed Nelson's redactional theory of the priests in the so-called DH, arguing the Dtr shared an "intrinsic interest in the priesthood."

and, at times, the relationship between king and priest than with the larger Israelite priesthood. The Deuteronomic innovation requiring the Levitical priests to keep the king's copy of the law (17:18), though never explicitly stated, is insinuated with the increasing role of the high priest in the monarchy. The discovery of the law by Hilkiah during the cleaning of the temple suggests that at one point in Israel's history the priest served as the keeper of the king's law (2 Kgs 22:8-9). The active service of the Levitical priesthood at the central sanctuary, however, possibly never existed until the reforms of Josiah—possibly supported by the minor reference to the priests of the second order (=Levitical priests?) in 2 Kgs 23:4.

Whether 2 Kgs 23:4 is a reference to the Levitical priests or not, 2 Kgs 23:1-20 does align itself with the evolution of the priesthood during the united and divided monarchies. In 2 Kgs 23, Josiah exercises authority over the elders of Judah and Jerusalem (v. 1) and the priests and prophets (v. 2). Upon reading the book of the law, the king declares the keeping of the commandments of Yahweh, which the people in attendance joined in with the covenant (v. 3). What unfolds next coincides with the authority of the king over priests elsewhere in the so-called DH. Josiah commands the Hilkiah the high priest and the other priests to destroy and burn the vessels of Baal and Asherah (vv. 4-6) and destroy the houses of prostitutes, the pagan altars and high places of Solomon, Jeroboam, Ahaz, and Manasseh, and the multitude of shrines and altars in the land (vv. 7-20). Even though an argument can be made that Hilkah was keeping a copy of the king's law (cf. Deut 17:18-19), it would appear from the directives issued by Josiah that the king usurped, yet again, the delimiting of power prescribed in Deuteronomy.[39]

IMPLICATIONS

I began this study by describing the relationship between diachronic and synchronic readings of the HB. Much attention was given to diachronic and exegetical assessment of biblical texts. Though scholarship has proven

---

The priesthood and the monarchy shared a unique relationship in the Kings corpus. As a result, both institutions suffered greatly at the hands of the Babylonians; however, the priesthood superseded the Davidic synthesis following the demise of the nation. See McConville, "Priesthood in Joshua to Kings," 73-87.

39. Likewise, Monroe independently came to the same conclusion: "While a limited kingship may be Deuteronomy's prerogative, it is unlikely to have been Josiah's." See Monroe, *Josiah's Reform*, 114.

The Legislative Themes of Centralization

through source, form, and redaction criticism the various literary layers and traditions in the HB, a bridge must be built between the gap of historical and literary-critical approaches to the HB. Proponents of a synchronic approach and/or a final canonical form cannot ignore the historical-critical contributions of the diachronic approach. I have argued that a collaborative effort must be made to conjoin the fruits of the historical-critical methods and the literary readings of the HB.

My research has examined the five legislative themes associated with the Deuteronomic concept of centralization of the cult. Traditionally, each of these themes has been studied from a diachronic perspective, especially within the Pentateuch. Above, however, I showed the relationship that exists between the five themes and 2 Kgs 22–23. Through a synchronic reading of these themes, I was able to establish how an exilic audience would have perceived the material, particularly how they perceived the reforms of Josiah. Through a diachronic and synchronic analysis of these themes, I revealed that simply associating the Deuteronomic concept of centralization with the Josianic reforms ignores the rhetorical perspective, the so-called DH. Within the so-called DH, the narrator uses the five legislative themes as the rhetorical foundation of Israel's demise and destruction. The relative absence of the Deuteronomic innovations concerning tithes, Passover, and judicial officials symbolizes the failures at the civil and religious levels within the monarchy. The discovery of "the book of the law" by Hilkiah and the subsequent reforms of Josiah attest to the narrator's theological agenda. These legislative themes play a rhetorical role—i.e., social, political, and religious—in the so-called DH. Only the theme of idolatry permeates the Enneateuch.

The silence concerning tithes, Passover and the festival calendar, judiciary officials, and the priesthood in the so-called DH does not negate the overall value of this study. I would argue that it corroborates the findings of other scholars, but from a different approach to the Deuteronomic concept of centralization.[40] My research has highlighted the fact that Deuteronomy

---

40. For example, Schmid recognized the Deut 12 had little to no influence on Joshua–Judges. The absence of "reflective Deuteronomistic passages" in Joshua–Judges led Schmid to suggest multiple "Deuteronomistic Histories" in the Enneateuch. The first history, Samuel–2 Kings, was shaped by the centralization of the cult in Jerusalem rather than Deut 12. A second history was Exodus–Joshua + Samuel–2 Kings. This history was shaped by the first commandment and derived its "theological thrust" through Exod 32/1 Kgs 12 and the themes of "exodus from Egypt" and "return from Egypt" (2 Kgs 25:26). The final history was post-priestly and identified as Gen–2 Kings. See Schmid, "Deuteronomistic Histories," 28.

and the centralization of the cult had limited interest to the editors of Joshua–2 Samuel. In the opposite direction, there exists limited evidence of the Deuteronomic concept of the centralized cult in the Tetrateuch.[41] The seemingly lack of evidence for the five legislative themes in Joshua–2 Samuel does not weaken my research. In fact, I suggest it strengthens my hypothesis—the themes of centralization play a prominent role in the demise and destruction of Judah at the social, political, and religious levels.

Whether Deut 12–18 is prophetic in nature or an example of *vaticanum ex eventu*, the "story" is to be read prophetically due to its position within the Enneateuch. The fact that the Israelites deviate from the Pentateuchal regulations and, more specifically, the Deuteronomic mandate of centralizing the cult proves that the five legislative themes, particularly the abrogation of idolatry, become the reasons for the demise and destruction of Israel. These legislative themes are repositioned and reinterpreted in Deuteronomy. In doing so, the ancient traditions are systematically altered through the centralization of the cult. In other words, the social, political, and religious structure of the cult—i.e., Deut 12–18—never becomes a reality until the reforms of Josiah. The untimely death of Josiah, however, signifies the beginning of the end. The subsequent kings deviate from the reforms instituted by Josiah. The result was swift and brutal—the demise and destruction of the kingdom at the hands of the Babylonians. From an exilic point of view, the demise of the kingdom was multifaceted. The social stratum was decimated by political monarchy. The political stratum eroded due to the compromise of religion by the kings and the people. And, the religious stratum failed because the priests and the priesthood were subjugated under the power of the king. The demise of all three facets of Israelite life is tied to the theme of idolatry. The centralization mandate was never going to fully work because there were too many variables. Centralizing the government and cult would not, and ultimately did not, protect the Yahwism declared in Deuteronomy. Thus, the centralization of the cult, in the eyes of the exilic audience, was unattainable, making it a utopian desire.[42]

In conclusion, this study has reiterated what other scholars have already noted: Deuteronomy is the center of the Enneateuch.[43] The diachron-

---

41. Redaction critic, Pakkala came to the same conclusions, but from a different perspective and approach. See Pakkala, "Deuteronomy and 1–2 Kings," 133–62.

42. Concluding from a different perspective, Pitkänen explained, "The rhetoric of Deuteronomy serves to encourage the people to follow Yahweh so that ideal conditions can be attained" See Pitkänen, *Central Sanctuary*, 272.

43. For example, see Freedman, *Unity of the Hebrew Bible*, 1–15 and Newing,

ic and synchronic readings of the five legislative themes reveal how these themes were altered radically by the introduction of the Deuteronomic concept of centralization of the cult. The new social, political, and theological paradigm of Deuteronomy closes the Pentateuch and transitions into the demise of the nation in the so-called DH. The Deuteronomic innovation of centralization modifies the preexisting legislative themes in Israel's history in an effort to emphasize cultic unity (*Kultuseinheit*) and cultic purity (*Kultusreinheit*). The narrator capitalizes on the failure of the people to accomplish cultic unity and cultic purity through centralizing the cult. Thus, the narrator uses the new paradigm in Deut 12–18 as the rhetorical foundation of the so-called DH. The literary link between the Tetrateuch and Deuteronomy, as well as the rhetorical relationship of Deuteronomy and the so-called DH, validates an Enneateuchal theory from the perspective of the Deuteronomic concept of centralization of the cult.

This study has shown that Deuteronomy is theologically important from a cultic and canonical point of view. The legal innovations introduced in Deuteronomy close the Tetrateuch and prepare the readers for the next phase in Israel's history—the inhabitance of the land of Canaan. In this chapter, I have shown how the five themes of centralization contain a rhetorical relationship with the so-called DH.

"Rhetoric of Hope," 1–15.

9

Conclusion

THE SIGNIFICANCE OF DEUTERONOMY—THE book's unique language, theology, and ideology—continues to have a pervasive influence in the study of the HB. The promise of a central sanctuary in the land of Canaan—the focus of this study—radically changes the social, political, and religious paradigm in Israel's history. The "place which Yahweh will choose" is antithetical to the idolatrous forms of worship prevalent among the inhabitants of the land that Israel will conqueror. The basic ideological rationale related to the Deuteronomic concept of centralization is cultic unity and cultic purity at the local, tribal, and national levels. The future central sanctuary symbolizes Yahweh's commitment to the people of Israel. The ideological thrust of the concept of centralization, however, remains dormant until the reformative efforts of Kings Hezekiah and Josiah. Much of the scholarly discussion surrounding the origins of Deuteronomy is aligned closely with the reformative years of these two kings. Moreover, many scholars emphasize the literary-historical relationship between Deut 12 and 2 Kgs 22–23, which overshadows the literary importance of the Deuteronomic concept of centralization within the larger literary framework of the Enneateuch.

In the present endeavor, my study integrated diachronic assessments of relevant texts related to each of the five themes as well as a synchronic reading of each legislative theme within the Enneateuch. In doing so, the innovative characteristics of the Deuteronomic concept of centralization became apparent, not only historically but also theologically. By studying these themes within the larger literary framework of the Enneateuch, I

The Legislative Themes of Centralization

introduced some new literary and theological considerations in the ever-expansive field of Deuteronomic and Deuteronomistic studies. From a canonical perspective, the Deuteronomic concept of centralization in Deut 12–18, functionally speaking, contains a prophetic undertone—the legislative themes represent the foundational and substantive failures of the Israelites in the so-called DH. In other words, there can be no coincidence that the legislative themes associated with the concept of centralization became detrimental to the survival of the people. This study has presented enough evidence to suggest the impregnability of the Israelites ceased with the contravention of the Deuteronomic covenant, specifically the five legislative themes in Deut 12–18.

The importance of this study might well be the beginning of a new way of thinking about Deuteronomic concept of centralization. I hopefully provided a viable, alternative method for examining and interpreting the concept of centralization in Deuteronomy. The study was not intended to dismiss the scholarly contributions to the discussion from the last one hundred and fifty years. It should encourage others to break free from the historical constraints of simply equating Deuteronomy with the reforms of Hezekiah or Josiah.

Obviously, the next developmental stage is going beyond a "theology of" the concept of centralization. Thus, the first stage is to examine the rhetorical relationship between the five themes and the kingship laws in Deut 17:14–20. In the kingship laws, the phrase, "You may indeed set a king over you whom the Lord your God will choose" (v. 15), appears to be modified centralization motif. This phrase, in many ways, controls the constitutional elements of Deut 16:18—18:22. Given my research, there does seem to exist a rhetorical relationship between the centralization mandate and the kingship. A second avenue for further research must be the examination of the centralizing language and ideology in the Enneateuch. An in-depth assessment of texts and traditions where centralization of worship occurs in Israel's history is needed (e.g., Bethel, Shechem, Shiloh, Nob, Gilgal, etc.), particularly utilizing the integrated method of diachronic and synchronic aspects. Such an assessment will determine whether the local shrines represent centralized locations for worshiping Yahweh, or if the literary history of the Enneateuch reveals an abhorrent syncretism at various local shrines with no individual shrine ever functioning as the central sanctuary for worshiping Yahweh. Many scholars quickly dismiss the former suggestion, but reexamining the biblical texts and traditions could be beneficial.

Conclusion

Third, in the development of the "theology of" centralization is the relationship between cultic unity and cultic purity and the office of the prophet. The literary structure of Deut 16:18—18:22 is no coincidence. Judiciary officials and priests are responsible for regulating the social and political milieu of Israelite life—both at the local and national levels (16:18—17:7). Additionally, the future kingship is part of this social and political stratum (17:14-20). The religious stratum counterbalances the potential abuse of power within the social and political milieu. Interwoven within the Israelite religious life are the priesthood (17:8-13; 18:1-8) and the office of prophet (18:15-18). The office of prophet, though not associated with the concept of centralization, is related to the constitutional program (16:18—18:22) since it is an integral component in the relationship between the civil and religious offices. Together, these two branches of Israelite government provide a civil, moral, and religious paradigm for living in the land of Canaan. The relationship between civil and religious offices, specifically the office of prophet, provides the rationale for the next stage of development of the "theology of" centralization: How does the office of prophet relate to the Deuteronomic concept of centralization? Does the narrator incorporate the office of prophet as the spiritual legislator of the Deuteronomic law code, specifically the breaches of five legislative themes?

The additional stages above will continue the quest for determining a comprehensive "theology of" the centralization. A pursuit for a holistic understanding of the Deuteronomic concept of centralization must continue to integrate diachronic and synchronic aspects. To this end, my work hopes to revisit afresh the discussion of the historical, literary, and theological implications of the Deuteronomic concept of centralization.

Bibliography

Abba, Raymond. "Priests and Levites in Deuteronomy." *VT* 27 (1977) 257–67.
Aberbach, Moses, and Leivy Smolar. "Aaron, Jeroboam, and the Golden Calves." *JBL* 86 (1967) 129–40.
Albertz, Rainer. *A History of Israelite Religion in the Old Testament Period. Volume I: From the Beginnings to the End of the Monarchy*. Translated by John Bowden. OTL. Louisville: Westminster John Knox, 1994.
Albright, William Foxwell. *From the Stone Age to Christianity*. 1940. Reprint. Garden City: Doubleday, 1957.
———. *Yahweh and the Gods of Canaan: A Historical Analysis of Two Contrasting Faiths*. Winona Lake, IN: Eisenbrauns, 1994.
Alexander, Lewis V. *The Origin and Development of the Deuteronomistic History Theory and Its Significance for Biblical Interpretation*. Ann Arbor, MI: UMI, 1993.
Alexander, T. Desmond. *From Paradise to the Promised Land: An Introduction to the Pentateuch*. 2nd ed. Grand Rapids: Baker, 2002.
Alt, Albrecht. "The Origins of Israelite Law." In *Essays on Old Testament History and Religion*. Translated by Robert A. Wilson, 101–71. Garden City, NY: Doubleday, 1967.
Alter, Robert. *The Art of Biblical Narrative*. Jackson, TN: Basic, 1981.
———. *The Five Books of Moses: A Translation with Commentary*. New York: Norton, 2008.
Amir, Yehoshua. "The Decalogue according to Philo." In *The Ten Commandments in History and Tradition*, 121–60. Jerusalem: Magnes, 1990.
Anbar, Moshé. *Josué et l'alliance de Sichem: Josué 24:1–28*. Beiträge zur biblischen Exegese und Theologie 25. Frankfurt: Lang, 1992.
The Anchor Bible Dictionary. 6 vols. Edited by David Noel Freedman. New York: Doubleday, 1992.
Anderson, Gary A. *Sacrifices and Offerings in Ancient Israel: Studies in their Social and Political Importance*. Harvard Semitic Monographs 41. Atlanta: Scholars, 1987.
Armerding, Carl E. "Festivals and Feasts." In *DOTP*, 300–13.
Ash, Paul S. "Jeroboam I and the Deuteronomistic Historian's Ideology of the Founder." *CBQ* 60 (1998) 16–24.
Ashley, Timothy R. *The Book of Numbers*. NICOT. Grand Rapids: Eerdmans, 1993.
Astruc, Jean. *Conjectures sur les memoires originaux dont il paroit que Moyse s'est servi pour composer le livre de la Genese*. Brussels: Chez Fricx, 1753.

Bibliography

Auld, Alan Graeme. "The Deuteronomists and the Former Prophets, or What Makes the Former Prophets Deuteronomistic?" In *Those Elusive Deuteronomists: The Phenomenon of Pan-Deuteronomism*, 116–26. Sheffield, UK: Sheffield Academic, 1999.

———. *Joshua, Moses and the Land: Tetrateuch-Pentateuch-Hexateuch in a Generation since 1938*. Edinburgh: T. & T. Clark, 1980.

Aurelius, Erik. *Zukunft jenseits des Gerichts: Eine redaktionsgeschichtliche Studie zum Enneateuch*. Beihefte zur Zeitschrift für die alttestamentliche Wissenschaft 319. Berlin: de Gruyter, 2003.

Averbeck, Richard. "מעשׂר." In *NIDOTTE* 2:1035–55.

Baker, David L. *Tight Fists or Open Hands? Wealth and Poverty in Old Testament Law*. Grand Rapids: Eerdmans, 2009.

Bakon, Shimon. "Centralization of Worship." *JBQ* 26 (1998) 26–33.

Bar-Efrat, Shimon. *Narrative Art in the Bible*. London: T. & T. Clark, 2004.

Barker, Paul A. "Contemporary Theological Interpretation." In *Interpreting Deuteronomy: Issues and Approaches*, edited by David G. Firth and Philip S. Johnston, 60–90. Downers Grove, IL: InterVarsity, 2012.

Barmash, Pamela. "The Narrative Quandary: Cases of Law in Literature." *VT* 54 (2004) 1–16.

Barr, James. "Childs' Introduction to the Old Testament as Scripture." *JSOT* 16 (1980) 12–23.

———. *The Concept of Biblical Theology: An Old Testament Perspective*. Minneapolis: Fortress, 1999.

———. "The Synchronic, the Diachronic and the Historical: A Triangular Relationship?" In *Synchronic or Diachronic? A Debate on Method in Old Testament Exegesis*, edited by Johannes Cornelis De Moor, 1–14. Oudtestamentische Studiën 34. Leiden: Brill, 1995.

Barton, John. *Reading the Old Testament: Method in Biblical Study*. Louisville: Westminster John Knox, 1996.

Baumgarten, Joseph M. "On the Non-Literal Use of *MA'ĀŚĒR/DEKATĒ*." *JBL* 103 (1984) 245–51.

Becking, Bob. "From Apostasy to Destruction: A Josianic View on the Fall of Samaria (2 Kings 17,21–23)." In *Deuteronomy and Deuteronomic Literature: Festschrift C. H. W. Brekelmans*, edited by Marc Vervenne and Johan Lust, 279–97. Bibliotheca ephemeridum theologicarum lovaniensium 133. Leuven: Leuven University Press, 1997.

Begg, Christopher T. "The Destruction of the Golden Calf Revisited (Exod 32,20/Deut 9,21)." In *Deuteronomy and Deuteronomic Literature: Festschrift C. H. W. Brekelmans*, edited by Marc Vervenne and Johan Lust, 469–79. Bibliotheca ephemeridum theologicarum lovaniensium 133. Leuven: Leuven University Press, 1997.

Bekken, Per Jarel. *The Word is Near You: A Study of Deuteronomy 30:12–14 in Paul's Letter to the Romans in a Jewish Context*. Beihefte zur Zeitschrift für die neutestamentliche Wissenschaft und die Kunde der aelteren Kirche 144. Berlin: de Gruyter, 2007.

Berger, Robert D. *1, 2 Samuel*. NAC 7. Nashville: Broadman & Holman, 1996.

Berlin, Adele. *Poetics and Interpretation of Biblical Narrative*. Winona Lake, IN: Eisenbrauns, 1983.

Berrigan, Daniel. *No Gods but One*. Grand Rapids: Eerdmans, 2009.

Bewer, Julius A. "The Case for the Early Date of Deuteronomy." *JBL* 47 (1928) 305–21.

Biddle, Mark E. *Deuteronomy*. SHBC. Macon, GA: Smyth and Helwys, 2003.
Blenkinsopp, Joseph. "The Baal Peor Episode Revisited (Num 25,1–18)." *Bib* 93 (2012) 86–97.
———. *The Pentateuch: An Introduction to the First Five Books of the Bible*. Anchor Bible Reference Library. New York: Doubleday, 1992.
Block, Daniel I. "The Burden of Leadership: The Mosaic Paradigm of Kingship (Deut 17:14–20)." *BSac* 162 (2005) 259–78.
———. *Deuteronomy*. NIVAC. Grand Rapids: Zondervan, 2013.
———. "The Joy of Worship: The Mosaic Invitation to the Presence of God (Deut 12:1–14)." *BSac* 162 (2005) 131–49.
———. *Judges*. NAC 6. Nashville: Broadman & Holman, 1999.
Bluedorn, Wolfgang. *Yahweh versus Baalism: A Theological Reading of the Gideon Abimelech Narrative*. Journal for the Study of the Old Testament Supplement Series 329. Sheffield, UK: Sheffield Academic, 2001.
Blum, Erhard. *Studien zur Komposition des Pentateuch*. Beihefte zur Zeitschrift für die alttestamentliche Wissenschaft 189. Berlin: de Gruyter, 1990.
Bokser, Baruch M. "The Feasts of Unleavened Bread and Passover." In *ABD* 6:755–65.
Boling, Robert G. *Joshua*. AB 6. Garden City, NY: Doubleday, 1981.
Boorer, Suzanne. "The Importance of a Diachronic Approach: The Case of Genesis-Kings." *CBQ* 51 (1989) 195–208.
Braulik, Georg. *Deuteronomium 1—16:17*. NEchtB. Würzburg: Echter Verlag, 1986.
———. *Deuteronomium 16:18—34:12*. NEchtB. Würzburg: Echter Verlag, 1992.
———. "The Joy of the Feast." In *The Theology of Deuteronomy: Collected Essays of Georg Braulik, O.S.B.* Translated by Ulrika Lindblad, 27–66. North Richland Hills, TX: Bibal, 1994.
———. "The Sequence of the Laws in Deuteronomy 12–26 and in the Decalogue." In *A Song of Power and the Power of Song: Essays on the Book of Deuteronomy*, 313–35. Sources for Biblical and Theological Study 3. Winona Lake, IN: Eisenbrauns, 1993.
———. "'Die Weisung und das Gebot' im Enneateuch." In *Das Manna fällt auch heute noch: Beiträge zur Geschichte und Theologie des Alten, Ersten Testaments: Festschrift für Erich Zenger*, edited by Frank-Lothar Hossfeld and Ludger Schwienhorst-Schönberger, 115–40. New York: Herder, 2004.
Bright, John. *A History of Israel*. 4th ed. Louisville: Westminster John Knox, 2000.
Brown, Francis, S. R. Driver, and Charles A. Briggs. *Hebrew and English Lexicon of the Old Testament*. Oxford: Clarendon, 1907.
Brueggemann, Walter. *Deuteronomy*. AOTC. Nashville: Abingdon, 2001.
———. *First and Second Samuel*. IBC. Louisville: John Knox, 1990.
Budd, Philip J. *Numbers*. WBC 5. Waco: Word, 1984.
Campbell, Anthony F. *1 Samuel*. FOTL 7. Grand Rapids: Eerdmans, 2003.
Campbell, Anthony F., and Mark A. O'Brien. *Unfolding the Deuteronomistic History: Origins, Upgrades, and Present Text*. Minneapolis: Fortress, 2000.
Carmichael, Calum M. *The Laws of Deuteronomy*. London: Cornell University Press, 1974.
Cassuto, Umberto. *A Commentary on the Book of Exodus*. Translated by Israel Abrahams. Jerusalem: Magnes, 1997.
Chavel, Simeon. "The Second Passover, Pilgrimage, and the Centralized Cult." *HTR* 102 (2009) 1–24.
Childs, Brevard S. *The Book of Exodus*. OTL. Philadelphia: Westminster, 1974.
———. *Introduction to the Old Testament as Scripture*. Philadelphia: Fortress, 1979.

Bibliography

———. *Old Testament Theology in a Canonical Context*. Philadelphia: Fortress, 1989.
Chisholm Robert B., Jr. "A Rhetorical Use of Point of View in Old Testament Narrative." *BSac* 159 (2002) 404–14.
Christensen, Duane L. *Deuteronomy 1:1—21:9*. WBC 6A. Dallas: Word, 1991.
———. "The *Numeruswechsel* in Deuteronomy 12." In *A Song of Power and the Power of Song: Essays on the Book of Deuteronomy*, 394–402. Sources for Biblical and Theological Study. Winona Lake, IN: Eisenbrauns, 1993.
Clements, Ronald E. "The Book of Deuteronomy." In *NIB* 2:271–538.
———. "The Deuteronomic Law of Centralisation and the Catastrophe of 587 B.C.E." In *After the Exile: Essays in Honor of Rex Mason*, edited by John Barton and David J. Reimer, 5–25. Macon, GA: Mercer University Press, 1996.
———. "The Deuteronomistic Interpretation of the Founding of the Monarchy in 1 Samuel VIII." *VT* 24 (1974) 398–410.
———. *Deuteronomy*. Old Testament Guides. Sheffield, UK: JSOT, 1989.
———. "Deuteronomy and the Jerusalem Cult Tradition." *VT* 15 (1965) 300–312.
———. *Exodus*. CBC. Cambridge: Cambridge University Press, 1972.
Clines, David J. A. "Beyond Synchronic/Diachronic." In *Synchronic or Diachronic? A Debate on Method in Old Testament Exegesis*, edited by Johannes Cornelis De Moor, 52–71, Oudtestamentische Studiën 34. Leiden: Brill, 1995.
———. *The Theme of the Pentateuch*. 2nd ed. Journal for the Study of the Old Testament Supplement Series 10. Sheffield, UK: Sheffield Academic, 1996.
Clines, David J. A., and J. Cheryl Exum. "The New Literary Criticism." In *The New Literary Criticism and the Hebrew Bible*, edited by J. Cheryl Exum and David J. A. Clines, 11–25. Journal for the Study of Old Testament Supplement Series 143. Sheffield, UK: Sheffield Academic, 1993.
Coats, George W. *Genesis*. FOTL 1. Grand Rapids: Eerdmans, 1983.
Cody, Aelred. *A History of Old Testament Priesthood*. Analecta biblica 35. Rome: Pontifical Biblical Institute, 1969.
Coggins, Richard. "What Does 'Deuteronomistic' Mean?" In *Those Elusive Deuteronomists: The Phenomenon of Pan-Deuteronomism*, edited by Linda S. Schearing and Steven L. McKenzie, 23–35. Journal for the Study of the Old Testament Supplement Series 268. Sheffield, UK: Sheffield Academic, 1999.
Cohen, Matty. "M^{e}KĒRŌTĒHEM (Genèse XLIX 5)." *VT* 31 (1981) 472–82.
Cole, R. Dennis. *Numbers*. NAC 3B. Nashville: Broadman & Holman, 2000.
Coleran, James E. "The Sacrifice of Melckisedek." *TS* 1 (1940) 27–36.
Collier, Gary D. "The Problem of Deuteronomy: In Search of Perspective." *ResQ* 26 (1983) 215–33.
Collins, John J. *Introduction to the Hebrew Bible*. Minneapolis: Fortress, 2004.
Cooper, Alan, and Bernard R. Goldstein. "Exodus and Massôt in History and Tradition." *Maarav* 8 (1992) 15–37.
Cotterell, Peter, and Max Turner. *Linguistics and Biblical Interpretation*. Downers Grove, IL: InterVarsity, 1989.
Cowley, A. E. *Aramaic Papyri of the Fifth Century B.C.* Oxford: Clarendon, 1923.
Craigie, Peter C. *The Book of Deuteronomy*. NICOT. Grand Rapids: Eerdmans, 1976.
Crim, Keith, ed. *The Interpreter's Dictionary of the Bible: Supplementary Volume*. 3rd ed. Nashville: Abingdon, 1982.
Cross, Frank Moore. *Canaanite Myth and Hebrew Epic: Essays in the History of Religion of Israel*. Cambridge: Harvard University Press, 1973.

Bibliography

Croteau, David A. "The Post-Tithing View: Giving in the New Covenant." In *Perspectives on Tithing: Four Views*, 57–83. Nashville: B. & H. Academic, 2012.

Crüsemann, Frank. *The Torah: Theology and Social History of Old Testament Law.* Translated by Allan W. Mahnke. Minneapolis: Fortress, 1996.

Dahood, Mitchell J. "*MKRTYHM* in Genesis 49,5." *CBQ* 23 (1961) 54–56.

Daube, David. *Studies in Biblical Law.* Cambridge: Cambridge University Press, 1947.

Davis, Dale Ralph. "Rebellion, Presence, and Covenant: A Study in Exodus 32-34." *WTJ* 44 (1982) 71–87.

Dorsey, David A. *The Literary Structure of the Old Testament: A Commentary on Genesis-Malachi.* Grand Rapids: Baker, 1999.

Douglas, Mary. "The Forbidden Animals in Leviticus." *JSOT* 59 (1993) 3–23.

———. "Justice as the Cornerstone: An Interpretation of Leviticus 18-20." *Int* 53 (1999) 341–50.

———. *Leviticus as Literature.* Oxford: Oxford University Press, 1999.

———. "Poetic Structure in Leviticus." In *Pomegranates and Golden Bells: Studies in Biblical, Jewish, and Near Eastern Ritual, Law and Literature in Honor of Jacob Milgrom*, edited by David P. Wright et al., 239–56. Winona Lake, IN: Eisenbrauns, 1995.

———. *Purity and Danger: An Analysis of Concept of Pollution and Taboo.* 1966. Reprint. London: Routledge Classics, 2005.

Dozeman, Thomas B. "The Composition of Exodus 32 within the Context of the Enneateuch." In *Auf dem Weg zur Endgestalt von Genesis bis II Regum: Festschrift für Hans-Christoph Schmitt zu seinem 65*, edited by Martin Beck and Ulrike Schorn, 175–89. Beihefte zür Zeitschrift fur de alttestamentliche Wissenschaft 370. Berlin: de Gruyter, 2006.

Dozeman, Thomas B., et al. *Pentateuch, Hexateuch, or Enneateuch: Identifying Literary Works in Genesis through Kings.* Ancient Israel and Its Literature 8. Atlanta: Society of Biblical Literature, 2011.

Driver, Samuel R. *The Book of Exodus.* Cambridge: Cambridge University Press, 1953.

———. *Deuteronomy.* ICC. Edinburgh: T. & T. Clark, 1965.

———. *Introduction to the Literature of the Old Testament.* 10th ed. International Theological Library. New York: Scribner's Sons, 1961.

Duhm, Bernhard D. *Das Buch Jesaia.* Handkommentar zum Alten Testament. 2nd ed. Göttingen: Vandenhoeck und Ruprecht, 1902.

Duke, Rodney K. "The Portion of the Levite: Another Reading of Deuteronomy 18:6-8." *JBL* 106 (1987) 193–201.

———. "Priests and Priesthood." In *DOTP* 646–55.

Durham, John I. *Exodus.* WBC 3. Waco: Word, 1987.

Dutcher-Walls, Patricia. "The Circumscription of the King: Deuteronomy 17:16-17 in Its Ancient Social Context." *JBL* 121 (2002) 601–16.

Edelman, Diana. *Opening the Books of Moses.* BibleWorld. Sheffield, UK: Equinox, 2012.

Eichrodt, Walther. *Theology of the Old Testament.* Translated by J. A. Baker. 2 vols. Philadelphia: Westminster, 1961–67.

Eissfeldt, Otto. *The Old Testament: An Introduction.* Translated by Peter Ackroyd. New York: Harper and Row, 1965.

Emerton, John A. "Gideon and Jerubbaal." *JTS* 27 (1976) 289–312.

———. "Priests and Levites in Deuteronomy: An Examination of Dr. G. E. Wright's Theory." *VT* 12 (1962) 128–39.

Bibliography

———. "The Riddle of Genesis XIV." *VT* 21 (1971) 403–39.

Eslinger, Lyle. *Into the Hands of the Living God*. Journal for the Study of the Old Testament Supplement Series 84. Sheffield, UK: Almond, 1989.

Falk, Ze'ev W. *Hebrew Law in Biblical Times: An Introduction*. 2nd ed. Winona Lake, IN: Eisenbrauns, 2001.

Fohrer, Georg. *Introduction to the Old Testament*. Translated by David Green. London: SPCK, 1970.

Frankena, Rintje. "The Vassal Treaties of Esarhaddon and the Dating of Deuteronomy." OtSt 14 (1965) 122–54.

Freedman, David Noel. "Canon of the OT." In *IDBSup*, 130–36.

———. "The Law and the Prophets." In *Congress Volume: Bonn 1962*, edited by Gary W. Anderson et al., 250–66. Supplements to Vetus Testamentum 9. Leiden: Brill, 1962.

———. *The Unity of the Hebrew Bible*. Distinguished Senior Faculty Lecture Series. Ann Arbor, MI: University of Michigan Press, 1993.

Fretheim, Terence E. *The Pentateuch*. Interpreting Biblical Texts. Nashville: Abingdon, 1996.

Fried, Lisbeth S. "The High Places (*Bamôt*) and the Reforms of Hezekiah and Josiah: An Archaeological Investigation." *JAOS* 122 (2002) 437–65.

Friedman, Richard Elliott. "The Deuteronomistic School." In *Fortunate the Eyes That See: Essays in Honor of David Noel Freedman in Celebration of His Seventieth Birthday*, edited by Astrid B. Beck et al., 70–80. Grand Rapids: Eerdmans, 1995.

Fritz, Volkmar. *1 & 2 Kings*. A Continental Commentary. Translated by Anselm Hagedorn. Minneapolis: Fortress, 2003.

Galil, Gershon. "The Sons of Judah and the Sons of Aaron in Biblical Historiography." *VT* 35 (1985) 488–95.

Gammie, John G. "Loci of the Melchizedek Tradition of Genesis 14:18–20." *JBL* 90 (1971) 385–96.

Geddes, Alexander. *The Holy Bible: Or the Books Accounted Sacred by Jews and Christians; Otherwise Called the Books of the Old and New Covenants I*. London: Davis, 1792.

Gesenius, William. *Gesenius' Hebrew and Chaldee Lexicon to the Old Testament Scriptures*. Translated by Samuel Prideaux Tregelles. Grand Rapids: Eerdmans, 1981.

———. *Gesenius' Hebrew Grammar*. Edited by E. Kautzsch. Translated by A. E. Cowley. 1910. Reprint, Mineola, NY: Dover, 2006.

Giblin, Charles H. "Structural Patterns in Jos 24,1–25." *CBQ* 26 (1964) 50–69.

Gignilliat, Mark S. *A Brief History of Old Testament Criticism: From Benedict Spinoza to Brevard Childs*. Grand Rapids: Zondervan, 2012.

Goldstein, Bernard R., and Alan Cooper. "The Festivals of Israel and Judah and the Literary History of the Pentateuch." *JAOS* 110 (1990) 19–31.

Grabb, Lester L. *Prophets, Diviners, and Sages: A Socio-Historical Study of Religious Specialists in Ancient Israel*. Valley Forge, PA: Trinity, 1995.

———. "Scribes and Synagogues." In *The Oxford Handbook of Biblical Studies*, edited by J. W. Rogerson and Judith M. Lieu, 362–71. New York: Oxford University Press, 2006.

Graf, Karl H. "Die sogenannte Grundschrift des Pentateuchs." In *Archiv für wissenschaftliche Erforschung des Alten Testaments* I, 466–77. Halle: n.p., 1869.

Gray, George Buchanan. *Numbers*. ICC. Edinburgh: T. & T. Clark, 2001.

Bibliography

Greenberg, Moshe. "The Decalogue Tradition Critically Examined." In *The Ten Commandments in History and Tradition*, edited by B. Segal and G. Levi, 83–120. Jerusalem: Magnes, 1985.

Gros Louis, Kenneth R. R., et al. *Literary Interpretations of Biblical Narratives*. 2 vols. Nashville: Abingdon, 1974.

Gunn, David M. "New Directions in the Study of Hebrew Narrative." *JSOT* 39 (1987) 65–75.

Guthrie Jr., Harvey H. "Tithe." In *IDB* 4:654–55.

Haag, Herbert. "Gideon–Jerubbaal–Abimelek." *ZAW* 79 (1967) 305–14.

Hagedorn, Anselm C. "Deut 17,8–13: Procedure for Cases of Pollution?" *ZAW* 115 (2003) 538–56.

Halbe, Jörn. "Erwägungen zu Ursprung und Wesen des Massotfestes." *ZAW* 87 (1975) 324–46.

———. "Passa-Massot im deuteronomischen Festkalender: Komposition, Entstehung und Programme von Dtn 16:1–8." *ZAW* 87 (1975) 147–68.

Halpern, Baruch. "The Centralization Formula in Deuteronomy." *VT* 31 (1981) 20–38.

———. "Jerusalem and the Lineages in the Seventh Century BCE: Kinship and the Rise of Individual Moral Liability." In *Law and Ideology in Monarchic Israel*, edited by Baruch Halpern and Deborah W. Hobson, 11–107. Journal for the Study of the Old Testament Supplement Series 124. Sheffield, UK: JSOT, 1991.

Hamilton, Victor P. *The Book of Genesis: Chapters 1–17*. NICOT. Grand Rapids: Eerdmans, 1990.

———. *Exodus: An Exegetical Commentary*. Grand Rapids: Baker, 2011.

Haran, Menahem. "Festivals." In *EncJud* 6:1237–46.

———. *Temples and Temple Service in Ancient Israel: An Inquiry into the Character of Cult Phenomena and the Historical Setting of the Priestly School*. 1978. Reprint. Winona Lake, IN: Eisenbrauns, 1985.

Harrelson, Walter. *The Ten Commandments and Human Rights*. Overtures to Biblical Theology. Philadelphia: Fortress, 1989.

Hartley, John E. *Leviticus*. WBC 4. Dallas: Baker, 1992.

Hayes, John H., and Frederick Prussner. *Old Testament Theology: Its History and Development*. Atlanta: John Knox, 1985.

Heard, R. Christopher. "Narrative Criticism and the Hebrew Scriptures: A Review and Assessment." *ResQ* 38 (1996) 29–43.

Heiser, Michael S. "Monotheism, Polytheism, Monolatry, or Henotheism? Toward an Assessment of Divine Plurality in the Hebrew Bible." *BBR* 18 (2008) 1–30.

Hermann, Siegfried. "Die Konstruktive Restauration, Das Deuteronomium als Mitte biblischer Theologie." In *Probleme biblischer Theologie: Festschrift for Gerhard von Rad*, edited by Hans Wolff, 155–70. Munich: Kaiser, 1971.

Herron, Roy Brasfield. "The Land, the Law, and the Poor." *WW* 6 (1986) 76–84.

Hertzberg, Hans Wilhelm. *I and II Samuel: A Commentary*. OTL. Philadelphia: Westminster, 1964.

Hess, Richard S. *Israelite Religions: An Archaeology and Biblical Survey*. Grand Rapids: Baker, 2007.

Hjelm, Ingrid. "Cult Centralization as a Device of Cult Control." *SJOT* 13 (1999) 298–309.

Hobbs, T. Raymond. *2 Kings*. WBC 13. Waco: Word, 1985.

Holladay, William L. "Elusive Deuteronomists, Jeremiah, and Proto-Deuteronomy." *CBQ* 66 (2004) 55–77.

Bibliography

Horton, Fred L., Jr. *The Melchizedek Tradition: A Critical Examination of the Sources to the Fifth Century A.D. and in the Epistle to the Hebrews.* Cambridge: Cambridge University Press, 1976.

Hyatt, J. Philip. "The Deuteronomic Edition of Jeremiah." In *Vanderbilt Studies in the Humanities,* edited by Richmond C. Beatty et al., 71-95. Nashville: Vanderbilt University Press, 1951.

———. *Exodus.* NCBC. Grand Rapids: Eerdmans, 1983.

———. "Jeremiah and Deuteronomy." *JNES* 1 (1942) 156-73.

The Interpreter's Dictionary of the Bible. 4 vols. Edited by George Arthur Buttrick. Nashville: Abingdon, 1962.

The Interpreter's Dictionary of the Bible. Supplementary Volume. Edited by Keith Crim. Nashville: Abingdon, 1976.

Jagersma, Henk. "The Tithe in the Old Testament." In *Remembering All the Way: A Collection of Old Testament Studies Published on the Occasion of the Fortieth Anniversary of the Oudtestamentische Werkgezelschap in Nederland,* edited by A. S. van der Woude, 116-28. Oudtestamentische Studiën 21. Leiden: Brill, 1981.

Janzen, J. Gerald. "The Character of the Calf and Its Cult in Exodus 32." *CBQ* 52 (1990) 597-607.

Jepsen, Alfred. *Die Quellen des Königsbuches.* 2nd ed. Halle: Niemeyer, 1956.

Johnstone, William. "The Two Theological Versions of the Passover Pericope in Exodus." In *Text as Pretext: Essays in Honour of Robert Davidson,* edited by Robert P. Carroll, 160-78. Journal for the Study of the Old Testament Supplement Series 138. Sheffield, UK: JSOT, 1992.

Joüon, Paul. *A Grammar of Biblical Hebrew.* 1923. Translated by T. Muraoka. Rome: Pontifical Biblical Institute, 2005.

Kaiser, Otto. "The Law as Center of the Hebrew Bible." In *"Sha'arie Talmon": Studies in the Bible, Qumran, and the Ancient Near East Presented to Shemaryahu Talmon,* edited by Michael Fishbane and Emanuel Tov, 93-103. Winona Lake, IN: Eisenbrauns, 1992.

Kaufman, Stephen. "The Structure of the Deuteronomic Law." *Maarav* 1/2 (1979) 105-58.

Kaufmann, Yehezkel. *The Religion of Israel: From Its Beginnings to the Babylonian Exile.* Translated by Moshe Greenberg. New York: Schocken, 1972.

Keszler, Werner. "Die Literarische, Historische und Theologische Problematik des Dekalogs. *VT* 7 (1957) 1-17.

Keulen, Percy S. F. van. *Manasseh through the Eyes of the Deuteronomists: The Manasseh Account (2 Kings 21:1-18) & the Final Chapters of the Deuteronomistic History.* Oudtestamentische studiën. Leiden: Brill, 1996.

Kilchör, Benjamin. "Passah und Mazzot—Ein Überblick über die Forschung seit dem 19. Jahrhundert." *Bib* 94 (2013) 340-67.

Kim, Young Hye. "The Finalization of Num 25,1-5." *ZAW* 122 (2010) 260-64.

Kitchen, Kenneth A. "The Fall and Rise of Covenant, Law and Treaty." *TynBul* 40 (1989) 118-35.

———. *On the Reliability of the Old Testament.* Grand Rapids: Eerdmans, 2003.

Klein, Ralph. *1 Samuel.* WBC 10. 2nd ed. Nashville: Thomas Nelson, 2008.

Kline, Meredith G. *Treaty of the Great King: Covenantal Structure of Deuteronomy.* Grand Rapids: Eerdmans, 1963.

Klingbeil, Gerald A. "Priests and Levites." In *DOTHB* 811-19.

Knauf, Ernest Axel. "Does 'Deuteronomistic Historiography' (DH) Exist?" In *Israel Constructs Its History: Deuteronomistic Historiography in Recent Research,* edited by

Albert de Pury et al., 388–98. Journal for the Study of the Old Testament Supplement Series 306. Sheffield, UK: Sheffield Academic, 2000.

Knoppers, Gary N. "Aaron's Calf and Jeroboam's Calves." In *Fortunate the Eyes That See: Essays in Honor of David Noel Freedman in Celebration of His Seventieth Birthday*, edited by Astrid B. Beck et al., 92–104. Grand Rapids: Eerdmans, 1995.

———. "The Deuteronomist and the Deuteronomic Law of the King: A Reexamination of a Relationship." *ZAW* 108 (1996) 329–46.

———. "Rethinking the Relationship between Deuteronomy and the Deuteronomistic History: The Case of Kings." *CBQ* 63 (2001) 393–415.

———. *Two Nations under God: The Deuteronomistic History of Solomon and the Dual Monarchies*. 2 vols. Harvard Semitic Monographs 52/53. Atlanta: Scholars, 1993–94.

Koehler, Ludwig, et al. *The Hebrew and Aramaic Lexicon of the Old Testament*. Translated by M. E. J. Richardson. Leiden: Brill, 1999.

Koopmans, William T. *Joshua 24 as Poetic Narrative*. Journal for the Study of the Old Testament Supplement Series 93. Sheffield, UK: JSOT, 1990.

Kratz, Reinhard G. *The Composition of the Narrative Books of the Old Testament*. Translated by John Bowden. London: T. & T. Clark, 2005.

———. "The Growth of the Old Testament." In *The Oxford Handbook of Biblical Studies*, edited by John W. Rogerson and Judith Lieu, 459–88. Oxford: Oxford University Press, 2006.

Kraus, Hans-Joachim. "Zur Geschichte des Passah-Massot-Festes im Alten Testament." *EvT* 18 (1958) 47–67.

———. *Gottesdienst in Israel: Grundriss einer Geschichte des alttestamentlichen Gottesdienstes*. Beiträge zur evangelischen Theologie 19. Munich: Kaiser, 1962.

Krüger, Thomas. "Anmerkungen zur Frage nach den Redaktionen der grossen Erzählwerke im Alten Testament." In *Les dernières rédactions du Pentateuque, de L'Hexateuque et de L'Ennéateuque*, edited by Thomas Römer and Konrad Schmid, 46–66. Bibliotheca ephemeridum theologicarum lovaniensium 203. Leuven: Peeters, 2007.

Kutsch, Ernst. "Erwägungen zur Geschichte der Passafeier und des Massot-festes." *ZTK* 55 (1958) 1–35.

Lasine, Stuart. "Manasseh as Villain and Scapegoat." In *The New Literary Criticism and the Hebrew Bible*, edited by J. Cheryl Exum and David J. A. Clines, 163–83. Journal for the Study of the Old Testament Supplement Series 143. Sheffield, UK: JSOT, 1993.

LaSor, William, et al. *Old Testament Survey: The Message, Form, and Background of the Old Testament*. 2nd ed. Grand Rapids: Eerdmans, 1996.

Latvus, Kari. *God, Anger and Ideology: The Anger of God in Joshua and Judges in Relation to Deuteronomy and the Priestly Writings*. Journal for the Study of the Old Testament Supplement Series 279. Sheffield, UK: Sheffield Academic, 1998.

Leithart, Peter J. "Attendants of Yahweh's House: Priesthood in the Old Testament." *JSOT* 85 (1999) 3–24.

Leuchter, Mark. "Why is the Song of Moses in the Book of Deuteronomy?" *VT* 57 (2007) 295–317.

Levenson, Jon D. *The Hebrew Bible, the Old Testament, and Historical Criticism: Jews and Christians in Biblical Studies*. Louisville: Westminster John Knox, 1993.

Levine, Baruch A. "The Cultic Scene in Biblical Religion: Hebrew 'al panai and a Ban on Divine Images." In *In Pursuit of Meaning: Collected Studies of Baruch A. Levine*, 1:283–99. Winona Lake, IN: 2011.

———. *Numbers 1–20*. AB 4A. New York: Doubleday, 1993.

Bibliography

———. *Numbers 21–36*. AB 4B. New York: Doubleday, 2000.
Levinson, Bernard M. *Deuteronomy and the Hermeneutics of Legal Innovation*. Oxford: Oxford University Press, 1997.
———. "The Hermeneutics of Tradition in Deuteronomy: A Reply to J. G. McConville." *JBL* 119 (2000) 269–86.
———. "The Reconceptualization of Kingship in Deuteronomy and the Deuteronomistic History's Transformation of Torah." *VT* 51 (2001) 511–34.
———. "Recovering the Lost Original Meaning of ולא תכסה עליו (Deuteronomy 13:9)." *JBL* 115 (1996) 601–20.
———. "The Right Chorale: From the Poetics to the Hermeneutics of the Hebrew Bible." In *"Not in Heaven": Coherence and Complexity in Biblical Narrative*, edited by Jason P. Rosenblatt and Joseph C. Sitterson, Jr., 130–48. Indiana Studies in Biblical Literature. Bloomington, IN: Indiana University Press, 1991.
Linafelt, Tod. "Prolegomena to Meaning, or, What Is 'Literary' about the Torah?" *TS* 69 (2008) 62–79.
Lincicum, David. *Paul and the Early Jewish Encounter with Deuteronomy*. Grand Rapids: Baker Academic, 2013.
Lindars, Barnabas. "Gideon and Kingship." *JTS* 16 (1965) 315–26.
Lohfink, Norbert. "The Cult Reform of Josiah of Judah: 2 Kings 22–23 as a Source for the History of Israelite Religion." In *Ancient Israelite Religion: Essays in Honor of Frank Moore Cross*, edited by Patrick D. Miller et al., 459–75. Philadelphia: Fortress, 1987.
———. "Culture Shock and Theology." *BTB* 7 (1977) 12–22.
———. "The Decalogue in Deuteronomy 5." In *Theology of the Pentateuch: Themes of the Priestly Narrative and Deuteronomy*. Translated by Linda M. Maloney, 248–64. Minneapolis: Fortress, 1994.
———. "Zur deuteronomischen Zentralisationsformel." In *Studien zum Deuteronomium und zur deuteronomistischen Literatur II*, 147–77. Stuttgart: Katholisches Bibelwerk, 1991.
———. *Das Deuteronomium: Entstehung, Gestalt und Botschaft*. Bibliotheca ephemeridum theologicarum lovaniensium 68. Leuven: Uitgeverij Peeters, 1985.
———. "Deuteronomy." In *IDBSup* 229–32.
———. "Distribution of the Functions of Power: The Laws concerning Public Offices in Deuteronomy 16:18—18:22." In *A Song of Power and the Power of Song: Essays on the Book of Deuteronomy*, edited by Duane L. Christensen, 336–52. Sources for Biblical and Theological Study 3. Winona Lake, IN: Eisenbrauns, 1993.
———. "Ich bin Jahwe, dein Arzt." In *"Ich will euer Gott werden." Beispiele bibliscer Redens von Gott*, edited by Norbert Lohfink et al., Stuttgarter Bibelstudien 100, 29–41. Stuttgart: Verlag Katholisches Bibelwerk, 1981.
———. "Kultzentralisation und Deuteronomium: Zu einem Buch von Eleonore Reuter." In *Zeitschrift für altorientalische und biblische Rechtsgeschichte*, edited by Eckart Otto, 1:117–48. Wiesbaden: Harrassowitz, 1995.
———. *Lectures on Deuteronomy 12–14*. Rome: Pontifical Biblical Institute, 1983.
———. "Recent Discussion on 2 Kings 22–23: The State of the Question." In *A Song of Power and the Power of Song: Essays on the Book of Deuteronomy*, edited by Duane L. Christensen, 36–61. Sources for Biblical and Theological Study 3. Winona Lake, IN: Eisenbrauns, 1993.
———. "Die Sicherung der Wirksamkeit des Gotteswortes durch das Prinzip der Schriftlichkeit der Tora und durch das Prinzip der Gewaltenteilung nach den

Ämtergesetzen des Buches Deuteronomium (Dt 16,18–18,22)." In *Testimonium Veritati: Festchrift Wilhelm Kempf*, edited by H. Wolter, 143–55. Frankfurt: Knecht, 1971.

———. "Was There a Deuteronomistic Movement?" In *Those Elusive Deuteronomists: The Phenomenon of Pan-Deuteronomism*, edited by Linda S. Schearing and Steven L. McKenzie, 36–66. Journal for the Study of the Old Testament Supplement Series 268. Sheffield, UK: Sheffield Academic, 1999.

Long, Burke O. *2 Kings*. FOTL 10. Grand Rapids: Eerdmans, 1991.

Lundbom, Jack R. *Deuteronomy: A Commentary*. Grand Rapids: Eerdmans, 2013.

———. "Lawbook of the Josianic Reform." *CBQ* 38 (1976) 293–302.

Margalith, Othniel. "*M^eKĒRŌTĒHEM* (Genesis XLIX 5)." *VT* 34 (1984) 101–2.

Master, Jonathan. "Exodus 32 as an Argument for Traditional Theism." *JETS* 45 (2002) 585–98.

Mauchline, John. *1 and 2 Samuel*. NCBC. London: Oliphants, 1971.

Mayes, Andrew D. H. "Deuteronomistic Ideology and the Theology of the Old Testament." In *Israel Constructs Its History: Deuteronomistic Historiography in Recent Research*, edited by Albert de Pury et al., 456–80. Journal for the Study of the Old Testament Supplement Series 306. Sheffield, UK: Sheffield Academic, 2000.

———. *Deuteronomy*. NCBC. London: Oliphants, 1979.

———. "On Describing the Purpose of Deuteronomy." *JSOT* 58 (1993) 13–33.

McBride, Samuel Dean, Jr. "Deuteronomic Name Theology." Ph.D. diss., Harvard University, 1969.

———. "The Essence of Orthodoxy: Deuteronomy 5:6–10 and Exodus 20:2–6." *Int* 60 (2006) 133–51.

———. "Polity of the Covenant People: The Book of Deuteronomy." *Int* 41 (1987) 229–44.

McCarter, P. Kyle, Jr. *I Samuel*. AB 8. New York: Doubleday, 1980.

———. *II Samuel*. AB 9. New York: Doubleday, 1984.

McCarthy, Dennis J. *Treaty and Covenant: A Study in Form in the Ancient Oriental Documents and in the Old Testament*. Analecta biblica 21. Rome: Pontificio Instituto Biblico, 1963.

McConville, J. Gordon. "Abraham and Melchizedek: Horizons in Genesis 14." In *He Swore an Oath: Biblical Themes from Genesis 12–50*. 2nd ed., edited by Richard S. Hess et al., 93–188. Grand Rapids: Baker, 1994.

———. *Deuteronomy*. Apollos Old Testament Commentary. Downers Grove, IL: InterVarsity, 2002.

———. "Deuteronomy's Unification of Passover and Maṣṣôt: A Response to Bernard M. Levinson." *JBL* 119 (2000) 47–58.

———. *God and Earthly Power. An Old Testament Political Theology: Genesis–Kings*. Library of Hebrew Bible 454. London: T. & T. Clark, 2006.

———. "God's 'Name' and God's 'Glory.'" *TynBul* 30 (1979) 149–63.

———. *Judgment and Promise: An Introduction of the Book of Jeremiah*. Winona Lake, IN: Eisenbrauns, 1993.

———. "King and Messiah in Deuteronomy and the Deuteronomistic History." In *King and Messiah in Israel and the Ancient Near East: Proceedings of the Oxford Old Testament Seminar*, edited by John Day, 271–95. Journal for the Study of the Old Testament Supplement Series 270. Sheffield, UK: Sheffield Academic, 1998.

———. *Law and Theology in Deuteronomy*. Journal for the Study of the Old Testament Supplement Series 33. Sheffield, UK: JSOT, 1984.

Bibliography

———. "Priesthood in Joshua to Kings," *VT* 49 (1999) 73–87.
———. "Time, Place and the Deuteronomic Altar-Law." In *Time and Place in Deuteronomy*, edited by David J. A. Clines and Philip R. Davies, 89–139. Journal for the Study of the Old Testament Supplement Series 179. Sheffield, UK: Sheffield Academic, 1994.
McKenzie, Tracy J. *Idolatry in the Pentateuch: An Innertextual Strategy*. Eugene, OR: Pickwick, 2010.
Mendenhall, George E. "Ancient Oriental and Biblical Law." *BA* 17 (1954) 26–44.
———. "Covenant Forms in Israelite Traditions." *BA* 17 (1954) 50–76.
Merrill, Eugene H. *Deuteronomy*. NAC 4. Nashville: Broadman & Holman, 1994.
Milgrom, Jacob. *Leviticus 1–16*. AB 3A. New York: Doubleday, 1991.
———. *Leviticus 17–22*. AB 3B. New York: Anchor Yale Bible, 2000.
———. *Leviticus 23–27*. AB 3C. New York: Doubleday, 2001.
———. *Numbers*. JPSTC. Philadelphia: Jewish Publication Society: 1989.
Miller, Patrick D. "Constitution or Instruction? The Purpose of Deuteronomy." In *Constituting the Community: Studies on the Polity of Ancient Israel in Honor of S. Dean McBride Jr.*, edited by John T. Strong and Steven S. Tuell, 125–41. Winona Lake, IN: Eisenbrauns, 2005.
———. *Deuteronomy*. IBC. Louisville: John Knox, 1990.
———. *The Religion of Ancient Israel*. Library of Ancient Israel. Louisville: Westminster John Knox, 2000.
———. *The Ten Commandments*. IBC. Louisville: Westminster John Knox, 2009.
Moeller, Henry R. "Four Old Testament Problem Terms." *BT* 13 (1962) 219–22.
Monroe, Lauren A. S. *Josiah's Reform and the Dynamics of Defilement: Israelite Rites of Violence and the Making of a Biblical Text*. New York: Oxford University Press, 2011.
Moran, William. "Ancient Near Eastern Background of the Love of God in Deuteronomy." *CBQ* 25 (1963) 77–87.
Morrow, William S. "'To Set the Name' in the Deuteronomic Centralization Formula: A Case of Cultural Hybridity." *JSS* 60 (2010) 365–83.
Moulton, Warren J. "Passover." In *DB* 3:684–92.
Mowinckel, Sigmund. *Zur Komposition des Buches Jeremia*. Christiania: Dewed, 1914.
———. *Tetrateuch, Pentateuch, Hexateuch: Die Berichte über die Landnahme in den drei Altisraelitischen Geschichtswerken*. Berlin: Töpelmann, 1964.
Moyise, Steve, and Maarten J. J. Menken. *Deuteronomy in the New Testament: The New Testament and the Scriptures of Israel*. Library of New Testament Studies 358. London: T. & T. Clark, 2007.
Muilenburg, James. "Form Criticism and Beyond." *JBL* 88 (1969) 1–18.
Na'aman, Nadav. "The Law of the Altar in Deuteronomy and the Cultic Site Near Shechem." In *Rethinking the Foundations: Historiography in the Ancient World and in the Bible: Feschrift John Van Seters*, edited by John Van Seters et al., 141–62. Beihefte für Zeitschrift fur die alttestamentliche Wissenschaft 294. Berlin: de Gruyter, 2000.
Nelson, Richard D. *Deuteronomy*. OTL. Louisville: Westminster John Knox, 2002.
———. *The Double Redaction of the Deuteronomistic History*. Journal for the Study of the Old Testament Supplement Series 18. Sheffield, UK: JSOT, 1981.
———. "The Double Redaction of the Deuteronomistic History: The Case Is Still Compelling," *JSOT* 29 (2005) 319–37.
———. "Josiah in the Book of Joshua." *JBL* 100 (1981) 531–40.
———. *Raising Up a Faithful Priest: Community and Priesthood in Biblical Theology*. Louisville: Westminster John Knox, 1993.

---. "The Role of the Priesthood in the Deuteronomistic History." In *Congress Volume: Leuven 1989*, edited by John A. Emerton, 132–47. Supplement to Vetus Testamentum 43. Leiden: Brill, 1989.
Newing, Edward G. "The Rhetoric of Hope: The Theological Structure of Genesis–2 Kings." *Colloq* 17 (1985) 1–15.
Nicholson, Ernest. "Centralization of the Cult in Deuteronomy." *VT* 13 (1963) 380–89.
---. *Deuteronomy and Tradition*. Oxford: Blackwell, 1967.
---. *The Pentateuch in the Twentieth Century: The Legacy of Julius Wellhausen*. Oxford: Clarendon, 1998.
Nicole, Emile. "בחר." In *NIDOTTE* 1:638–42.
Niditch, Susan. *Judges*. OTL. Louisville: Westminster John Knox, 2008.
Niehaus, Jeffrey. "Central Sanctuary: Where and When?" *TynBul* 43 (1992) 3–30.
Nielsen, Eduard. *Deuteronomium*. HAT I/6. Tübingen: Mohr, 1995.
---. *Shechem: A Traditio-Historical Investigation*. 2nd ed. Copenhagen: Atelier Elektra, 1959.
Nihan, Christophe. "The Torah between Samaria and Judah: Shechem and Gerizim in Deuteronomy and Joshua." In *The Pentateuch as Torah: New Methods for Understanding Its Promulgation and Acceptance*, edited by Gary N. Knoppers and Bernard M. Levinson, 187–223. Winona Lake, IN: Eisenbrauns, 2007.
Noth, Martin. *Das Buch Josua*. HAT 7. Tübingen: Mohr Siebeck, 1953.
---. *Deuteronomistic History*. Journal for the Study of the Old Testament Supplement Series 15. Translated by Jane Doull. Sheffield, UK: JSOT, 1981.
---. *Exodus*. Translated by James S. Bowden. OTL. Philadelphia: Westminster, 1962.
---. *A History of Pentateuchal Traditions*. Translated by Bernhard W. Anderson. Englewood Cliffs, NJ: Prentice-Hall, 1972.
---. *Numbers*. Translated by James D. Martin. OTL. Philadelphia: Westminster, 1968.
North, Robert G. "עשׂר." In *TDOT* 11:404–8.
Nurmela, Risto. *The Levites: Their Emergence as a Second-Class Priesthood*. South Florida Studies in the History of Judaism. Atlanta: Scholars, 1998.
O'Brien, Mark A. "The Book of Deuteronomy." *CurBS* 3 (1995) 95–128.
Oestreicher, Theodor. *Das deuteronomische Grundgesetz*. Beiträge zur Förderung christlicher Theologie 27. Gütersloh: Bertelsmann, 1923.
Olson, Dennis T. *Deuteronomy and the Death of Moses*. Overtures to Biblical Theology. Minneapolis: Fortress, 1994.
Oswalt, John N. "בחר." In *TWOT* 100–101.
Otto, Eckart. "Altorientalische Kontexte der deuteronomischen Namenstheologie." *ZAW* 13 (2007) 237–48.
---. *Das Deuteronomium: Politische Theologie und Rechtsreform in Juda und Assyrien*. Beihefte zur Zeitschrift für die alttestamentliche Wissenschaft 284. Berlin: de Gruyter, 2000.
---. *Das Deuteronomium im Pentateuch und Hexateuch: Studien zur Literaturgeschichte von Pentateuch und Hexateuch im Lichte des Deuteronomiumrahmens*. Forschungen zum Alten Testament 30. Tübingen: Mohr Siebeck, 2000.
---. "פסח." In *TDOT* 12:1–23.
Pakkala, Juha. "Deuteronomy and 1–2 Kings in the Redaction of the Pentateuch and Former Prophets." In *Deuteronomy in the Pentateuch, Hexateuch, and the Deuteronomistic History*, edited by Konrad Schmid and Raymond F. Person, Jr., 133–62. Forschungen zum Alten Testament 2. Reihe 56; Tübingen: Mohr Siebeck, 2012.

Bibliography

Patrick, Dale. *Old Testament Law*. Atlanta: John Knox, 1985.
———. *The Rhetoric of Revelation in the Hebrew Bible*. Overtures to Biblical Theology. Minneapolis: Fortress, 1999.
Pedersen, Johannes. *Israel: Its Life and Culture*. London: Oxford University Press, 1973.
———. "Passahfest und Passahlegende." *ZAW* 52 (1934) 161–75.
Person, Raymond F. *The Deuteronomic School: History, Social Setting, and Literature*. Society of Biblical Literature Studies in Biblical Literature 2. Atlanta: Society of Biblical Literature, 2002.
———. *Second Zechariah and the Deuteronomic School*. Journal for the Study of the Old Testament Supplement Series 167. Sheffield, UK: JSOT, 1993.
Peter, Michal. "Wer sprach den Segen nach Genesis XIV 19 über Abraham aus?" *VT* 29 (1979) 114–20.
Pitkänen, Pekka. *Central Sanctuary and Centralization of Worship in Ancient Israel: From the Settlement to the Building of Solomon's Temple*. Gorgias Dissertations: Near Eastern Studies 5. Piscataway, NJ: Gorgias, 2003.
Polzin, Robert. *Biblical Structuralism: Method and Subjectivity in the Study of Ancient Texts*, edited by William A. Beardslee. SEMEIA Supplement. Philadelphia: Fortress, 1977.
———. *David and the Deuteronomist: A Literary Study of the Deuteronomistic History*. Indiana Studies in Biblical Literature. Bloomington, IN: Indiana University Press, 1993.
———. *Moses and the Deuteronomist: A Literary Study of the Deuteronomic History*. New York: Seabury, 1980.
———. *Samuel and the Deuteronomist: A Literary Study of the Deuteronomistic History*. Indiana Studies in Biblical Literature. Bloomington, IN: Indiana University Press, 1993.
Preuss, Horst D. *Deuteronomium*. EdF 164. Darmstadt: Wissenschaftliche Buchgesellschaft, 1982.
Propp, William H. C. *Exodus 19–40*. AB 2B. New York: Yale University Press, 2006.
Rad, Gerhard von. *Deuteronomy*. Translated by Dorothea Barton. OTL. Philadelphia: Westminster, 1966.
———. "The Form-Critical Problem of the Hexateuch." In *Problem of the Hexateuch and Other Essays*. Translated by E. W. Trueman Dicken, 1–78 London: Oliver & Boyd, 1966.
———. *Genesis*. Translated by John H. Marks. OTL. Philadelphia: Westminster, 1972.
———. *God at Work in Israel*. Translated by John H. Marks. Nashville: Abingdon, 1980.
———. *Old Testament Theology*. Translated by David M. G. Stalker. 1962–1965. Reprint, Peabody, MA: Prince, 2005.
———. *Studies in Deuteronomy*. Translated by David M. G. Stalker. London: SCM, 1961.
Rainey, Anson F. "Sacrifice and Offerings." In *ZPEB* 5:194–211.
Rehm, Merlin D. "Levites and Priests." In *ABD* 4:297–310.
Rendtorff, Rolf. "The Paradigm Is Changing: Hopes—and Fears." *BibInt* 1 (1993) 34–53.
Reuter, Eleonore. *Kultzentralisation: Entstehung und Theologie von Dtn 12*. Bonnerbiblische Beiträge 87. Frankfurt: Anton Hain, 1993.
Richter, Sandra L. *The Deuteronomistic History and the Name Theology: l^{e}šakkēn š^{e}mô šām in the Bible and the Ancient Near East*. Beihefte zür Zeitschrift fur de alttestamentliche Wissenschaft 318. Berlin: De Gruyter, 2002.
———. "The Place of the Name in Deuteronomy." *VT* 57 (2007) 342–66.

Bibliography

———. "Placing the Name, Pushing the Paradigm: A Decade with the Deuteronomistic Name Formula." In *Deuteronomy in the Pentateuch, Hexateuch, and the Deuteronomistic History*, edited by Konrad Schmid and Raymond F. Person, Jr. 64–78. Forschungen zum Alten Testament 2. Reihe 56. Tübingen: Mohr Siebeck, 2012.

Roberts, Kathryn L. "Exodus 20:1–6." *Int* 60 (2006) 60–62.

Robson, James. "The Literary Composition of Deuteronomy." In *Interpreting Deuteronomy: Issues and Approaches*, edited by David G. Firth and Philip S. Johnston, 19–59. Downers Grove, IL: InterVarsity, 2012.

Rofé, Alexander. "The Book of Deuteronomy: A Summary." In *Deuteronomy: Issues and Interpretation*, edited by David J. Reimer, 1–13. Old Testament Studies. London: T. & T. Clark, 2002.

———. "The Strata of Law about the Centralization of Worship in Deuteronomy and the History of the Deuteronomic Movement." In *Congress Volume: Uppsala 1971*, edited by P. A. H. de Boer et al., 221–26. Supplements to Vetus Testamentum 22. Leiden: Brill, 1972.

Rogerson, John W. *W. M. L. de Wette, Founder of Modern Biblical Criticism: An Intellectual Biography*. Journal for the Study of the Old Testament Supplement Series 126. Sheffield, UK: Sheffield Academic, 1992.

Römer, Thomas. "The Book of Deuteronomy." In *The History of Israel's Traditions: The Heritage of Martin Noth*, edited by Steven L. McKenzie and M. Patrick Graham, 178–212. Journal for the Study of the Old Testament Supplement Series 182. Sheffield, UK: Sheffield Academic, 1994.

———. "La construction du Pentateuque, de l'Hexateuque et de l'Ennéateuque: Investigations préliminaries sur la formation des grandes ensembles littéraires de la Bible hébraïque." In *Les dernières rédactions du Pentateuque, de L'Hexateuque et de L'Ennéateuque*, edited by Thomas Römer and Konrad Schmid, 9–34. Bibliotheca ephemeridum theologicarum lovaniensium 203. Leuven: Peeters, 2007.

———. "Cult Centralization in Deuteronomy 12: Between Deuteronomistic History and Pentateuch." In *Das Deuteronomium zwischen Pentateuch und Deuteronomistischem Geschichtswerk*, edited by Eckart Otto and Reinhard Achenbach, 168–80. Forschungen zur Religion und Literatur des Alten und Neuen Testaments 206. Göttingen: Vandenhoeck & Ruprecht, 2004.

———. "Le Deutéronome à la quête des origins." In *Le Pentateuque: Débats et recherches*, edited by Pierre Haudebert, 65–98. Lectio divina 151. Paris: Cerf, 1992.

———. "The Form-Critical Problem of the So-Called Deuteronomistic History." In *The Changing Face of Form Criticism for the Twenty-First Century*, edited by Marvin A. Sweeney and Ehud Ben Zvi, 240–52. Grand Rapids: Eerdmans, 2003.

———. *The So-Called Deuteronomistic History: A Sociological, Historical, and Literary Introduction*. London: T. & T. Clark, 2007.

Römer, Thomas, and Albert de Pury. "Deuteronomistic Historiography (DH) History of Research and Debated Issues." In *Israel Constructs Its History: Deuteronomistic Historiography in Recent Research*, edited by Albert de Pury et al., 24–141. Journal for the Study of the Old Testament Supplement Series 306. Sheffield, UK: Sheffield Academic, 2000.

Römer, Thomas, and Konrad Schmid. *Les dernières rédactions du Pentateuque, de L'Hexateuque et de L'Ennéateuque*. Bibliotheca ephemeridum theologicarum lovaniensium 203. Leuven: Peeters: 2007.

Bibliography

———. "Introduction: Pentateuque, Hexateuque, Ennéateuque: Exposé du problème." In *Les dernières rédactions du Pentateuque, de L'Hexateuque et de L'Ennéateuque*, edited by Thomas Römer and Konrad Schmid, 1–7. Bibliotheca ephemeridum theologicarum lovaniensium 203. Leuven: Peeters, 2007.

Rooker, Mark. *The Ten Commandments: Ethics for the Twenty-First Century*. NAC Studies in Bible & Theology. Nashville: B. & H., 2010.

Rose, Martin. *Deuteronomist und Jahwist: Untersuchungen zu den Beruhrungspunkten beider Literaturwerke*. Abhandlungen zur Theologie des Alten und Neuen Testaments 67. Zurich: Theologischer Verlag, 1981.

———. "Deuteronomistic Ideology and Theology of the Old Testament." In *Israel Constructs Its History: Deuteronomistic Historiography in Recent Research*, edited by Albert de Pury et al., 424–55. Journal for the Study of the Old Testament Supplement Series 306. Sheffield, UK: Sheffield Academic, 2000.

Rösel, Hartmut N. "Why 2 Kings 17 Does Not Constitute a Chapter of Reflection in the 'Deuteronomistic History.'" *JBL* 128 (2009) 85–90.

Rost, Leonhard. "Weidewechsel und altisraelitischen Festkalendar." *ZDPV* 66 (1943) 205–16.

Rowley, Harold H. "Hezekiah's Reform and Rebellion." *BJRL* 44 (1961–62) 395–431.

———. "Papyri from Elephantine." In *Documents from Old Testament Times*, edited by D. Winton Thomas, 256–69. New York: Thomas Nelson, 1958.

———. "The Prophet Jeremiah and the Book of Deuteronomy." In *Studies in Old Testament Prophecy: Festschrift Theodore H. Robinson*, edited by Harold H. Rowley, 157–74. Edinburgh: T. & T. Clark, 1950.

———. *Worship in Ancient Israel: Its Forms and Meaning*. Philadelphia: Fortress, 1967.

———. "Zadok and Nehustan." *JBL* 58 (1939) 113–41.

Ryken, Leland, and Tremper Longman III, eds. *A Complete Literary Guide to the Bible*. Grand Rapids: Zondervan, 1993.

Rylaarsdam, J. C. "Passover." In *IDB* 3:663–68.

Sailhamer, John H. *The Pentateuch as Narrative: A Biblical-Theological Commentary*. Library of Biblical Interpretation. Grand Rapids: Zondervan, 1992.

Sanders, Paul. *The Provenance of Deuteronomy 32*. Oudtestamentische Studiën 37. Leiden: Brill, 1996.

Sarna, Nahum M. *Exodus*. JPSTC. Philadelphia: Jewish Publication Society, 1991.

Schenker, Adrian. "Jeroboam and the Division of the Kingdom in the Ancient Septuagint: LXX 3 Kingdoms 12.24 a-z, MT 1 Kings 11–12; 14 and the Deuteronomistic History." In *Israel Constructs Its History: Deuteronomistic Historiography in Recent Research*, edited by Albert de Pury et al., 214–57. Journal for the Study of the Old Testament Supplement Series 306. Sheffield, UK: Sheffield Academic, 2000.

Schmid, Konrad. "Buchtechnische und sachliche Prolegomena zur Enneateuchfrage." In *Auf dem Weg zur Endgestalt von Genesis bis II Regum: Festschrift Hans-Christoph Schmitt zum 65*, edited by Martin Beck and Ulrike Schorn, 1–14. Beihefte zur Zeitschrift für die alttestamentliche Wissenschaft 370. Berlin: de Gruyter, 2006.

———. "Deuteronomy within the 'Deuteronomistic Histories' in Genesis–2 Kings." In *Deuteronomy in the Pentateuch, Hexateuch, and the Deuteronomistic History*, edited by Konrad Schmid and Raymond F. Person, Jr., 8–30. Forschungen zum Alten Testament 2. Reihe 56; Tübingen: Mohr Siebeck, 2012.

———. *Erzväter und Exodus: Untersuchungen zur doppelten Begründung der Ursprünge Israels innerhalb der Geschichtsbücher des Alten Testaments*. Wissenschaftliche

Monographien zum Alten und Neuen Testament 81. Neukirchen-Vluyn: Neukirchener Verlag, 1999.

———. "Une grande historiographie allant de Genèse à 2 Rois a-t-elle un jour existé?" In *Les dernières rédactions du Pentateuque, de L'Hexateuque et de L'Ennéateuque*, edited by Thomas Römer and Konrad Schmid, 35–46. Bibliotheca ephemeridum theologicarum lovaniensium 203. Leuven: Peeters, 2007.

Schmitt, Has Christoph. "Die Erzählung von Goldenen Kalb Ex. 32 und das Deuteronomistische Geschichtwerk." In *Rethinking the Foundations: Historiography in the Ancient World and in the Bible; Essays in Honour of John Van Seters*, edited by Steven L. McKenzie and Thomas Römer, 235–50. Beihefte zur Zeitschrift für die alttestamentliche Wissenschaft 294. Berlin: de Gruyter, 2000.

Seebass, Horst. "בחר." In *TDOT* 2:73–87.

Segal, Judah B. *The Hebrew Passover: From the Earliest Times to A.D. 70*. London Oriental Series 12. London: Oxford University Press, 1963.

Segal, Moses H. "The Book of Deuteronomy." *JQR* 48 (1958) 315–51.

Sellin, Ernest. *Geschichte des Israelitisch-jüdischen Volkes*. 2 vols. Leipzig: Deichert, 1924–1932.

———. *Gilgal: Ein Beitrag zur Geschichte der Einwandering Israels in Palästina*. Leipzig: Deichert, 1917.

Siegfried Hermann, "Die Konstruktive Restauration, Das Deuteronomium als Mitte biblischer Theologie." In *Probleme biblischer Theologie. Festschrift for Gerhard von Rad*, edited by Hans Wolff, 155–70. Munich: Kaiser, 1971.

Ska, Jean-Louis. *Introduction to Reading the Pentateuch*. Winona Lake, IN: Eisenbrauns, 2006.

Skinner, John. *Genesis*. 2nd ed. ICC. Edinburgh: T. & T. Clark, 1938.

Slayton, Joel C. "Baal-Peor." In *ABD* 1:553.

Smend, Rudolf, Jr. "Das Gesetz und die Volker: Ein Beitrag zur deuteronomistischen Redaktionsgeschichte." In *Problem biblischer Theologie: Gerhard von Rad zum 70. Geburtstag*, edited by Hans W. Wolff, 495–509. Munich: Kaiser, 1971.

Smith, Robert H. "Abram and Melchizedek (Gen 14:18–20)." *ZAW* 77 (1965) 129–53.

Snaith, N. H. *Leviticus and Numbers*. NCBC. London: Thomas Nelson, 1967.

Soggin, J. Alberto. *Introduction to the Old Testament: From Its Origins to the Closing of the Alexandrian Canon*. Translated by John Bowden. OTL. Philadelphia: Fortress, 1980.

Sonnet, Jean-Pierre. *The Book within the Book: Writing in Deuteronomy*. Biblical Interpretation Series 14. Leiden: Brill, 1997.

Speiser, Ephraim A. *Genesis*. AB 1. Garden City, NY: Doubleday, 1964.

Spronk, K. "Baal of Peor." In *DDD* 147–48.

Stackert, Jeffrey. *Rewriting the Torah: Literary Revision in Deuteronomy and the Holiness Code*. Forschungen zum Alten Testament 52. Tübingen: Mohr Siebeck, 2007.

Steinberg, Naomi. "The Deuteronomic Law Code and the Politics of State Centralization." In *The Bible and Liberation: Political and Social Hermeneutics*, edited by Norman K. Gottwald and Richard A. Horsley, 365–75. London: SPCK, 1993.

Sternberg, Meir. "The Bible's Art of Persuasion: Ideology, Rhetoric, and Poetics in Saul's Fall." *HUCA* 54 (1983) 45–82.

———. *Expositional Modes and Temporal Ordering in Fiction*. Bloomington, IN: Indiana University Press, 1993.

———. *The Poetics of Biblical Narrative: Ideological Literature and the Drama of Reading*. Bloomington, IN: Indiana University Press, 1985.

Bibliography

Stevens, Marty E. *Temples, Tithes, and Taxes: The Temple and the Economic Life of Ancient Israel*. Grand Rapids: Baker, 2006.

Strawn, Brent A. "Deuteronomy." In *Theological Bible Commentary*, edited by Gail R. O'Day and David L. Peterson, 63–76. Louisville: Westminster John Knox, 2009.

Suzuki, Yoshihide. "'The Place Which Yahweh Your God Will Choose' in Deuteronomy." In *Problems in Biblical Theology: Essays in Honor of Rolf Knierim*, edited by Henry T. C. Sun and Keith L. Eades, 338–52. Grand Rapids: Eerdmans, 1997.

Sweeney, Marvin A. *I & II Kings*. OTL. Louisville: Westminster John Knox, 2007.

———. *King Josiah of Judah: The Lost Messiah of Israel*. Oxford: Oxford University Press, 2001.

Theological Dictionary of the Old Testament. 14 vols. Edited by G. Johannes Botterweck and Helmer Ringgren. Translated by Geoffrey W. Bromiley et al. Grand Rapids: Eerdmans, 1974–2004.

Thiessen, Matthew. "The Form and Function of the Song of Moses (Deuteronomy 32:1–43)." *JBL* 123 (2004) 401–24.

Tigay, Jeffrey H. *Deuteronomy*. JPSTC. Philadelphia: Jewish Publication Society, 1996.

Timmer, Daniel C. "Small Lexemes, Large Semantics: Prepositions and Theology in the Golden Calf Episode (Exodus 32–34)." *Bib* 88 (2007) 92–99.

Tov, Emanuel. *Textual Criticism of the Hebrew Bible*. 2nd ed. Minneapolis: Fortress, 2001.

Tsumura, David Toshio. *The First Book of Samuel*. NICOT. Grand Rapids: Eerdmans, 2007.

Van Seters, John. *Abraham in History and Tradition*. New Haven, CT: Yale University Press, 1975.

———. "Cultic Laws in the Covenant Code (Exodus 20,22—23,33) and Their Relationship to Deuteronomy and the Holiness Code." In *Studies in the Book of Exodus: Redaction-Reception-Interpretation*, edited by Marc Vervenne, 319–46. Bibliotheca ephemeridum theologicarum lovaniensium 125. Leuven: Leuven University Press, 1996.

———. "Deuteronomy between Pentateuch and the Deuteronomistic History." *HvTSt* 59 (2003) 947–56.

———. "The Formula *leshakken shemo sham* and the Centralization of Worship in Deuteronomy and DH," *JNSL* 30 (2004) 1–18.

———. "Law and the Wilderness Rebellion Tradition: Exodus 32." *SBLSP* 29 (1990) 583–91.

———. "Law (Torah)." In *The Hebrew Bible Today: An Introduction to Critical Issues*, edited by Steven L. McKenzie and M. Patrick Graham, 206–24. Louisville: John Knox, 1998.

———. *The Life of Moses: The Yahwist as Historian in Exodus-Numbers*. Louisville: Westminster, 1994.

———. "The Place of the Yahwist in the History of Passover and Massot." *ZAW* 95 (1983) 167–82.

———. *Prologue to History: The Yahwist as Historian in Genesis*. Louisville: Westminster John Knox, 1992.

Vater, Johann S. *Commentar über den Pentateuch mit Einleitungen in den einzelnen Abschnitten der eingeschalteten Übersetzung von Dr. Alexander Geddes's merkwürdigeren critischen und exegetischen Anmerkungen und einer Abhandlung über Moses und die Verfasser des Pentateuchs*. 4 vols. Halle: Waisenhaus Buchhandlung, 1802–5.

Bibliography

Vaux, Roland de. *Ancient Israel: Its Life and Institutions*. Translated by John McHugh. Biblical Resource Series. Grand Rapids: Eerdmans, 1961.

———. *The Early History of Israel*. Translated by David Smith. Philadelphia: Westminster, 1978.

Veijola, Timo. *Das fünfte Buch Mose (Deuteronomium) Kapitel 1,1–16,17*. Das Alte Testament Deutsch 8.1. Göttingen: Vandenhoeck & Ruprecht, 2004.

———. *Das Konigtum in der Beurteilung der deuteronomistischen Historiographie: Eine redaktionsgeschichtliche Untersuchung*. Annales Academiae scientiarum fennicae, Series B, 198. Helsinki: Suomalainen Tiedeakatemia, 1977.

———. *Die ewige Dynastie: David und die Entstehung seiner Dynastie nach der deuteronomistischen Darstellung*. Annales Academiae scientiarum fennicae, Series B, 193. Helsinki: Suomalainen Tiedeakatemia, 1975.

Verhoef, Pieter A. "Tithing—A Hermeneutical Consideration." In *The Law and the Prophets: Old Testament Studies in Honor of O. T. Allis*, edited by J. H. Skilton, 115–27. Nutley, NJ: P. & R., 1974.

Vogt, Peter T. "Centralization and Decentralization in Deuteronomy." In *Interpreting Deuteronomy: Issues and Approaches*, edited by David G. Firth and Philip S. Johnston, 118–38. Downers Grove, IL: InterVarsity, 2012.

———. *Deuteronomic Theology and the Significance of Torah: A Reappraisal*. Winona Lake, IN: Eisenbrauns, 2006.

Waaler, Erik. *The Shema and the First Commandment in First Corinthians: An Intertextual Approach to Paul's Re-reading of Deuteronomy*. Wissenschaftliche Untersuchungen zum Neuen Testament 2/253. Tübingen: Mohr Siebeck, 2008.

Wagner, Volker. "Das Pesach ist 'zwischeneingekommen' (Dtn 16,1–8)." *Bib* 91 (2010) 481–98.

Waltke, Bruce K. *Genesis*. Grand Rapids: Zondervan, 2001.

Waltke, Bruce K., and Michael Patrick O'Connor. *An Introduction to Biblical Hebrew Syntax*. Winona Lake, IN: Eisenbrauns, 1990.

Walton, John. "The Decalogue Structure of the Deuteronomic Law." In *Interpreting Deuteronomy: Issues and Approaches*, edited by David G. Firth and Philip S. Johnston, 93–117. Downers Grove, IL: InterVarsity, 2012.

Wambacq, Benjamin N. "Les Massôt." *Bib* 61 (1980) 31–54.

———. "Les origines de la *Pesah* Israélite." *Bib* 57 (1976) 206–24.

———. "Pesach–Massôt." *Bib* 62 (1981) 499–518.

Watts, John D. W. "Deuteronomic Theology." *RevExp* 74 (1977) 321–36.

———. "The Torah as the Rhetoric of Priesthood." In *The Pentateuch as Torah: New Methods for Understanding Its Promulgation and Acceptance*, edited by Gary N. Knoppers and Bernard M. Levinson, 319–31. Winona Lake, IN: Eisenbrauns, 2007.

Webb, Barry G. *The Book of Judges*. NICOT. Grand Rapids: Eerdmans, 2012.

Weimar, Peter. "Pascha und Massot: Anmerkungen zu Dt 16,1–8." In *Recht und Ethos im Alten Testament-Gestalt und Wirkung*, 61–72. Neukirchen-Vluyn: Neukirchener, 1999.

Weinberg, Joel. "Das BÊ IT 'ĀḆŌT im 6.–4. Jh. V. U. Z." *VT* 23 (1973) 400–414.

Weinfeld, Moshe. "ברית." In *TDOT*, 2:253–79.

———. "Cult Centralization in Israel in the Light of a Neo-Babylonian Analogy." *JNES* 23 (1964) 202–12.

———. *Deuteronomy 1–11*. AB 5. New York: Doubleday, 1991.

———. "Deuteronomy: The Present State of Inquiry." *JBL* 86 (1967) 249–62.

Bibliography

———. *Deuteronomy and the Deuteronomic School*. 1972. Reprint. Winona Lake, IN: Eisenbrauns, 1992.

———. "Deuteronomy's Theological Revolution." *BRev* 12 (1996) 38–44.

———. "Judge and Officer in Ancient Israel and in the Ancient Near East." *IOS* 7 (1977) 65–88.

———. "The Origin of the Humanism in Deuteronomy." *JBL* 80 (1961) 241–47.

———. "Tithe." *EncJud* 15:1156–62.

Weippert, Helga. "Die Atiologie des Nordreiches und seiner Konigshauser (1 Reg 11,29–40)." *ZAW* 95 (1983) 344–75.

Welch, Adam C. *The Code of Deuteronomy: A New Theory of Its Origin*. London: James Clark, 1924.

Wellhausen, Julius. *Die Composition des Hexateuchs und der historischen Bucher des Alten Testament*. Berlin: Druck, 1889.

———. *Prolegomena to the History of Ancient Israel*. Translated by J. S. Black and A. Menzies. 1885. Reprint. Eugene, OR: Wipf and Stock, 2003.

Wenham, Gordon J. *The Book of Leviticus*. NICOT. Grand Rapids: Eerdmans, 1979.

———. "Deuteronomic Theology of the Book of Joshua." *JBL* 90 (1971) 140–48.

———. "Deuteronomy and the Central Sanctuary." *TynBul* 22 (1971) 103–18.

———. *Genesis 1–15*. WBC 1. Waco, TX: Word, 1987.

Westermann, Claus. *Genesis 12–36: A Commentary*. Translated by John J. Scullion. Minneapolis: Augsburg, 1985.

Wette, Wilhelm Martin Leberecht de. "Dissertatio critica qua Deuteronomium diversum a prioribus Pentateuchi libris, alius cuiusdam recentiori auctoris opus esse demonstrator." Th.d. diss., University of Jena, 1805.

———. *Opuscula Theologica*. Berlin: Berolini, 1830.

Wijngaards, John N. M. *The Dramatization of Salvific History in the Deuteronomic Schools*. Oudtestamentische Studiën 16. Leiden: Brill, 1969.

Williams, Ronald J., and John C. Beckman. *Hebrew Syntax: An Outline*. 3rd ed. Toronto: University of Toronto Press, 2007.

Wilson, Ian. "Divine Presence in Deuteronomy." *TynBul* 43 (1992) 403–6.

———. *Out of the Midst of the Fire: Divine Presence in Deuteronomy*. Society of Biblical Literature Dissertation Series 151. Atlanta: Scholars, 1995.

Wilson, J. Christian "Tithe." In *ABD* 6:578–79.

Wilson, Jeffrey R. *Blessing for the Nations and the Curse of the Law: Paul's Citations of Genesis and Deuteronomy in Gal 3:8–10*. Wissenschaftliche Untersuchungen zum Neuen Testament 2/133. Tübingen: Mohr Siebeck, 2001.

Wilson, Robert. R. "Deuteronomy, Ethnicity, and Reform: Reflections on the Social Setting of the Book of Deuteronomy." In *Constituting the Community: Studies on the Polity of Ancient Israel in Honor of S. Dean McBride Jr.*, edited by John T. Strong and Steven S. Tuell, 107–23. Winona Lake, IN: Eisenbrauns, 2005.

———. "Who Was the Deuteronomist? (Who Was Not the Deuteronomist?) Reflections on Pan-Deuteronomism." In *Those Elusive Deuteronomists: The Phenomenon of Pan-Deuteronomism*, edited by Linda S. Schearing and Steven L. McKenzie, 67–82. Journal for the Study of the Old Testament Supplement Series 268. Sheffield, UK: Sheffield Academic, 1999.

Wright, George Ernest. "The Lawsuit of God: A Form-Critical Study of Deuteronomy 32." In *Israel's Prophetic Heritage*, edited by Bernard W. Anderson and Walter Harrelson, 26–67. New York: Harper and Brothers, 1962.

———. "The Levites in Deuteronomy." *VT* 4 (1945) 325–30.
Young, Dwight Wayne. "A Ghost Word in the Testament of Jacob (Gen 49:5)?" *JBL* 100 (1981) 335–42.
Zehnder, Markus. "Building on Stone? Deuteronomy and Esarhaddon's Loyalty Oaths (Part I) Some Preliminary Observations." *BRB* 19 (2009) 341–74.
———. "Building on Stone? Deuteronomy and Esarhaddon's Loyalty Oaths (Part II) Some Additional Observations." *BRB* 19 (2009) 511–35.
Zvi, Ehud Ben. "Looking at the Primary (Hi)story and the Prophetic Books as Literary/Theological Units within the Frame of the Early Second Temple: Some Considerations." *SJOT* 12 (1998) 26–43.

Scripture Index

Genesis

1	53
4:4	143
6:2	162
8:20	143
12–22	77
12–13	90
12	62
12:6	90
12:7	62
12:8–9	90
13	86
13:2–4	90
13:11	162
14	85, 86, 87, 88, 90
14:1–16	85
14:1–15	88
14:16	88
14:17–24	84–90, 91, 100
14:17	84, 85, 86, 88, 89, 90
14:18–20	85, 86, 91
14:18	85, 89
14:19–20	84, 87, 89
14:20	81, 82, 83, 84, 87, 89, 90, 91
14:21–24	85, 86
14:21	88, 89
14:22–24	87, 89
14:22–23	87
14:22	91
14:27–29	85
18–19	86
18:25	125
19:9	125
22:1–13	143
28	90
28:10–22	90, 91
28:12–15	90
28:17	90
28:18–22	84, 90–91, 100
28:22	82, 83, 91
29:34	144, 158
31:30	112
31:53	125
31:54	143
34:22	144
34:25–31	144
34:25–26	144
34:25	144
34:28	144
44	141
46:11	144
49:5	144

Exodus

1–15	108
2:1–11	145, 158
2:14	125
2:23—4:17	158
3	48
3:8	48
3:17	48
4:14	147, 158
4:27–31	147
5	125
5:1—11:10	147
5:6	125
5:10	125

Exodus *(continued)*

Reference	Pages
5:14	125
5:15	125
5:19	125
5:21	125
6:13–30	147
6:16–25	144
6:23–25	149
6:23	147
9:20	62
9:30	62
9:31–32	107
12–13	29, 104, 105, 106, 107, 108, 110
12	106, 107, 108, 111–13, 118, 121–23, 124, 143
12:1–28	108, 109
12:1–20	107, 110, 111, 121
12:1–13	115
12:1–10	112
12:3	111–12, 115, 123
12:5	122
12:11–13	112
12:11	112
12:12–13	112
12:12	125
12:13	105
12:14–20	113
12:15	106
12:16	106
12:17–20	110, 113
12:18–19	106
12:18	106
12:19	106
12:21–28	111
12:21–27	115
12:21–23	107, 111
12:23	105
12:24–27	111
12:27	105, 107, 111, 112
12:28	107
12:29–39	107
12:40–51	107
12:43	147
13	107
13:1–16	146
13:1–2	107
13:3–10	110, 117
13:4	111, 121
13:6–7	106
14	43
14:31	62
15	109
15:1–18	43
15:22–27	43–44, 78
15:22–25	44
15:25–26	44
15:25	43, 44
15:26	44
17	126, 127
17:8–15	126
18	126, 127, 135
18:1–12	126
18:12	143
18:13–27	126–27, 128, 129, 134, 135, 136
18:13	126
18:15–16	126, 127, 135
18:16	127
18:18	127, 136
18:19–20	127
18:20–25	54, 78
18:21	127
18:22–23	127
18:25	162
19	126
19:1–2	126
19:5	1
19:24	147
20	45
20:1–17	45, 77
20:2–17	42
20:2	45
20:3–6	48, 78
20:3–5	42, 43, 45–47
20:3	45, 46
20:4–6	49, 53
20:5	45, 46, 47, 60
20:23—23:19	23, 77, 78
20:22–26	28
20:24	37, 39
22:19	42, 43
22:29–30	146
23	47, 48
23:13	43

Scripture Index

23:14–19	105, 111, 113–14, 115, 122	34:14	48
23:14–17	103, 104, 117	34:17	46
23:14	106, 114, 115	34:18–26	103, 106, 111, 113–14, 115, 117, 122
23:15–18	117	34:18–23	104
23:15	103, 113, 114	34:18	103
23:16	70	34:22	70
23:17	114, 115	34:23	114
23:18	114, 122	34:24	114, 115
23:20–25	43, 47–48	34:25	114, 122
23:20–22	47	34:29–35	127
23:21	47	38:21	146, 158
23:23	48	39:1–31	147
23:24	48, 114		
23:25	48		

Leviticus

24	48, 145	1–16	157
24:1–8	145	1–7	148
27:21	147	1:1—6:7	148
28	147, 148	1	145, 148
28:2–40	147	2	148
28:28–30	147	3	148
28:41	147	6:8—7:38	148
29–31	148	8–10	148
29	147, 148	8	148
29:7–9	147	10	148
29:10–14	147	11–15	149
29:15–18	148	13–14	157
29:19–34	148	13:2–3	157
29:35–41	148	16	149
29:42–46	148	17–26	50, 91
32–34	49	17	28
32	48, 49, 69, 70, 78, 145, 146, 148	17:1–16	149
32:1–35	148	17:7	42, 43
32:1–30	49	18	51
32:4	49	18:1–4	43, 50–51, 78
32:7–20	43, 48–49	18:4	50, 51
32:14	49	18:22	51
32:25–29	145	18:25	51
32:30–35	145	18:28	51
33:1–3	48	19	51
33:2	48	19:4	46
33:7–11	127	19:14	62
34	48, 107	19:30	63
34:11–16	43, 50, 56, 78	19:32	63
34:11	48, 50	20	51
34:12–17	42	20:22–26	43, 51, 78
34:12	50	20:22	51
34:13	56, 66		

211

Scripture Index

Leviticus (continued)

20:23	51
20:24	51
20:25	51
21:6	149
23	103, 105, 111, 115, 116, 117
23:3	115
23:4–22	115
23:5	112, 115
23:6	106, 115
23:7–8	106
23:10–12	115
23:23–25	115
23:26–32	115
23:33–43	70
23:33–36	115
23:34	115
25:32–34	146
26:1	46
26:2	63
26:46	43, 44
27	83, 100
27:30–33	83, 84, 85, 91–92, 98
27:30	81, 83, 91, 100
27:31	81, 91, 101
27:32	81, 92, 100

Numbers

1:2	112
1:3	147
1:4	112
1:18	112
1:20	112
1:22	112
1:24	112
1:26	112
1:28	112
1:30	112
1:32	112
1:34	112
1:36	112
1:38	112
1:40	112
1:42	112
1:44	112
1:45	112
1:47–51	146
1:47–49	146
1:47	146
1:49	146
2:2	112
2:32	112
2:33	146
3–4	101, 150
3:1–3	149
3:4	148
3:5–10	149
3:5–9	146, 158
3:6	146
3:11–13	146
3:15	112
3:17–39	144
3:20	112
3:21–37	158
3:21–25	144
3:27–32	144
3:32	146, 158
3:33–37	145
3:38–39	147, 149
3:41	146
3:45	146
4:1–3	147
4:2	112
4:4–20	144, 147, 149
4:20	150
4:22–34	158
4:22–27	144
4:22	112
4:28	144
4:29–34	145
4:29	112
4:34–37	147
4:34	112
4:38	112
4:40	112
4:42	112
4:46	112
6:22–27	147
7:9	145, 158
8:5–13	149
8:13	146, 158
8:14–19	146
9	115, 123

Scripture Index

9:1–14	111, 115–16, 122	18:29	93
9:2–14	106	18:31	92
9:2–5	115	19–26	149
9:2	112	20:22–29	149
9:12–13	116	22–24	51, 128
9:20	149	24:15–24	52
10:6	149	25	135
11	127	25:1–5	51–52, 78, 126, 128
11:1–17	126, 127–28	25:1–3	42, 43, 51, 52
11:1–15	135	25:1–2	52, 128
11:1–6	127	25:1	52
11:10–15	128	25:2	52
11:14	128, 129, 136, 175	25:3–5	52
11:16–22	128	25:4–5	129, 135, 175
11:16–17	128, 135	25:5	52, 128
11:16	125	25:15	52
11:17	128, 129, 136, 175	26:2	112
11:24–25	128	26:57–63	144
12:1–11	149	26:58	142
12:10–15	157	26:62	146, 155
14:1–45	2	28–29	103, 111, 116–17
16:1–50	145	28	116
16:7–11	150	28:16	112
16:9–10	145	28:21–32	83
16:40	145, 150	31:25–31	85
17:3	146	31:30	146
17:8	146	31:47	146
17:16–28	145, 149, 158	32:50	149
17:17	112	33:3	106, 115
17:18	145	33:50–56	43, 53, 78
17:21–23	145	34:14	112
17:21	112	35:1–6	146
18	92, 93, 95, 96		
18:1–7	150	## Deuteronomy	
18:1–6	146, 158		
18:1	150	1–28	26
18:2	146	1–4	76
18:7	150	1	135
18:20–32	92, 101, 102	1:5	2, 165
18:20	149	1:8–12	135, 175
18:21–30	83	1:8–9	136
18:21–28	84, 92–93, 101	1:9–18	126, 128–29
18:21–24	92, 96	1:9–12	136
18:21	81, 83, 85	1:9	128
18:24	81	1:12	128
18:25	92	1:13–17	135, 136
18:26	81, 92	1:13	128
18:28	81, 92	1:15–16	135

Scripture Index

Deuteronomy (continued)

Reference	Pages
1:15	125, 135
1:39	51
3:22	63
4–6	78
4	5, 6, 32, 43, 53
4:1–8	52
4:1	43, 53
4:5	43
4:8	2, 43
4:14–35	42
4:14	43
4:15–31	53
4:15–19	53
4:19	53
4:25–26	53
4:25	64
4:26–28	53
4:27–31	176
4:40	45
4:44—28:68	33
4:45	43
5	45
5:1	43, 157
5:3–7	54
5:5–8	70
5:6–21	42
5:6–10	43, 45–47
5:6	45
5:7–10	78
5:7	45, 46
5:8–10	49, 53
5:8	46
5:9	45, 46, 47, 60
5:31	43, 51
6	43, 53
6:1	43
6:2	63
6:3	157
6:4–5	54, 63, 74, 170
6:4	157
6:5	54
6:13–15	54
6:20–24	62
6:20	43
6:24	63
7	43, 54, 55, 79
7:1–5	54, 55
7:1–2	54, 65
7:1	54
7:2–5	43
7:3–4	54
7:5	55, 56, 66
7:6–11	54
7:11	43
7:16	43
7:25–26	43
8:19–20	43
9:1	157
9:12–21	43, 48–49
9:18	64
10:8	151
10:9	96, 146, 150, 151
10:12	63
10:13	76
11	33
11:16	43, 133
11:26–32	61
11:28	43
11:31	51
11:32	43
12–26	2, 18, 61, 166
12–18	4, 5, 6, 19, 20, 30, 36, 40, 70, 161, 164, 165, 166, 168, 169, 170, 172, 181, 182, 184
12–13	72, 74, 75
12	5, 23, 28, 38, 39, 55, 57, 70, 166, 167, 170, 171, 172, 180, 183
12:1–28	171
12:1–5	43, 54, 55–56, 57, 78, 79
12:1–4	50, 53, 56, 65, 66, 70, 76, 79, 166, 171
12:1	43, 55, 166
12:2–7	38, 55
12:2–4	75
12:2–3	43
12:2	72, 165
12:3	55, 56, 66, 165
12:4–28	37
12:5–14	167
12:5–7	165
12:5	25, 29, 53, 55, 79, 93, 164, 166, 167

Scripture Index

12:6	81, 83	14:24–27	92
12:8–12	38, 55	14:24–26	83, 95
12:10–11	84, 93–94, 173	14:24	29, 95, 164
12:11	29, 81, 164, 167	14:26	83
12:12	83, 146, 150, 151	14:27–29	95, 97, 102, 173
12:13–19	38, 55, 94	14:27	146, 150, 151
12:13	165	14:28–29	95
12:14	39, 94, 165	14:28	81, 83, 93, 173
12:15–25	167	14:29	146, 150, 151, 154
12:15–18	84, 93–94, 173	15	107
12:15	55	15:1–23	165
12:17	81, 83	15:4	51
12:18	94, 150, 151	15:5	44
12:19	95, 101, 146, 150, 151	15:20	167
12:20–28	38, 55, 94	16	43, 58–59, 107, 115, 120–23, 124, 174
12:20–23	94	16:1–17	103, 104, 111, 117–19, 174
12:21	29, 55, 164, 167	16:1–16	105
12:24–27	107	16:1–8	29, 106, 117, 123
12:25	72	16:2	29, 112, 118, 121, 122, 164, 167
12:26	167		
12:29–32	79, 166, 171	16:3–8	118, 174
12:29–31	75	16:3–4	103, 106, 118
12:30–31	43	16:4	118
13–18	37	16:5–8	118
13	43, 56–58, 76	16:5–7	118
13:1–18	79	16:6	29, 115, 121, 164, 167
13:1–15	43	16:7–8	106
13:1	56	16:7	121, 167
13:2–6	57	16:8	103, 106
13:3–16	107	16:9–17	118
13:3	57	16:11	29, 150, 151, 154, 164, 168
13:4	57	16:13–17	165
13:5–6	57	16:13–16	71
13:7–12	57	16:14	150, 151, 154
13:9–10	57	16:15	168
13:9	57	16:16	114, 168
13:10	58	16:17	119
13:13–18	58	16:18—18:22	134, 136, 176, 184, 185
13:15	58	16:18—17:7	185
13:19	44, 72	16:18–20	126, 129–30, 136, 175
14	94, 95, 102, 167	16:18	125, 129, 130, 133
14:2	164, 165	16:20	129
14:22–29	84, 92, 93, 94–96, 101	16:21—17:7	171, 172
14:22–27	95, 96	16:21–22	28, 43
14:22–26	173	17	130, 136, 152
14:22–23	94	17:1–13	79, 130–31, 136
14:22	82, 83		
14:23	63, 81, 92		

215

Scripture Index

Deuteronomy *(continued)*

17:1–7	136
17:2–7	126, 129, 130, 175
17:2–3	43, 130
17:2	64
17:3	130
17:8–13	129, 130, 136, 151–52, 172, 175, 185
17:8–9	136
17:8	152, 168
17:9–13	151, 152
17:10	168
17:9	131, 150, 151
17:12	131, 150
17:14–20	79, 129, 136, 151, 164, 171, 176, 184, 185
17:14	51
17:15	164, 184
17:16–18	152
17:18–19	171, 179
17:18	2, 150, 151–52, 177, 179
17:19–20	152
17:19	2, 63
18	43, 58–59, 102, 136
18:1–8	58, 79, 84, 93, 96–97, 102, 129, 152–56, 177, 178, 185
18:1–5	151
18:1–2	153, 155
18:1	99, 146, 150, 152, 153
18:2	96, 99
18:3–5	153, 155
18:3	150
18:5	164, 165
18:6–8	153, 155
18:6–7	151
18:6	96, 150, 155
18:7	150
18:8	96, 99, 173
18:9–14	43, 58, 79, 171
18:13	59
18:15–22	129
18:15–18	75, 76, 136, 185
19:2	51
19:14	51
19:17–18	130, 136, 175
19:17	131, 150, 151
19:18	131
20	156
20:1	63, 156
20:2–4	156
20:2	150
20:3–4	151
20:3	157
20:4	156
20:5–7	156
20:5	125
20:8	125
20:9	125, 156
20:17–18	43, 54
20:17	65
21:1	51
21:5	150, 151, 164
21:9	72
23:17	165
24:8	150, 151, 157
24:9	157
25:1–3	126, 131, 136
25:1	125
25:2	131
25:19	51
26	97
26:1	46, 51
26:2	4, 29, 164, 165
26:3	150
26:4	150
26:5–9	62, 70, 74, 97
26:10–11	97
26:11–13	151, 154
26:11	150, 151
26:12–27	84, 93, 97, 102
26:12–15	151
26:12–13	95
26:12	81, 83, 93, 97, 150, 173
26:13	150
26:14	44
26:16	43
26:17	43
27	28, 33, 61
27:1–10	157–58
27:1–4	157
27:3	2
27:4–5	137
27:5–8	33
27:5–7	157
27:5	43

27:8	2, 157	32:4–9	60
27:9	150, 151, 157	32:10–14	60
27:10	44, 45, 157	32:15–18	60, 79
27:14	150, 151	32:16–21	43
27:19	129	32:19–43	60
27:21	43	32:19–25	60, 79
27:25	129	32:19–24	61
27:26	2	32:21–25	61
28–30	5	32:26–35	60
28:1–14	2	32:36–43	60
28:1	44	32:43	61, 79
28:2	44	32:44	61
28:15–68	43	32:46	2
28:15	44, 45, 76	33:8	141, 151
28:36	43, 176		
28:45	44, 45, 76		
28:58	2, 63		

Joshua

28:61	2, 4
28:62	44
28:63–68	176
29:1–29	171
29:9	125
29:17–18	43
29:20	2, 4
29:27	176
29:28	2
30:1–10	176
30:10	2, 4, 44, 45, 76, 133
30:16	45, 76
30:17	43
31:7–8	61, 171
31:9	2, 150, 151
31:11	2, 4, 165
31:12	2, 63
31:13	63
31:16–22	59, 79
31:16–20	43
31:16–18	59
31:19–22	59
31:23–29	61
31:24	2
31:25	150, 151
31:26	2
31:28	125, 136
31:29	43, 64
32–34	61
32	26, 59–61, 136
32:1–3	60

1–5	61
1:2	64
1:8	2, 171
1:10	125
1:11	51
2:9	170
2:11	170
2:24	63
3	178
3:2	125
3:3	150, 152
3:6	145, 159
3:10	54
4	178
5–9	61
5	119, 120, 124, 174
5:1–12	111, 119–20
5:1–2	170
5:3–4	119
5:3	119
5:9	119
5:10–11	106, 109, 174
5:11	120
5:13—11:23	170
6–12	61
6	178
6:4	158
6:8	158
6:9	158
6:13	158
6:16	158

Scripture Index

Joshua (continued)

7:1–5	152
7:11	130
7:15	130
8:30–35	152
8:33	125, 137, 150, 152
9:27	164
13:6–7	171
13:14	96, 146
13:33	96, 146
14:1	177
14:3	146
18:7	146
19:51	177
21	146, 149, 177
21:43	51
22:13	177
22:25	63
22:31	177
22:32	177
23:2	125, 137
23:5	171
23:6–9	171
23:11–13	176
23:15	176
23:16	130
24	43, 61–63, 79
24:1–28	79
24:1–13	63, 171
24:1	125, 137
24:2–13	62
24:2	63
24:5	149, 177
24:11–13	171
24:11	54
24:14–23	63
24:14	62, 63, 133
24:15	63, 66, 171
24:16–18	63
24:16	63
24:19–28	2
24:19–24	63, 79
24:19	63
24:21	63
24:22	63
24:23	63, 133
24:24	63
24:25–28	63
24:25	43
24:28	64
24:29–30	64
24:33	149, 177

Judges

1–2	43, 63–65, 79
1	64, 172
1:1	64
2	64, 75
2:6–9	64
2:6	64
2:10–11	65
2:10	64, 66
2:11–23	126, 131–32
2:11–19	66
2:11–15	172
2:11	64
2:12–15	65
2:16–23	172
2:16–20	130
2:16–19	125
2:16–17	65, 132, 137
2:17	125
2:18–19	132, 137
2:18	131
2:19	131
3:5–7	65
3:7—16:31	43, 65–67
3:7–11	65, 66
3:7	64
3:10	125, 132
3:12–30	65
3:12	64, 76
3:41	76
4	178
4:1—5:31	65
4:1	64
4:4	125
6:1—8:35	65
6:1	64
6:19	118
6:25–26	66
6:26	143
6:31–32	56
8:27–32	66

Scripture Index

8:27	66	2:22–25	67
10:2–3	125	3–4	97
10:6—12:7	65	3	172
10:6–16	66	3:1	67, 132, 159
10:6	64, 76	3:2–21	159
10:16	133	3:13	125
11:27	125, 131	4:18	125
11:31	143	6:15	146
12:8	125	7:3–17	172
12:9	125	7:3–6	126, 132–33
12:11	125	7:3	133, 137
12:13	125	7:5	97
12:14	125	7:6	125, 133
13:1—16:31	65	7:13–14	133
13:1	64, 76	7:15–17	126, 132–33
13:3	132	7:15	125
13:4–5	132	7:16–17	175
13:6	132	7:16	125
13:16–23	143	7:17	125
14:1	132	8	98, 102, 133, 173
14:6	132	8:1–5	125, 137
14:19	132	8:1–3	126, 132–33, 134
15:14	132	8:1	125, 133
15:20	125	8:2	125
16:31	125	8:3	133
17–20	159	8:4–5	133
17:6	44, 65, 66	8:5–6	175
17:7–13	143	8:5	125, 133
18	143	8:6–18	133
18:1	66	8:6	125
18:5	141	8:11–17	82, 84, 97–98
19–20	143, 177	8:11–12	98
19:1	66	8:13	98
20:28	149, 177	8:14–15	98
21:19	110	8:15–17	173
21:25	44, 65, 66	8:15	83, 98
		8:16	98
		8:17	83, 98
		8:20	125

1 Samuel

1–3	177	10:17–19	133
1–2	177	12:1–2	133
1:1—2:10	159	12:6–8	133
1:1	177	12:6	149, 177
1:5	132	12:8	149, 177
1:11	132	12:9–12	133
1:26–27	132	12:14	63
2:12–17	67	12:24	63
2:13	118	12:25	176

219

Scripture Index

1 Samuel (continued)

13:9–12	143
14:18–42	141
15:4	125
15:19	64
17:40	162
22:10–15	141
23:9–12	141
25:28	71
30:7	141
30:25	43

2 Samuel

4:4	105
6:1–3	146
6:9	63
7	33, 176
7:11	125
8:15	176
8:17	71
8:18	177
15:1–6	126, 133–34, 137, 175, 176
15:3	134
15:4–6	134
15:4	125
15:24–29	178
15:24	71, 146
17:15	178
18:18	88
19:12	178
20:25	178
22:20–23	178
24:22	143

1 Kings

1–11	67
1:7	178
1:8	71, 178
1:19	178
1:25	178
1:26	178
1:32	178
1:34	178
1:42	178
2:4	176
2:22	178
2:35	71, 178
3	126, 134
3:2	35
3:4	143
3:9	125, 134, 137, 138
3:14	45
3:16–27	125, 134, 137, 175, 176
3:28	125, 134
4:5	178
6:11–13	176
7:7	125, 134
8:1—9:9	33
8:3–4	146
8:16	164
8:25	176
8:29	164
8:46–53	176
8:58	43
8:61	45
9:3	33, 164
9:4–9	176
9:4	43
9:6	76
11–14	75
11:1—12:33	67–71, 79
11:1–13	67
11:6	64
11:7	51
11:13	68, 69
11:14–27	68
11:26—12:33	68
11:26—12:23	68
11:26—12:20	68
11:29–40	71
11:31–33	67
11:31	68, 69
11:33	68, 133
11:34–36	68
11:34	76
11:36	33, 164, 176
11:38	68, 71
11:40	68
12	49, 69, 180
12:1–19	68
12:20	69
12:21–24	69
12:25–33	68, 69, 70, 78

12:25	69	21:25	64, 76
12:26–31	69	22:8–28	176
12:26–30	70	22:43	72
12:26	69	22:53	64
12:27	69		
12:28–29	69	## 2 Kings	
12:28	70		
12:29	69	3:2	64
12:31–32	178	4:1	63
12:31	178	7–12	76
12:32–33	70	8:18	64
12:32	143, 178	8:19	176
13–14	75	8:27	64
13	43, 71–72	9:1–10:31	43, 73
13:1–4	71	9:6–10	73
13:2–5	176	10:18–28	73
13:2	178	10:25	143
13:25	176	10:31	71, 73
13:33	178	11–12	178
14:16	71	12:2	72
14:17–11	176	13:2	64, 71
14:21–23	43, 72	13:11	64, 71
14:21	33, 164	14:3	72
14:22	64, 72	14:24	64, 71
14:23	58, 72	15:3	72
15:4	176	15:9	64, 71
15:11	72	15:10–15	72
15:26	64	15:18	64, 71
15:30	71	15:24	64, 71
15:34	64	15:28	64, 71
16:1–4	176	15:34	72
16:19	64, 76	16:13–15	143
16:21–22	72	17	43, 74–76, 80, 176
16:25	64	17:1–23	176
16:30	64	17:1–6	74
16:31	71	17:2	74
18–19	43, 73, 80	17:7–23	74, 75
18:3	63	17:7–8	74
18:12	63, 130	17:9–12	75
18:13–16	27	17:10	58, 72
18:20–39	56, 66, 143	17:13–18	75
18:21	105	17:13–14	76
18:25	162	17:13	76
18:26	105	17:14	75
19:15–18	73	17:15–18	75
20:42	176	17:16	76
21:17–29	176	17:17	64, 76
21:20	64, 76	17:19–20	76

2 Kings (continued)

17:19	176
17:22	71, 76
17:25–33	76
17:25	63
17:27–28	178
17:28	63
17:32	63
17:34	63
17:37	43
17:41	63
18–20	40
18:3–7	77
18:3	72
18:4	58
18:9–14	58
18:12	44, 130
18:13–16	27
19:19	77
20:17	176
21–22	32
21	76–77
21:1–9	24
21:1	76
21:2–15	176
21:2–9	80
21:2	64, 76
21:3–6	77
21:3–5	77
21:4	164
21:6	64, 76, 77
21:7	58, 77, 164
21:9	77
21:12–15	77
21:16	64, 76
21:20	64
21:21–22	77
21:22	133
22–23	3, 26, 38, 40, 120, 124, 180, 183
22:1—23:30	80
22:1—23:25	176
22	120, 173
22:2	72
22:3–7	174
22:3–6	173
22:3	178
22:8–9	179
22:8	3, 4, 23, 106, 166
22:11	4
22:12	178
22:16–20	26
23	120, 124, 174, 179
23:1–20	179
23:1–14	176
23:1–4	176
23:1	178, 179
23:2	179
23:3	179
23:4–6	179
23:4	178, 179
23:7–20	179
23:8–9	178
23:14	58
23:20	178
23:21–23	111, 120–21, 124, 174
23:21–22	107
23:21	118, 120, 174, 178
23:22	125, 131, 174
23:23	106, 120, 121
23:25–27	176
23:25	133
23:27	164
23:32	64
23:37	64
24–25	40, 80
24:9	64
24:19	64
25:13–18	178
25:26	180

1 Chronicles

5:13	112
5:15	112
5:24	112
5:34	178
6:1–15	144
7:2	112
7:4	112
9:2	150
9:9	112
9:13	112
9:19	112
12:31	112

Scripture Index

18:17	177
23:11	112
23:13	144
23:24	112
24:4	112
24:30	112
26:6	112
26:13	112

2 Chronicles

5:5	150
6:20	164
8:13	106
12:13	164
17:14	112
19:5–11	130
23:18	150
25:5	112
30	106
30:18	112
30:27	150
31:5–12	83
31:5	83
31:17	112
35:1–19	106
35:4	112
35:6	112
35:12	112

Ezra

6:19	106
10:5	150
10:16	112

Nehemiah

9:8	54
10:29	150
10:35	112, 150
10:37–39	83
11:20	150
12:44–47	83
12:44	83
12:47	83
13:4–14	83
13:5	83
13:12	83

Job

7:15	163

Psalms

135:20	146

Isaiah

1:17	125
16:5	125
30:29	106
31:5	105
40:20	163

Jeremiah

2:20	72
2:23	133
3:25	44
5:28	125
7:28	44
7:30	65
8:8	35
26:13	44
26:24	35
30:3	51, 65
42:6	44
42:13	44
42:21	44
52:2	65

Lamentations

3:59	125

Ezekiel

7:27	125
16:38	125
23:24	125
23:45	125
43:19	150
44:15	150
44:24	125

Scripture Index

Ezekiel *(continued)*

45:21	106
46:24	118

Hosea

1:8	60
2:11	106
6:1	133
7:10	133
9:5	106
14:3	133

Amos

4	82
4:4	83
5:21	106
8:10	106

Zechariah

7:9	125
8:16	125
12:13	146

Malachi

3:8–10	83

www.ingramcontent.com/pod-product-compliance
Lightning Source LLC
Chambersburg PA
CBHW051639230426
43669CB00013B/2371